American Polar Bears
in Russia

ALSO BY WILLIAM THOMAS VENNER
AND FROM McFARLAND

*The 30th North Carolina Infantry in the Civil War:
A History and Roster* (2018)

*The 11th North Carolina Infantry
in the Civil War: A History and Roster* (2015)

*The 7th Tennessee Infantry in the Civil War:
A History and Roster* (2013)

American Polar Bears in Russia

Soldiers of the 339th Infantry and the Archangel Campaign, 1918–1919

William Thomas Venner

McFarland & Company, Inc., Publishers
Jefferson, North Carolina

LIBRARY OF CONGRESS CATALOGUING-IN-PUBLICATION DATA

Names: Venner, William Thomas, 1950– author.
Title: American Polar Bears in Russia : Soldiers of the 339th Infantry and the Archangel Campaign, 1918–1919 / William Thomas Venner.
Other titles: Soldiers of the 339th Infantry and the Archangel Campaign, 1918–1919
Description: Jefferson, North Carolina : McFarland & Company, Inc., Publishers, 2023 | Includes bibliographical references and index.
Identifiers: LCCN 2022055547 | ISBN 9781476686509 (paperback : acid free paper) ∞
ISBN 9781476648385 (ebook)
Subjects: LCSH: Polar Bear Expedition, 1918–1919. | Soviet Union—History—Allied intervention, 1918–1920. | United States. Army. Infantry Regiment, 339th—Biography. | United States. Army. American Expeditionary Force, North Russia. | BISAC: HISTORY / Wars & Conflicts / World War I | HISTORY / Russia & the Former Soviet Union
Classification: LCC DK265.42.U5 V46 2023 | DDC 947.084/1—dc23/eng/20221116
LC record available at https://lccn.loc.gov/2022055547

BRITISH LIBRARY CATALOGUING DATA ARE AVAILABLE

ISBN (print) 978-1-4766-8650-9
ISBN (ebook) 978-1-4766-4838-5

© 2023 William Thomas Venner. All rights reserved

No part of this book may be reproduced or transmitted in any form or by any means, electronic or mechanical, including photocopying or recording, or by any information storage and retrieval system, without permission in writing from the publisher.

Front cover: *inset* Officers of Company M, April 5, 1919. [L–R] Clarence Primm, Milton Carpenter, Robert Wieczorek, Wesley Wright, James Donovan, George Stoner, and Joel Moore (U.S. Army Signal Corps); Company M moving southward from verst 468 on September 11, 1918, just moments before coming under artillery fire (U.S. Army Signal Corps)

Printed in the United States of America

McFarland & Company, Inc., Publishers
Box 611, Jefferson, North Carolina 28640
www.mcfarlandpub.com

To Paul K. Shreve.
Grandpa Paul was there
to guide me in the right direction.
It was his stories that led me to
the Polar Bears and their families.
May their memories never fade.

Table of Contents

Preface   1
Introduction   5

1. Camp Custer, Michigan—The 339th Infantry Is Formed   7
2. The 339th Heads to the Western Front   15
3. Why America Sent Troops to Russia   23
4. First American Troops in Russia   29
5. The Americans Settle In   40
6. A Muddled Assault   49
7. Assault on Verst 455   60
8. A Change in Strategy   72
9. The Great War Ends   77
10. Archangel   83
11. On the Front Lines   91
12. The March to Pinega   99
13. The Pinega Campaign   107
14. Winter on the Railroad Front   118
15. A Mutiny in Name Only   126
16. The Fight for Bolshie Ozerki   134
17. Prisoners   147
18. Spring 1919   154
19. Homeward Bound   163
20. Bringing Home the Fallen   175

Chapter Notes   187
Bibliography   203
Index   207

Preface

Paul K. Shreve was my grandmother's third husband; however, to me, he was Grandpa Paul. He was born December 24, 1898, to his parents Otto and Mattie Shreve. His life started hard, as he bounced back and forth between divorced parents. At best, Paul completed one year of high school before venturing out on his own, and by the time he was sixteen, he established himself as a decent rough carpenter in Grand Rapids, Michigan.

In 1917 Paul enlisted in the army and served in France during World War I. He came home from the war, married Elizabeth Siegel in 1919, and commenced working as a carpenter in the Grand Rapids area. Unfortunately the Depression destroyed their dreams. They moved around, eventually ending up in Oklahoma City, Oklahoma, but by this time their marriage was on the rocks and they divorced.

Paul met my grandmother, Waunita Cherington. She had already ground her way through two divorces, though not before having a daughter (my mother, Beverly). Paul and Waunita married in 1948 and soon after moved to Daggett, California, to live just a few houses away from where my parents, Bill and Beverly Venner, were raising my sister, Mary, and me. Paul secured a job as the maintenance man for the local water company while Waunita worked as a short-order cook at a nearby roadside diner. I do not remember much about those early years of my life, except Granny (as I called her) could whip up the best pancakes and Paul's workshop contained the most marvelous mysteries.

Grandpa Paul became my hero; whenever we were visiting, Mary and I were like his shadows. We relished his enchanting shop; it was crammed with extraordinary treasures and exciting intrigues. Paul's shop was filled with every kind of carpentry tool imaginable, plus machinery parts for the water company's equipment, innumerable coffee cans filled with nuts, nails and bolts and other unnamable prizes, including a dry washer for mining gold. Each tool had a purpose, and most important, Paul had a story for every tool. His world existed in that shop, and like the man himself, was completely beguiling.

By the time I entered high school, Paul and Granny moved to Goldfield, Nevada. At first, they operated a greasy-spoon restaurant, attached to a worn-carpet, faded-curtain motel. Granny cooked and served the meals while Paul kept the equipment running and the motel rooms habitable. But their business didn't survive. The bank ended up owning it, so the two retired to a small house with a nearby workshop. We often visited, and I have pleasant memories of that little place—especially the odors of cigarette smoke, fresh coffee, pancakes, and Grandpa Paul's shop, its whiffs of cleaning solvents, oils, sawdust, and tantalizing secrets.

Paul realized I loved the outdoors, so he loaded me into his Jeep and took me to the town's historic dump. Here, he showed me how to dig for purple-glass bottles. What a world he opened up—digging in the ground for treasure! There is little wonder why, when I declared a major in college, archaeology would play a prominent part. Years later I would attend Southern Utah State College in Cedar City, Utah, a school only a couple hundred miles away from Goldfield, and there were many times when I would spend the weekend with my grandparents. By now, Paul was in his late sixties and his health was not the best. He seldom accompanied me when I took his Jeep to dig for bottles, but instead he and I spent more time sitting together on his front porch. Here, Paul would smoke his Camel cigarettes and, most wondrously, tell stories. Grandpa Paul was a gifted storyteller. Granny would find us on the porch and shake her head. I reveled in Paul's entertaining accounts, but Granny's comment about his yarns were simply "he's just a damned liar."

Eventually, as Paul's health deteriorated, his stories changed; it was like he needed to share with me secrets from when he was a young man. Paul began talking about his experiences in World War I, something he had never mentioned before. He told me about the trenches, their rats, their stench, their horror, and about what it was like to be gassed. Paul described watching men jump out of burning observation balloons and falling to their deaths. He also narrated how he and his comrades would chalk circles on the blade of a shovel and then bet on the different circles. Someone would hold the shovel up, above the top of the trench, and an obliging German sniper would shoot at it. Whoever had picked the circle in which the sniper's bullet plowed through would reap the betting pool.

But then one night, while we sat on the porch, Paul chain-smoking and me gazing at the stars, he began to tell a different set of stories. He described sleeping on top of large brick stoves, days spent floundering in waist-deep snow, enduring temperatures so low trees would burst, and cold so intense that bullet and artillery wounds would freeze before a person had the chance to bleed to death. These tales puzzled me; what was he talking about? I feared interrupting. I did not want to break the spell that seemed to have enveloped my grandfather—it was like something was driving him to speak. I remained silent and took in all he had to say. I could ask later.

As a graduate student with a number of European history classes among my transcripts I was aware that America had sent soldiers into Russia in 1918. Paul's unusual narratives fit with this knowledge; however, I never got the chance to question him about his stories—the moment was lost. A year after that—Christmas 1973—Paul gave away all of his tools. He died three months later. My life went on; as the years passed, I became a teacher, archaeologist, husband, father, and, ultimately, grandfather. But when I retired from teaching, Paul's stories bubbled back up to haunt me.

Thankfully, by the time I retired, the internet had transformed access to information; I had an easy avenue to pursue Grandpa Paul's stories. I learned

Preface

Paul K. Shreve enlisted on July 7, 1917, and was shipped to France on February 18, 1918, as a private in Company L, 127th National Guard Regiment. His regiment was amalgamated into the 337th Infantry Regiment. Then, the war ended and the 337th Infantry came home. The records were all there; I had physical evidence. Paul served in France during the Great War but did not go to Russia. So why in some of our final conversations had he bared his soul and talked about what only could have occurred in Russia?

I excavated deeper into the archives and discovered 162 men were transferred from Paul's 337th Regiment in September 1918 as replacements for the American regiment that had been sent to northern Russia. And in a further analysis of those 162 doughboys, I learned eight men came from Paul Shreve's Company L! The odds of Paul knowing some or all of these men was quite likely. Thus, the stories Paul told me as we sat on the front porch of his little house were most likely derived from conversations Paul had with these army buddies. Therefore, my initial interest in the men who became the American Polar Bears is based upon a collection of stories told to me by a man who felt it important to share the memories of his friends. Maybe, maybe he was acutely aware of how few people knew about America's Polar Bears and he wanted me to honor their memories? I will never know.

My perspective, however noteworthy, is quite different from those of descendants of those soldiers. All I have are third-person narratives; descendants have both a genetic connection as well as the possibility of oral histories. Sadly, many descendants know little about their family members' involvement in the Russian Revolution, even though they carry within their bones stories of their ancestors' experiences. Fortunately, though, a small collection of descendants is quite active in remembering and honoring their ancestors. One of the most dynamic members of this special community is Mike Grobbel of Shelby Township, Michigan. His connection to the Northern Russian Expedition is through his grandfather, Cpl. Clement Grobbel, Co. I, 339th Infantry. Mike Grobbel is the president of the "Detroit's Own" Polar Bear Memorial Association, a website providing vast amounts of information about the lives and times of the Americans in northern Russia. Mike also is "the keeper of the keys" with access to countless volumes of letters, journals, military records, and photographs, all of which he has graciously made available. Researching and writing this work on the American Polar Bears in Russia could not have been completed without Mike Grobbel's generosity and support.

In closing, my grandfather, a man so special in my heart, may have been more of a fiction storyteller than a spreader of the truth, and I'll never know why he felt it important to speak of northern Russia as he did, but he did, passing on to me the memories of men whose experiences had been silenced by time. Maybe it is as simple as that; Paul believed it was necessary that the sufferings of those doughboys not be forgotten. That's good enough for me. However, there is no doubt Mike Grobbel believes it is vital to keep these ancestors' memories vibrant—his actions speak loudly. I agree with both Grandpa Paul and Mike Grobbel: the memories of our American Polar Bears should be kept alive. This work is my way of saying to both Grandpa Paul and Mike Grobbel that we must honor the lives of these brave Americans.

Introduction

American Polar Bears in Russia: Soldiers of the 339th Infantry and the Archangel Campaign, 1918–1919 is similar to a couple of recently written books about the American involvement in Russia, 1918–1919; however, from that point on, it varies tremendously. Robert L. Willett (2003) and James C. Nelson (2019) have both created solid, "big-picture" histories. They focus on the battlefronts and the fighting—Willett examines America's involvement in both eastern Russia and northern Russia while Nelson only studies the Americans in northern Russia, as he explores the Americans' activities on three battlefronts—the Dvina River, the Emtsa River, and the Railroad front. Willett and Nelson's overall point of view is top-down, though they do include personal accounts as American soldiers battle against the Bolsheviks.

American Polar Bears in Russia provides a detailed description of what life is like for the men on just one of northern Russia's battlefronts—the Railroad front. It will immerse the reader into the soldiers' lives from a ground-level point of view. The weight of this book is carried by the words of the riflemen, NCOs, and officers from Companies I and M of the 339th Infantry. We will listen as these men describe how they felt and what they did, while being trapped in a dangerous and confusing situation, far from home, and seemingly abandoned by their nation.

Though these American soldiers occasionally fight the Bolsheviks, most of the time they are just trying to get enough to eat and to survive an Arctic winter's perilous hardships. But they are Americans, resilient, resourceful and optimistic, raised to deal with problems, and forever hopeful of returning to their families.

Each chapter of *American Polar Bears in Russia* highlights a soldier, focusing on who he is and how he came to be in northern Russia. We'll hear his thoughts, see his reactions, thus giving us the opportunity to wear his combat boots, slog through the mud and snow, struggle to survive the cold, and, finally, battle against hordes of attacking Bolsheviks.

These doughboys wrote about their experiences; unfortunately, not all were good with pen and ink. Many of their passages come with literary shortfalls, and because of this, I have at times been forced to insert identifying words, change tenses, add subjects, modify pronouns, and include relevant punctuation marks. My goal has been to enable easier access to these soldiers' thoughts. Hopefully I have not distorted what they wrote, but if that circumstance occurs, I apologize; that was never my intention. My goal has always been to honor these amazing young men and to give them a voice in how their experiences are to be remembered. In *American Polar Bears in Russia*, it is these soldiers' memories that are most important!

Chapter 1

Camp Custer, Michigan— The 339th Infantry Is Formed

June 28, 1918: First Lieutenant Clarence J. Primm (Co. M) had a problem. The 32-year-old glanced at his cadre of sergeants, milling about, smoking cigarettes and griping to each other. It was late in the afternoon; if the train didn't arrive soon, they would be up late, an unpleasant circumstance. Primm had been in the army for over six months now and in that short time discovered the old adage was true—"hurry up and wait." Originally, he was from South Dakota, the son of Sarah and John Primm, a physician practicing out on the frontier. However, while Primm was still quite young, his family had moved to Door, Illinois, and there, C.J., as he was known, attended primary schools and finished high school. He went to Park College, Illinois, and graduated with high honors.[1] The young scholar continued his education, earning a master's degree from the University of Kansas in political science, economics, and sociology. C.J. took a job as a teacher and soon afterward married Marguerite Christensen, an accomplished 21-year-old woman with a degree from the University of Chicago.[2] The couple moved to New York and in 1913 had a son. Then they moved to Wisconsin, where Primm became the secretary

First Lieutenant Clarence J. Primm earned a master's degree before attending Officer Candidate School (Carol Primm and Peter Stuntz Collection).

for the First Manitowoc Chamber of Commerce. Nonetheless, when America entered the Great War, he kissed Marguerite good-bye, passed the military exam to become an officer, and today, idly stood, waiting for a late-arriving train. This train, which was just one of many of Michigan Central's daily scheduled arrivals at Camp Custer's depot, carried within its passenger cars another batch of young men from Michigan.

These men, draftees and recruits, were coming to Camp Custer ready to be transformed from civilians to soldiers. Camp Custer had been quickly constructed, a massive cantonment named after Michigan's famous Civil War and Indian fighter George Custer. The facility had begun its existence in July 1917 as a collection of hurriedly printed blueprints. It was to be "a national university that takes young men from the farm, the shop and office and in a few short months graduates soldiers ... ready to fight the battles for democracy."[3] Nearly 8,000 construction workers had been transported three and a half miles west of Battle Creek, Michigan, and in six months hammered together a sprawling four-square-mile training center, consuming enough materials to "fill a freight train thirty-six miles long."[4] This base contained nearly 2,000 buildings and had its own water system, sewer system, central heating plant, laundry facilities, and theater that could seat 5,000 as well as miles of paved roads. In effect it was an instantly built modern city.

Michigan's volunteers and draftees were to be housed in barracks capable of quartering 30,000 men and could be fed in mess halls supported by a bakery able to furnish bread for a city of 40,000. Hundreds of acres were allocated for drilling, maneuvers, rifle practice, parades, and playing baseball. A hospital large enough to accommodate 2,200 patients substantiated the fact this military base was prepared for any need the soldiers might have.

Lieutenant Primm's sergeants suddenly looked up; the train was arriving. Soon, it rumbled to a stop, its brakes screeching, amid clouds of hissed steam. The

Camp Custer train depot. Camp Custer could house 30,000 soldiers at a time (Library of Congress).

sergeants clambered aboard the passenger cars, and moments later, bewildered young men poured from the train, herded by the bellowing NCOs; they were "in the Army now"! It did not take long before the disoriented recruits found themselves standing in a rough formation, facing NCOs armed with clipboards and scowls.

These men that were to make up the 339th Infantry Regiment were mainly from Michigan; in fact, so many hailed from Detroit and its suburbs the regiment became known as "Detroit's Own." They were factory workers, auto assembly-line men, clerks, taxi drivers, salesmen, machinists, bartenders, construction workers, railroad linemen, bookkeepers, truck drivers, repairmen, tailors, barbers, students, and farm workers. Though the majority were United States citizens, a sizeable number of these were first-generation Americans; plus, there was a good sprinkling of immigrants—Polish, Swedish, Italian, Norwegian, Danish, Finnish, Greek, and Russian. They spoke a variety of languages as well as attended Catholic, Lutheran, Greek Orthodox, and Jewish houses of worship. In all, the June 1918 recruits being assembled to form the 339th Infantry numbered nearly 5,000 men.[5]

The 339th's trainees arrived all telling the same story; they had received their draft notice to report, said their farewells to loved ones, traveled to Camp Custer by train, and then found themselves facing rough-speaking drill instructors. Trainee George Petropoulos, a 25-year-old immigrant from Greece, remarked, "I got the green card, a notice to be drafted, two weeks before the drafting. Then I got the red card; they give me 24 hours. Next day, I had to go to the courthouse with a bunch of fellows. We took the train to Camp Custer."[6] He, along with countless others, had been ripped from civilian life without regard to their personal states of affairs. Many were like Radus Kemperman (Co. E) of Fremont, Michigan, who noted frankly, "I knew I had to go.... I just simply ... quit my job and left."[7] Others, like Matthew Grahek (Co. M), who would soon be promoted to sergeant due to his leadership and administrative skills, were not happy to have been snatched from their civilian pursuits. The 22-year-old Grahek of Calumet, Michigan, grumbled, "I wouldn't sign up to fight for anybody."[8] For the most part, the young soldiers' sympathies toward going off to war were positive; Russell Hershberger (MG Co.) of Muskegon, Michigan, wrote, "I wanted to get in [before getting drafted] ... but my mother was put in a snitch about it," while James Siplon (Co. I) stated, "I had no objection to being drafted."[9]

James F. Siplon, like many of Michigan's young men arriving at Camp Custer, had tried to get into the military right after America's declaring war on Germany in 1917. Siplon was born February 2, 1896, to Dutch-immigrant parents, Herman and Katherine. James' father worked at an office furniture factory in Muskegon, Michigan, while Katie labored as a housewife and dressmaker, and together the two provided a decent upbringing for James and his two brothers. James finished one year of high school before going to work at Muskegon's Campbell, Wyant and Cannon Foundry, a company bragging it was "the financial rock for thousands."[10] But then, with America's entrance into the Great War, he joined the U.S. Navy. James recalled, "I enlisted in the navy ... when we got to Great Lakes [Naval

Station, Illinois] ... they put us in uniform and ... put us out to drill for a few days." Navy recruit Siplon added, "Then they called us all back in for reexamination.... About half of [us] fellows that were registered for the draft were sent back home." He remarked, "And as they said, the Army will get you anyway."[11] Not long after being dumped by the Navy, Siplon was drafted. His draft registration card identified him as blue-eyed, of medium build, and with brown hair.[12]

The recruits standing before the depot were divided into smaller groups, each to be under the power of an NCO. Many of the young men, their adventure having now begun, looked about in anticipation. The 22-year-old Clement Grobbel (Co. I) of Warren, Michigan, noted, "Arrived safe and sound. Left Detroit at 2 o'clock, the train was ... late. We are going on a big hike tomorrow."[13] Others gawked about, taking in Camp Custer's impressive environs. One draftee, Godfrey Anderson of Grand Rapids, Michigan, recalled, "The train finally halted at the north end where we disembarked at what was called, I believe, the Depot Brigade. This was a large raw-looking unpainted building.... The camp seemed to extend for miles—a veritable city of barracks."[14]

The young men then began their first steps toward becoming soldiers. Fred Kooyers (Co. E) of Muskegon remembered, "We got into Camp Custer about 6 P.M., then we had to begin checking up and taking examinations, signing our names and standing in line until about two o'clock in the morning, then we got our blankets and mess kits and started for our barrack. We walked about a mile to our barracks."[15] Godfrey Anderson added, "Each of us ... was handed a blunt roll in which was tucked various articles including an aluminum mess kit holding a knife, fork and spoon with a cover snapped on and a folding cup." He continued, "We stumbled along like robots in a fog, dead tired, carrying suitcases in one hand and the bedroll over our shoulders." The young recruit resumed his first day's tale: "We were halted in front of an empty barracks off to one side and were herded up a stairway at one end to the second floor.... We were instructed to pick a cot at random.... It had been a long grueling day and everyone was dog tired."[16]

Reveille came early and the soldiers were rousted from their cots. Their day was a busy one, as they were herded from building to building like a bunch of sheep. Recruit Alfred Lewis (Co. M) of Muskegon recalled, "We were ushered into a large hall.... We took seats as directed and the officers up front [began] calling out for volunteers for the different duties ... one was for machine guns—the suicide squad." He continued, "[They asked] did any of [us] drive mules? And [other] various lines of civilian work, and ... men would respond and go up."[17] Another new soldier, Charles Grace (Co. D), added, "[I] talked to the captain ... he asked me what I had done. I told him I'd been in the food line since I was about 13 years old, and I was now 27 ... 'You're going in the kitchen tomorrow morning,' he said.... In a very few days.... I was detailed as a [mess] sergeant."[18]

The 24-year-old Frey Kooyers (Co. E) wrote, "We spent most of our time checking up, telling our past life, vaccinations and insurance."[19] Kooyers reminisced, "We got a lecture about what we couldn't do [and] what we had to do ... what our officers ... could say to us and [that] we couldn't talk back." The raw novice continued, "I then thought of the way the Sergeant swore at us the night we got

The new recruits at Camp Custer line up for vaccinations (*Souvenir*, 1918).

into camp so I asked the officer what we could do.... The officer told me that [the sergeant] had no right to swear at the men. Shortly after he was through talking he told me I would be on K.P. duty the next day."[20] The newly drafted kitchen worker Kooyers added, "I had to go to the officers barracks about 6 A.M. [to] scrub floors, peel potatoes, and wash dishes until about 8 P.M."[21]

Thirty-year-old Alfred Lewis (Co. M) wrote, "[We went through] the preliminaries; hospital shots and vaccinations and such."[22] For Lewis, like many, getting vaccinated in a mass situation was a new experience. He, along with everyone else, was lined up, ordered to roll up his sleeves, and then approached a medical officer, who hammered him with needles. Getting shots, the 23-year-old Hugo Salchow (Co. E) remembered, "was something entirely new for me."[23] Another soldier, bothered by what was happening, remarked, "Boy.... I wish I were home."[24]

Soon, the trainees found themselves standing before drill officers. For many, this was another shock. Godfrey Anderson recalled, "We were lined up for our first drill in charge of a red headed, foul-mouthed sergeant."[25] Another, his comments reflecting an attitude of acceptance, wrote, "The officers took us out ... and just give us that 'squads right and left.'"[26] Fred Kooyers added, "We had to drill about eight hours a day.... I didn't like drill very well."[27]

Fortunately for the new recruits, not long after the men became accustomed to close-order drill, they were issued a M1903 Springfield, a five-round, magazine-fed, bolt action rifle, and marched out to the rifle range. For many of the soldiers, this was the first time they had ever fired a weapon. One of these recruits unfamiliar with a gun was 23-year-old Samuel Safer (Co. E). He was born August 10, 1894, in Wisconsin, his Russian-immigrant parents, Jacob and Ida, having arrived in America barely two years earlier. The Safers moved about, living in Milwaukee, Erie, Buffalo, and, finally, Flint, Michigan. Samuel's parents, like so many Jewish immigrants, scrambled to provide for their six children, yet insisted their kids attend school. Yiddish may have been spoken at home, but English was required for success in America. Samuel completed three years of high school before entering Flint's labor force, getting a job as a salesman, proud to bring cash into the Safer household budget. However, when the United States entered the war, Samuel Safer tried to enlist but was informed by the enlistment board "wait to be drafted." That event came June 27, 1918. Draftee Samuel Safer then entered Camp Custer's massive war-training maul, and when handed a weapon for the first time, he remarked, "I had never fired a rifle in my life."[28]

For others, though, time on the rifle range was enjoyable. Many of the men had grown up with guns in their homes and putting a rifle to one's shoulder was nothing new. New recruit Richard Zank (Co. L) boasted, "We got our guns. I always was a fairly good shot. I was out for rifle practice…. [They said,] 'You don't need any practice; you're good enough.'"[29] For others shooting was no big deal. Alfred Lewis (Co. M) summarized his day, recording, "Up early in the morning … the army is that way … they pushed us through all the tricks; target practice, bayonet drill, gas masks, and the works."[30]

The drilling pace was frantic, leaving the young soldiers little time to rest. Each day they received more of the equipment they would need for the Western Front. Fred Kooyers (Co. E) jotted into his diary, "We got our guns, packs, belts, clothes, and nearly everything we had to have to be equipped for service." He added, "Drilling was a lot harder because we had our packs and guns to drill with."[31] Kooyers also got another taste of unusual-to-him military discipline. He wrote, "We took a long hike with our … packs…. When we first started out the roads were kind of muddy and made the hiking quite hard." Kooyers continued, "They tried … on this hike to see how long we could go without a drink. We carried water with us but we wasn't (sic.) allowed to drink it without the officer's permission. On the way the men kept falling out along the road."[32]

As the days went by, the soldiers began to familiarize themselves with the other men in their company. The 339th was composed of twelve rifle companies—identified A through M—as well as an HQ company, a Supply company, and a Machine Gun company. The twelve rifle companies were divided into three battalions: First Battalion—A, B, C, and D; Second Battalion—E, F, G, and H; and Third Battalion—I, K, L, and M. Each battalion was commanded by a major, 1st BN James Corbley; 2nd BN Jesse Brooks Nichols; and 3rd BN Charles Young, with each company to be led by a captain and supported by five lieutenants.

The soldiers in the Third Battalion came to know their commander, and they quickly grew to dislike Major Charles Young. Private George Yohey (HQ Co.) described his first impression of their battalion commander: "He was a bugger…. When I got out to Camp Custer, he came over for inspection. I looked straight up to the end of the grounds. Out of the corner of my eye, I seen him down there, and he said, 'I'm talking to you…. You're supposed to be standing at attention.'" Yohey added, "I wondered, 'some guy's getting the hell bawled out of him.' 'I'm talking to you' [he said]. I'm looking straight; I say, 'Why you son-of-a-bitch! I'm standing at attention!' It's a wonder he didn't court-martial me."³³ Another enlisted man wrote, "Charles Young was … a rigid disciplinarian, he was hard on men in his command…. He apparently was dissatisfied [with] Pvt. Julius Stalinski … who polished Young's boots…. He was so annoyed with Stalinski that he pulled a gun and threatened to shoot the private unless he improved."³⁴

The Third Battalion's riflemen also were learning about their company commanders, and fortunately, all four captains earned their respect. But of course the men had comments to make about each officer. Horatio Winslow (Co. I) was described as "a noted author [who has] written a lot of books." Michael Donoghue (Co. K), nicknamed "Iron Mike," was known as "one of the toughest leaders." Grant Cherry, Jr. (Co. L) was referred to simply as "our investment banker." And Joel Moore (Co. M) earned the moniker "professor of economics."³⁵

The pace quickened even more and the men rose to the challenge. It was as if everyone knew they would soon be heading to war. They never had a moment to rest, a situation created both by the army's need for more troops and the military's regulations which stated, "men are not permitted to sit about in idleness during drill hours, as this indicates a lack of intelligent plans for the employment of available time."³⁶ Fortunately there was one moment when activity stopped—the playing of "Taps." Many of the troops relished the pomp that went with Camp Custer's nightly retreat. Fred Kooyers (Co. E) wrote, "I didn't mind reveille or retreat, there we had a good band and I always did like music."³⁷ Godfrey Anderson agreed, noting, "The most impressive moment of the day … was at sunset when the troops all over the camp stood at attention in front of their barracks, amid the bugle calls, while the bands played the national anthem and the flags came down."³⁸

The men knew they were preparing to go to France to fight the Germans, a fact constantly drilled into their brains. Their regiment, the 339th, was to be one of four regiments in the 85th Division, a formation scheduled for quick shipment to France. One soldier mentioned their marching chants: "As [we] changed from recruits into fighting units of the 85th Division … the officers and men roared out … 'Keep your head down, you dirty Hun.'"³⁹ Private Roy Tremaine (Co. M) voiced what nearly all his comrades knew to be true: he "thought [he] was going to Germany to fight the Hun."⁴⁰

No one knew when they were going to be shipped to France, though the mess halls and barracks were the hot house of gossip—everyone knew someone who knew. Nonetheless, the more observant soldiers began to notice changes. Private Donald Carey (Co. E) recorded, "The canteen closed last night; trains are loaded and coaches awaiting someone—probably our division."⁴¹ And then the drilling came to a halt and a new wave of frantic activity began. Instructions were given to turn in training materials, clean and sort equipment, pack gear, and police the grounds. Then, it became official; the 339th was leaving Camp Custer on July 14, 1918. Private James Siplon (Co. I), though cognizant of thousands of rumors, was surprised by the suddenness of departure. He remembered, "We thought we'd have our regular sixty days."⁴² But most of the men felt differently from Siplon. Their attitude was summed up by Alfred Lewis (Co. M): "I thought [I was] well-enough prepared."⁴³

Then, July 14, 1918, arrived. Private Fred Kooyers (Co. E) described the chaos in his diary: "We got ready that morning at 6:00 A.M. to board the train.... About nine o'clock A.M. we got our packs on our backs, got out in front of the barracks, and lined up to wait for orders." The 23-year-old continued, "We stood there until about half past ten. Then we took our packs off again and took lunch. About 11:00 A.M. we got ready again, we then would walk a little ways then stop, then walk again, then stop and wait. We did this until 1:00 P.M. We then boarded the train. About 1:30 P.M. the train started moving." Kooyers resumed his story: "Officers then came through the car and gave us lectures, telling us not to put our hands out of the windows, our heads out the windows, or speak or holler to any of the civilians that might be standing at stations where the trains stopped."[44]

Chapter 2

The 339th Heads to the Western Front

July 14, 1918: Captain Horatio G. Winslow glanced over at the 339th's sergeant major, 22-year-old David Van Dusen. The regiment's senior sergeant slapped the thick stack of paper attached to his clipboard and nodded; everyone was loaded aboard Michigan Central's railcars. Captain Winslow smiled. The 36-year-old officer, now acting as the 339th Regiment's adjutant, would now report to Lt. Col. George Stewart and inform him the regiment's equipment and troops were ready for transport to England.[1]

Horatio Winslow was born May 5, 1882, in Madison, Wisconsin, to Agnes and Judge John B. Winslow. Horatio's father, the chief justice of Wisconsin's Supreme Court, was a major player in Wisconsin's Democratic Party as well as a national Progressive-pushing force, aggressive enough that he had caught President Theodore Roosevelt's attention to the point Winslow was on TR's short list for Supreme Court nominee. With a high-ranking judge for a father, Horatio and his brother and four sisters grew up in a mansion in Madison's posh Langdon Street district. Horatio attended the elite private institute the Racine Academy and went on to earn his B.A. from the University of Wisconsin, Madison in 1904. Horatio, though, did not follow in his father's footsteps. The young Winslow had become a prolific writer for the *Wisconsin Alumni Magazine*.[2]

Captain Horatio Winslow (Co. I) had published a number of articles and books before entering the Army (*Detroit Free Press*, 1919).

The judge supported Winslow's choice of writing as a career and supported his son when the young writer ventured away to the publishing capital, New York City. Horatio acquired

15

an apartment in Brooklyn and became the copy editor for the activist magazine *The Masses* and in 1909 published his first book, *Rhymes and Meters: A Practical Guide for Versifiers*.[3] At this time he met a rambunctious young divorcée, Rosalind Guggenheim, who had published enough to simply refer to herself by her pen name—Jane Burr. The two married in 1911.

Winslow published a number of articles in *Munsey's*, a publication with a circulation of as many as 700,000 monthly subscribers, and *The Cavalier*, an edgy publication known for its sophisticated, colorized covers.[4] These publications were front runners in the new world of pulp magazines which sold for ten cents a copy and often had racy covers and lascivious illustrations, along with progressive ideas among their writings, and were "attacked for [their] half-dressed women and undressed statues."[5]

The couple, though, besides supporting themselves with their liberal/progressive writings, also lived what they promoted; they became known as "movers and shakers" in the "Greenwich Village group of artists, writers, and radicals."[6] Sadly, their marriage crumbled and in 1917 the two separated. Thus, when America entered the Great War, Horatio Winslow chose to turn his back on the literary world; he went into the military.

Winslow applied to become an officer, passed the examination and was sent to Ft. Sheridan, Illinois, for Officer Candidate School. He was commissioned a captain upon completion of the course, and in early 1918 he was sent to Camp Custer, where he eventually was slotted as a company commander in the 339th Infantry. And now, acting as the regiment's adjutant, and with his duties for the moment finished, Cpt. Winslow settled into a seat on a train headed east to New York City, the first step in a journey to France.

Winslow's excited men filled the Michigan Central train, exuberant and noisy; they were going to fight the Germans. None had any idea what the future had in store for them, but most were, as Pvt. Floyd Lewis (Co. M) proclaimed, "glad we were on the move." Later, Lewis would admit, "[We] had a lot to learn."[7] For many, the trip east filled their adventurous expectations. Private Godfrey Anderson noted that whenever their train came to a station, "there was an animated flirtation between the loquacious doughboys leaning out of the windows and the pretty girls giggling below."[8] Their train rumbled eastward into the night, and the day's exhilaration melted away. One private complained, "I had to stand up all night because there weren't enough seats to go around."[9]

The 339th's train arrived in New York City in the evening of July 15, 1918. For most of the boys from Michigan and Wisconsin this was their first time to see that famous city, and they were astounded. Anderson remarked, "I ... [was] completely dumbfounded, gaping spellbound at the magnificent scene."[10] The regiment's troops unloaded and crowded onto a ferry. They arrived on Long Island, and there, the men ended up doing nothing but waiting. The disgruntled 1st Sgt. Walter Dundon (Co. M) was not impressed. He recorded, "Arrived at Weehawken at 6:00 p.m. Took ferry to Long Island City at 6:30 p.m. Long delay there."[11] Finally, the regiment was transferred to their next location, Camp Mills, arriving at 1:30 a.m.

The men of the 339th wait to board transports to France, like millions of other American soldiers (U.S. Army Signal Corps).

Camp Mills was a massive tent city that originally had been used as a training facility for many New York divisions. However, once that first wave of troops had been shipped to France, the base become the main hub for transient troops being sent to the Western Front. Private Fred Kooyers (Co. E) recorded in his diary, "Camp Mills was a canvas city."[12] However, besides drill, there was little for the young men to do; the camp was over twenty miles from New York City and only officers or individuals with "pull" were able to wrangle passes. The regiment went into motion on July 20, 1918. That morning, before 4 o'clock, the men received orders to load their barracks bags, clean their equipment one last time, and ready themselves for transport. They marched to Long Island's depot, boarded ferries, cruised New York's harbor, and ended up at Hoboken's Pier 61. Private Kooyers scratched into his diary, "We arrived at the big dock where the Red Cross girls gave us ice cream ... we hadn't had anything to eat from 4:00 A.M."[13]

The 339th Infantry loaded its nearly 5,000 men onto three troopships, the U.S.S. *Plattsburg*, the U.S.S. *Northumberland*, and the U.S.S. *Harrisburg*. Captain Horatio Winslow, still acting as the regimental adjutant, went aboard the *Plattsburg*, along with Lt. Col. George Stewart and the rest of the headquarters personnel. Meanwhile, Winslow's Company I, under the command of 1st Lt. Albert May, plus the other companies of the Third Battalion, K, L, and M, tramped onto the *Harrisburg*. In Company M, Cpt. Joel Moore found himself berthed in a first-class cabin, while his lieutenants bunked together in another cabin. Moore's first sergeant, Walter Dundon, was assigned a single room; meanwhile, the rest of the company, 237 enlisted men and corporals, were all housed in third-class chambers.[14]

First Sergeant Dundon recorded, "Embarked on *U.S.S. Harrisburg* (the old *Philadelphia*) converted into an armored transport."[15] Then, the anxious-to-travel soldiers waited impatiently for their ship to push away from its pier and head for France. Private Kooyers (Co. E) grumbled, "We layed (*sic*) in [the] harbor until the next night."[16] Kooyers and the rest of the 339th's restless doughboys were not aware the Navy was assembling a convoy of ships to transport the entire 85th Division (the Custer Division), a force of nearly 30,000 men. The 339th Infantry's brother regiments, the 337th, 338th, and 340th Infantry, also filled troopships.

In all, the convoy would entail at least fifteen transport ships, a handful of battleships and cruisers, and a number of supporting vessels.[17]

The convoy steamed out of Hoboken on July 22, 1918, the ships' decks crammed with excited young men who watched as they passed the Statue of Liberty and then as they left the American skyline behind. Private Anderson recorded their movement, writing, "[We] were spread out in a formation occupying perhaps a square mile ... [with] two destroyers [keeping] pace with us."[18] The troop convoy sailed into the night. The men lined up for meals and were quick to discover the food was not to their liking. Private Frank Douma (Co. D), like countless others, griped, "The chow is rotten."[19] Then, with nothing else to do, the soldiers settled into their sleeping quarters. Some soldiers lucked out to have bunks while others had to sleep in hammocks; either way, though, the enlisted men were crowded together. Those men who suffered from seasickness packed the toilet facilities—"heads," the sailors called them. Soon, horrible odors filled their living quarters. Private Anderson wrote, "The odor below ... was disgusting."[20]

The hours passed slowly as the convoy sailed eastward. Frank Douma scribbled in his diary, "The bunks are fairly good.... I spent most of my time reading."[21] Others took refuge from the horrible smells below deck by taking their turn above deck. There was little to see, except watch the other ships in the convoy cut through the ocean's dark waters. First Sergeant Dundon recorded, "Sailed for England.... Navy protection tight." The ships passed through a summer storm that lasted for two days, July 26 and 27, 1918.[22] The turbulent waters caused many a doughboy to spew his meals, adding to the wretched stench permeating the enlisted men's compartments.

A few days later, on August 2, 1918, the sighting of a German submarine put the convoy's fighting ships into action. First Sergeant Dundon remarked, "All up and in boat drill position at 3:30 a.m. ... our sub-chasers evidently caught a submarine with depth charges."[23] Another Michigan soldier recorded, "A submarine was sighted, and our sub-chasers opened fire, giving 16 large boatloads of 'Green Yankees' their first experience with the 'Big Noise.'"[24] Then, the excitement ended. Private Anderson wrote, "Presently all was quiet again and we returned to the foredeck."[25]

The next day, August 3, 1918, the 339th's ships filed into Liverpool's harbor. Lieutenant George Stoner (Co. M) recorded the event, writing, "Dropped anchor at 7:30 AM."[26] Frank Douma (Co. D) noted, "There was a great reception for us in Liverpool. We paraded through the city and heard some very beautiful chimes in one of the largest churches as we passed."[27] Fred Kooyers (Co. E) added, "We paraded down the streets of Liverpool ... we were met by the Red Cross, we had cup cakes and coffee."[28] The 339th's men, once at the train station, climbed into the railcars, which rattled out of Liverpool and into the English countryside, following a route to a destination near the grounds outside Stoney Castle—Camp Aldershot. Douma recorded, "reached Camp [Aldershot] at 10:00 P.M. ... it is quite cold. We had small tents to sleep in without floors."[29] Private Anderson added, "There were no cots supplied and we spread our blankets on the bare ground and established ourselves as best we could."[30]

2. The 339th Heads to the Western Front 19

Camp Aldershot was a large tent city 32 miles outside of London (courtesy R.B. Layton Postcard Collection, Oakville Images).

The men formed for breakfast the next morning and received their next culture shock; British food was different from American. First Sergeant Dundon wrote, "First taste of British army rations. 'Baa Baa, old sheep.'"[31] Drill came next, which was followed by a long march. Private Douma noted in his diary on August 6, 1918, "We drilled from 7:30 to 11:30 and we hiked from 1:00 P.M. to 4:15." The young soldier also noted, "The roses in this country are the most beautiful I have ever seen."[32] The evening meal and the day's concluding ceremonial formation ended their activities.

The Michigan and Wisconsin soldiers bedded down, taking with them thoughts about their upcoming transfer to France. The U.S. Army, though, had other plans for the boys of the 339th Infantry. The army, acting upon decisions made by President Wilson and the State Department, required troops to be sent to northern Russia, and the 339th was culled out of the 85th Division as that unit. On August 16, 1918, a decree ordered that "winter clothing will be supplied ... [and] any American equipment now in the possession of the [339th Infantry], and not required, will be handed in at Aldershot ... [and] Russian rifles will be issued."[33]

The 339th's men did not know what was ahead. Instead, they got up each day, drilled, and went on lengthy endurance marches. Private James Siplon (Co. I) wrote, "Training was awfully hard, you know; close-order drill, bayonet drill, and the ten-mile hike every afternoon with your gas mask on, and a full steel helmet and full pack—about forty pounds." Siplon continued, "It was right in July ... and about ninety degrees ... and men were falling out like leaves.... They'd send a truck out behind ... and pick them up."[34] Godfrey Anderson also recalled their long marches, writing, "We would be marching along ... singing one of those ribald obscene songs such as soldiers have sung from time immemorial, when, rounding a turn, we would unexpectedly run into some small hamlet." He continued, "Immediately the officer shouted 'attention' and we marched thru the village in silence, only to resume the bawdy songs when we had passed through it."[35]

With drills complete and the day's marches finished, the young men sought the oh-so-coveted liberty passes to London. One of the lucky fellows to get a pass, Pvt. Frank Douma (Co. D), reminisced, "Got a pass for London ... we visited Westminster Abbey, Buckingham Palace, [the] Royal Stables, and The Strand. We had supper at Eagle Hut and went to the Gaiety Theatre [a theater excelling in burlesque] in the evening."[36] Private Fred Kooyers (Co. E) bragged, "We walked around London ... to Hyde Park. There we met a bunch of British girls ... we celebrated with them.... I arrived in Stoney Castle about 4:00 A.M. ... [I] didn't get much sleep that night."[37]

The excursions to London of 1st Lt. George Stoner (Co. M), while similar to those of the enlisted men, differed in that he had access to high society. Stoner recorded, "Left for London 1 P.M. Met Earl of Meath. Visited House of Parliament, West Minister Abbey. [I Watched] Chu Chin Chow ... [and] stayed at the Washington Inn."[38] The play Lt. Stoner attended, *Chu Chin Chow*, was greatly attended by troops on leave from the Western Front. One of this performance's attractions for the on-leave soldiers was its chorus of pretty, scantily clad young women. Complaints about the show, though never from the soldiers, resulted in the Lord Chamberlain (the British theater censor) viewing it and wishing "this naughtiness" to be stopped, which, of course, did not happen.[39]

The soldiers returned to Stoney Castle and Camp Aldershot for more drill and more marching. Private Floyd Lewis (Co. M) wrote, "The countryside seemed to me was divided up into small sectors of farms, each with its own produce or products; giving it different colors—sort of an interesting patchwork."[40] Private Cleo Colburn (Co. I) agreed, writing, "England was a beautiful country, especially their architectural design ... of masonry construction—mostly vine-covered. Beautiful, beautiful homes."[41]

And for those fortunate ones to get another pass to London, they returned to camp with more stories. Private Rudolph Marxer (Co. E) whined, "They had no ice in England. We had to drink that warm ale," while Frank Douma (Co. D) boasted, "[I] was in the finest saloon there. The bar tenders were all girls. Women drink in the saloon the same as men and also smoke a great deal."[42] Meanwhile Pvt. William Robbins (Co. I) came back with a great tale: "[Me] and a buddy were out and about seeing the sights of the city when a commotion was heard. 'The King is coming!' 'Bow, the King is coming!'" He continued, "Down the street came the King [in a vehicle]. [Me] and [my] friend knew that Americans bow to no king; however, [we] wished to be respectful and were in uniform, so as the regent approached, [we] saluted. King George V leaned out his window and returned the salute to [us]."[43] Finally, 1st Lt. Clarence Primm summed up the Americans' experiences in London, writing, "we were treated most cordially by the English everywhere and enjoyed our stay there. London is the same as New York in its habit of separating one from [his] money."[44]

Back in camp, the soldiers began to suspect something was amiss. Private Jan Sarosiek (Co. K) stated, "I come (*sic*.) here from [the] old country [Russia].... [One] morning [the captain] ... says, 'Turn in your rifles!' So, [we] turn in all [our] rifles. I see [a] wagon come, and I see [Russian lettering] on it. I say to top sergeant, 'Sarge, I bet you I can tell you now where we go.' He says, 'What the hell you know? Sure thing, they open that box and all of them were Russian rifles."[45]

The rifle exchange began in one company and spread to all twelve. First Sergeant Dundon (Co. M), when his company took its turn to hand in their American weapons, simply recorded, "Drill and drawing new equipment for Russia."[46] These Mosin-Nagant 7.62 mm rifles the Yanks were getting, ironically, were American made. First Lieutenant Harry Costello (MG Co.) reported, "[The] Mosin-Nagant 7.62 rifles—guns made in America, purchased by the ... Czar, and stored near Aldershot, [were] awaiting shipment to the Russian Imperial Army."[47] Lieutenant John Cudahy (Co. B), after watching his platoon struggle with the Russian equipment, remarked, "The[se] clumsy rifles that had been intended for Russian hands were long, awkward pieces, with [a] flimsy, bolt mechanism, that frequently jammed."[48] This development angered the doughboys, especially when they discovered these weapons' faults on the target range. Private John Peatling (Co. F) grumbled, "When we got the clips, the bullets, you couldn't put them down in from your clip. You had to take them out of the clip and put them in one-by-one."[49] Lastly, not only did the Americans dislike these rifles, but they also objected to the accompanying Russian bayonet. One soldier griped, "As [we] ... took hold of the[se] inferior rifles [we] were issued substandard corkscrew bayonets that did not serve a practical purpose."[50]

The Russian rifles provided a major hint the 339th was not going to France. Private Donald Carey (Co. E), like so many of his comrades, objected, saying, "What was the object of equipping American troops with such a rifle? Were we to fight alongside the Russians against the Huns?"[51] Regardless of the Americans' concerns the evidence of a Russian deployment continued to grow. This was followed by another clue. Lieutenant Costello, along with the rest of the 339th's officers, saw explicit foreshadowing when they were called to a regimental officers' meeting. He recorded, "Then the great hint came. It happened in the most casual way. It was merely an announcement that Sir Ernest Shackleton, the Antarctic explorer, was to deliver a series of lectures to us on how to care for ourselves in the Arctic regions."[52]

On August 18, 1918, the news became official; the 339th was being deployed to Russia. The men were dismayed. Captain Joel Moore wrote, "[My men were] keenly disappointed. We were ... told in England that we were not to join our Americans comrades who were fighting 'Fritz.'"[53] Private Levi Bartels (Co. K) complained, "[We] thought we were going to France.... We was counting on it.... [They] kept it a secret.... We was just kept dumb you might say ... we was like a bunch of sheep."[54] And Pvt. Albert "AJ" Slaugh (Co. D) stoically summed up their situation, remarking, "We were supposed to go to France.... I guess ... they didn't need us."[55]

The 339th's camp became one of frenzied activity. The companies spent more time on the rifle range, the men trying to zero their Russian rifles in at ranges of 200 and 300 yards. Then, on August 19, 1918, everyone was paid, and following that, the next few days were spent packing.[56] A few days later, the 339th Regiment formed up, marched to the rail station and boarded train cars. Private Fred Kooyers (Co. E) recorded in his diary, "August 25—Left Stoney Castle 8:30 A.M."[57] Private John Toornman (Co. G) added, "We got on the train and they locked us in—eight in each partition. [We] couldn't get out."[58] Kooyers continued, "Stopped at Doucaster, 3:30 P.M. Got to York at 4:00 P.M. Took supper with the Red Cross."[59] The trains continued to roll northward, reaching Newcastle. Here, the soldiers exited their train and climbed aboard ships. With that, their time in England had come to an end. First Lieutenant George Stoner simply recorded in his diary, "August 27, 1918—Convoy left at 5 P.M."[60]

Chapter 3

Why America Sent Troops to Russia

August 27, 1918: Colonel George E. Stewart stood before a contingent of his regiment's officers, his subordinates waiting for him to explain why the 339th was going to Russia and not to France. Everyone wrestled uneasily with this question, and its uncertainty troubled the entire regiment. Stewart, born August 2, 1872, in New South Wales, Australia, was a freshly minted colonel, with the date of his commission July 30, 1918.[1] He had grown up not far from Sydney, Australia, living in a lower-middle class neighborhood, his father making ends meet as a gardener. The young Stewart was not the best student in grade school, as he much preferred the outdoors, and once out of high school, he worked at odd jobs until 1890. Then, at the age of eighteen, the young man immigrated to America, landing in New York City.[2]

Colonel George E. Stewart was awarded the Medal of Honor for his actions in the Philippines in 1899 (Library of Congress).

The inexperienced immigrant knocked around New York City, taking odd jobs whenever he could, but he never seemed to get ahead. Seeing his prospects not matching his aspirations, Stewart, in October 1896, joined the U.S. Army and ended up as a private in Battery A, 5th Artillery. Private Stewart served in the battery with such distinction that when the Spanish American War began, he applied for an officer's position, and in April 1899, he was commissioned second lieutenant in the 19th U.S. Infantry.[3] Though the war with Spain did not last long, the situation in the Philippines

23

escalated into a full-blown conflict. Lieutenant Stewart, along with the 19th Infantry, was shipped to Manila in July 1899.

The Philippine insurgency was a very frustrating one for the American leadership. The Philippine fighters knew they could not match the U.S. Army's firepower, so they adapted a strategy of guerrilla warfare, one of ambush and hit and run. Lieutenant Stewart's company was tasked with patrolling the jungle, hunting for the elusive Filipinos, warding off ambushes, and trying to pin the guerrillas down long enough to destroy their combat abilities. Eventually Stewart's company found itself on a large island south of Manila's mainland—Panay. The region had just been battered by a seasonal typhoon that had washed out most of the area's roads as well as swelled all the rivers by as much as ten feet.[4] On November 26, 1899, Lt. Stewart's company pushed through the jungle not far from the village of Passi. The Americans came to the debris-choked and swollen Jalaur River and began fording the dangerous river. Filipino fighters on the opposite bank opened fire, their ambush brutally effective. A number of Americans were shot down before they could pull back to safety. One soldier, wounded and helpless, began to drown in the river's angry currents. George Stewart, ignoring the ambushers' machine gun and rifle fire, "plunged in and at the imminent risk of his own life, saved from drowning" the enlisted man. This feat of heroism earned 2d Lt. George E. Stewart the Medal of Honor.[5]

Lieutenant Stewart's company remained in the Philippines for the next two years, as the conflict slowly ground to a halt, and during this time he was promoted to first lieutenant. Then, once the army began sending troops home, the young officer was transferred to the 15th Infantry, a formation tasked with, as the official bulletins announced, "a pacification campaign called 'Policy of Attraction.'" He remained stationed in Manila, and for the next five years, he lead a platoon that did little more than guard American interests. Two years later Stewart, now a captain, met Elizabeth Wildman, the 38-year-old ex-wife of a Signal Corps officer. The isolated world of American officers and their wives in Manila was a small one, and when the two married in 1910, Stewart's future no longer glowed with the brightness his Medal of Honor had provided. Stewart was transferred from his company to the Quartermaster Corps, and this posting was eventually followed by reassignment to a military facility in Alaska. Stewart remained in Alaska until the United States declared war on Germany in 1917, and with that development, the army needed officers who had combat experience. Even though George Stewart had not led men into combat in sixteen years, in May 1917, he was promoted to major, and three months later, he was promoted to lieutenant colonel. Stewart was sent to Camp Custer and placed as second in command of the 339th Infantry. However, once the 339th Infantry's rosters were filled out, its original colonel, John W. Craig, was assigned elsewhere, leaving Stewart the senior officer. He was promoted to colonel and now, as his regiment steamed toward Russia, he stood before his officer corps to explain why they were not going to France.

The 339th Infantry was being shipped to northern Russia due to a handful of reasons, and these all revolved around the fact that Russia had withdrawn from the Great War. The Treaty of Brest-Litovsk on March 3, 1918, had been, as one American diplomat remarked, "a staggering blow to the Allies."[6] America's ambassador to Russia, David R. Francis, was quick to realize the Bolshevik regime (the leadership replacing the Kerensky government, which had replaced the czar's leadership) had no intentions of assisting the Allies and possibly was making plans to help the Germans. The Allies had been aiding the czar in his struggle against the Germans by shipping millions of dollars of supplies and munitions to Russia, and most of these war materials had arrived at Russia's two northern ports—Archangel and Murmansk. No one was certain what was going to happen to the military stores that sat in these cities. However, one fact was clear to the Allies: if they did nothing, those supplies would fall into the wrong hands. Therefore, the Allied Supreme Command at Versailles concluded that troops must be sent to Russia as a protection against German interests and as insurance against Bolshevik actions.

Archangel's port, Bakharitza, which because of its geographical location was only open during a few months of the year, had large numbers of massive warehouses, all of which had been filled with Allied supplies. America, Great Britain, and France had filled these storehouses with, as a diplomat noted, "in 1918 [alone] ... over two million tons [of supplies]."[7] The United States' contributions totaled millions of dollars in guns and equipment. A good amount of these supplies had been transported by railroad to Moscow but much still remained in Archangel. Ambassador Francis recorded, "[The Allies] shipped 210,000 rifles and 16,000,000 cartridges ... [with] 110,000 rifles remain[ing] in Archangel."[8] The Allies' conclusion was simple: troops had to be sent to Archangel to protect these valuable supplies.

Protection of property was something that the average American understood. When the 339th officers explained this as a reason for deployment in Russia, most of the enlisted men accepted this rationale. Private Joseph Sauter (Co. K) remarked, "We got orders that we're going up there [Archangel] to guard supplies. They had warehouses there, 300 feet long, 100 feet wide, 20 feet to the top ... all filled."[9] And the simple comment by Pvt. Will Rowers (Co. H) summed up what many of his comrades took to heart: "We were told ... we were going to Russia, they said it was to do guard duty."[10]

The Allies were also aware that Germany was considering sending troops to Finland. Ambassador David Francis believed he had intel supporting this knowledge and proclaimed, "The Germans will doubtless advance promptly with all [the] force [they] can command."[11] If German troops seized Murmansk, they would have gained access to a modern shipping port, a well-built rail system leading out of the city, and easy passage to any part of Russia. One Allied intelligence officer reported, "As the Allies had built this port from scratch to supply the Russian troops on the Eastern Front, they knew [all] too well of its critical importance and were not about to surrender the port."[12] Murmansk also contained sheltered locations perfect for submarine docks. German subs operated in the area, attacking transport ships traveling between the British Isles and France. A protected German submarine base centered around Murmansk would further hinder Allied supply movements. These facts left the Allies no alternative; they had to protect Murmansk. Private James Siplon (Co. I) agreed, writing, "We were protecting these ports to keep the Germans out [and] to keep their submarines from having bases in the White Sea and in the northern part of Russia."[13]

The Allied Supreme Command also had hopes of getting the Russians to return to the war. Ambassador David Francis, who had been close to the czar's political circle, realized that there were many Russians who had not wanted to surrender to Germany. Ambassador Francis cherished the belief it might be possible for the Allies to rebuild a Russian army and re-attack Germany. Francis wrote, "Sending American troops would provide support to millions of sensible Russian who only need encouragement to organize against the Bolsheviks." He added a warning: "[If] Allied troops [retreat], [it] will encourage thousands of Russians ... [to remain] inactive and permit Germany to ... gain a secure foothold."[14] Lieutenant Clarence Primm (Co. M) considered his ambassador's statements and concluded, "It seemed imperative for the success of the allies that the eastern front again be made active. A reorganized eastern front would cause Germany to withdraw some of the divisions massed on the western front."[15] Surprisingly, many Allied leaders were giddy with the thought of Russia re-opening the Eastern Front, and a number of senior officers let optimism outplay reality. One British officer proclaimed, "We'll just rush up there and re-establish the great Russian army—reorganize the vast forces of the Tsar."[16]

The Allied leaders also had to consider the Czecho-Slovakian situation. When the Russians signed the treaty at Brest-Litovsk, nearly 60,000 Czech-Slovak soldiers occupied positions deep within Russia, where they had fought the Central Powers' advances originating from Turkish-Ottoman lands. However, with Russia out of the war, these soldiers wanted to return home. Captain Joel Moore (Co. M) summarized this situation, recording, "Several thousand Czecho-Slovak troops formerly on the Eastern Front had been held there after the dissolution of the last Russian offensive in 1917.... These troops had desired to go back to their own country or to France and take part in the final campaign against the Germans." Moore continued, "Negotiations with the Bolshevist rulers of Russia ... brought promises of safe passage westward across central Russia and then northward to Archangel, thence by ship to France."[17] The Allied high command, though, sought to gain advantage from this situation; they planned to use this Czech-Slovak force as the core of their reorganized Russian army. Lieutenant Primm contemplated these designs, writing, "The Allied Supreme War Council urged a plan whereby an allied expedition of respectable size ... would be sent to Archangel early in 1918. This expedition would meet the Czechs, re-organize and re-equip them, rally about them a large North Russian army, and then proceed southward to re-open an eastern front against Germany."[18] President Woodrow Wilson, who had originally opposed involving Americans, eventually agreed to allow doughboys to be sent to Russia, though he argued "the only justifiable reason for entering Russia ... would be to ... consolidate the [czarist] forces, and to steady any effort at self-government or self-defense."[19] Private Alfred Larson (Co. D), when he learned this news, recalled, "There were stories about ... another army [in] ... Vladivostok and they ... would meet somewhere along the line. And then we would combine our forces."[20]

Finally, the last reason why the 339th Infantry sailed for northern Russia was pretty basic—the French and British no longer had any extra men. The British and French losses in four years of war had been so massive that no one was left. Captain Moore recorded, "A survey of the military resources of the European Allies had disclosed their utter lack of men for such an expedition and it was found that the only hope lay in drawing the bulk of the needed troops from the United States." Moore continued, "The French were able to send only part of a regiment, one battalion of Colonial troops and a machine gun company ... and the total number of British officers and men ... was less than 1,200."[21]

Immediately after President Wilson committed American troops to the Russian intervention, the British scraped together a small force and, buttressed by a strong show of naval forces and a platoon of American sailors, landed these men in Murmansk. The results were instantaneous; the Bolshevik government in northern Russia collapsed. Captain Moore recorded, "The arrival of [Allied] troops at the Murmansk coast, together with the promise of further to immediately follow, was to influence the Russian local government of the state of Archangel to break with the hated Reds. And so, on August 1st, a quiet *coup d'état* was effected.... The Provisional North Russia Government was organized."[22] Then, on August 2, 1918, a contingent of Allied troops landed in Archangel. Ambassador Francis wrote, "His majesty's Government have received a communication from ... [Archangel] reporting the city was occupied by British troops on August 2 without casualties."[23]

The Allied convoy's route took them into the North Atlantic, where they rounded Norway, and from there they steamed into the Barents Sea. Though the calendar stood at late August, the weather in these northern latitudes was already approaching winter. Lieutenant Clarence Primm recorded, "Outside it is cold and the sea is grey. The men of the guard are dancing on the deck to keep their blood circulating." The first lieutenant did admit, "Our salon is comfortable and light; green felt covers on the tables between meals. Cards, smoking and chess."[24] Unfortunately for the 339th's enlisted men this journey was not one of salons, felt-covered tables, and games of chess. For them, conditions grew bitter. The North Sea was frigid and rough, and freezing rain squalls and cold, biting wind assaulted any topside Yank. Private Alfred Larsen (Co. D) grumbled, "They put the infantrymen out on the boat, on guard. We were on iceberg guard duty—looking for icebergs."[25] Meanwhile, conditions inside the ship had deteriorated. The crowded conditions below deck, combined with the Arctic weather's influence on the North Sea, produced disaster. Private Rudolph Marxer (Co. E) wrote, "It was rough. Up and down ... [the boat] was a cork in the water. It was a rough affair." Marxer continued, "[We had] a catcher for Connie Mack's baseball team in Philadelphia, and he was a great big burly guy. I don't think he ate two meals the whole time we were on that damn boat.... He couldn't keep it down."[26] This fellow, Pvt. William Meyers (Co. L), had batted .235 in 62 games for the Philadelphia Athletics in 1917, but the army had other plans for him. He was drafted in early 1918 and now was headed to Russia.[27]

Private Godfrey Anderson, now a member of the 337th Field Hospital, the medical unit assigned to support Col. Stewart's regiment, noticed something else, something insidiously more serious than seasickness. Private Anderson observed, "[The] bunks were occupied by soldiers desperately ill, with raging fevers, [while] others lay on stretchers, the breathing of all a rasping wheeze."[28] The Spanish flu had swept over the ships like a choking cloud of smoke, taking down the soldiers in massive numbers. Private Floyd Lewis (Co. M) remembered, "Most everybody was coming down sick.... Our first sergeant would come down to announce sick call about nine o'clock in the morning, and more and more of [us] responded ... he would sound-off with, 'If any of you fellows are just gold-bricking, you're gonna (sic.) get double K.P.'"[29] Another rifleman, Pvt. Fred Kooyers (Co. E), said, "I know I was sick—half the time laying under the bunk." He added, "A doctor would come see you if they found you, but there was so many of us that half the time they didn't know where we were."[30] Captain Joel Moore (Co. M) recorded, "On the *Somali* ... every available bed was full on the fifth day out to sea. Congestion was so bad that men with temperatures of only 101 or 102 were not put into the hospital ... [and] to make matters worse, on the eighth day out all the flu medicines were exhausted."[31] Private Rudolph Marxer (Co. E) observed, "All we had was scotch whiskey. And ... [it could] cure a lot on the fly. That's what we did about three times a day."[32] Then, as the influenza ate its way through the soldiers, some began to die. Private Floyd Lewis (Co. M) recalled, "I said to the sergeant, 'Sir, we've got one fellow over here that isn't responding.' So [the first sergeant] right away got the aides rounded up and they got him out of there."[33] Private Alfred Larsen (Co. D) remembered, "There was also [an] Italian boat following along with us and we could see those guys going overboard every once in a while. They died, you know."[34] The 339th also suffered deaths aboard the ships. Private Albert Slaught (Co. D) recorded, "We had the flu.... There [were] three hundred sick on [our] boat ... [and] no medicine, nothing ... [so] some died," and Pvt. Levi Bartels (Co. K) observed, "Some [died of] the flu at the time. They dumped them overboard."[35] Medic Charles Simpson (337th Field Hospital) also noticed this sad fact: "The large plank is raised to the side-rail, your Buddy, draped in the American flag, slides from the plank into the ocean and the ship sails on.... Thank goodness there were but few funerals at sea."[36]

By the time the convoy entered the White Sea, over five hundred American soldiers had been stricken. Sadly, the *Somali* and the Italians' ship, the *Tsar*, suffered the worst.[37] However, now, as the troops ships slowly approached Dvina Bay and the port of Archangel, with "all bunks occupied by soldiers desperately ill, with raging fevers," the journey to Russia was coming to an end.[38] It was time for the Yanks to step foot on Russian soil, and it was time for Col. George Stewart to command his Americans in battle.

Chapter 4

First American Troops in Russia

September 4, 1918: Captain Joel R. Moore listened to the reports about American sailors in need of rescue. The 39-year-old was born July 2, 1879, to Emma and William Moore, a fairly prosperous couple who owned a grist mill in Litchfield, Michigan. Joel, like his three brothers, attended local schools. Joel discovered he relished competition, and even though he was not a big guy, the young man was lanky and agile. He excelled in track, football, and baseball. Plus, he possessed a skill for motivating, tutoring, and leading his teammates. Joel did well in school; thus, when he graduated from high school, the young scholar immediately enrolled at Albion College, Illinois.

Captain Joel R. Moore was a college instructor before the war (National Archives).

Joel went on to earn a degree in economics in 1908 and took a position as an assistant lecturer in the economics department at the University of Illinois as well as commenced a master's degree in economics. He would publish his thesis "Taxation of Corporations in Illinois" in 1914.[1] Joel Moore met the 25-year-old Mabel Olmstead and the two married in 1904. Mabel gave birth to a daughter two years later but, sadly, the infant died. Unfortunately, the pay at the University of Illinois was barely enough for survival, forcing Joel to seek employment elsewhere. He secured a teaching position at Great Falls High School, Montana, where he taught three history classes and coached the football team. Though he did well at Great Falls, the district did not renew his contract,

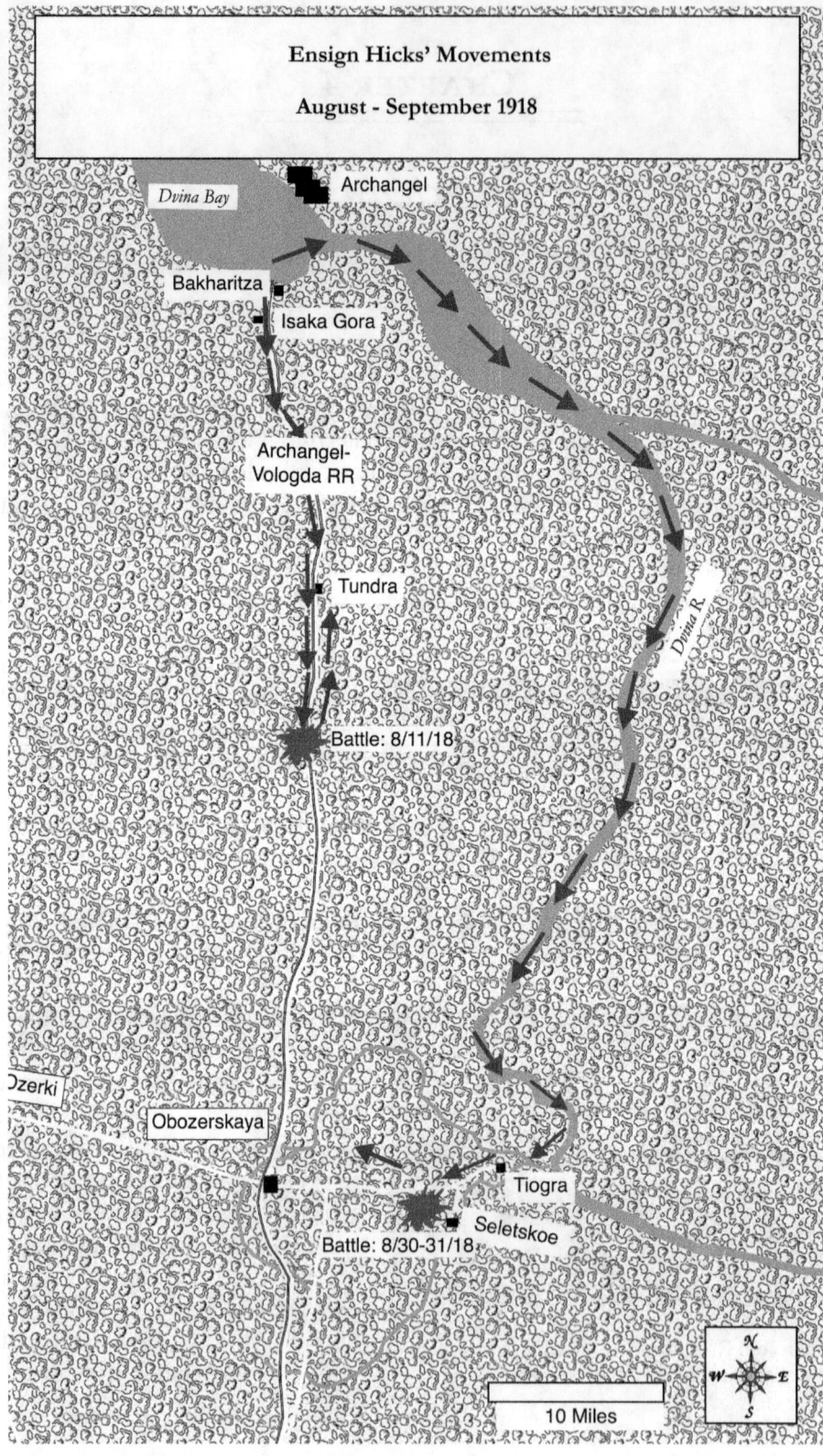

sending the Moores packing. Joel landed an instructor's slot at La Crosse State Teachers' College, Wisconsin, and was a coach for the school's football team.[2]

America's entry into the Great War on April 2, 1917, meant millions of young men would soon receive draft notices. Joel Moore, knowing the army's need for officers, applied for the officers' examination on May 2, 1917, a day before he was required to register for the draft. Moore's application was approved a week later, and he was ordered to Ft. Sheridan, Illinois, for Officer Candidate School. Three months later, August 6, 1917, Moore was commissioned captain. He was sent to Camp Custer, Michigan, and assigned to lead the 339th Infantry's Company M.[3] And now, as the *Somali* pulled into the docks at Bakharitza, Cpt. Moore gathered his lieutenants around him to discuss the military situation as it had been relayed to him.

The soldiers of the 339th Infantry were not the first American soldiers to step onto North Russian soil, and that was one reason why Col. Stewart and Third Battalion commander Maj. Charles Young were in such a hurry to get their men off the ship. A group of American sailors was trapped by the Bolsheviks and in danger of being wiped out. It would be the Third Battalion's immediate mission to rescue them. A month earlier, two dozen American sailors from the U.S.S. *Olympia* had stepped ashore. The leader of this band of sailors was 27-year-old ensign Donald M. Hicks, a young sailor assigned aboard the 5,580-ton cruiser. Hicks' ship steamed into Dvina Bay and on August 2, 1918, detached Ensign Hicks and twenty-five sailors, tasking them with dealing with the Bolsheviks. Ensign Hicks quickly organized transportation for his men, securing an old wood-burning locomotive the Bolsheviks had left behind with two flatcars attached to it. His sailors piled sandbags onto the flatcars to create breastworks, and armed with rifles and two Lewis machine guns, as Clarence Primm recorded, they "gave immediate chase to the Bolsheviks down the railroad."[4] They caught up with a Bolshevik train near the village of Issaka Gorka, a few miles south of Archangel, and in a quick exchange of gunfire routed a group of Russians. The Bolsheviks fled, with the Americans in close pursuit, both sides moving so quickly the Bolsheviks could not get an opportunity to destroy a bridge or trestle and delay the pursuers.

The Americans were slowed thirty miles south of Archangel near the village of Tundra. This situation gave the Bolsheviks enough time to get away from Hicks' band. The Americans fixed their problem and resumed pursuit. The Bolsheviks, though, had enough time to set fire to a trestle spanning a gulch forty miles further south and damaged it enough that when the Americans arrived the span was uncrossable. The Bolsheviks also had assembled an armed force that opened fire upon Hicks' approach, forcing the small detachment of sailors to dismount from their train. The sailors took cover and fired back but their wild ride southward had been halted. Later, Joel Moore would record, "[Hicks] went on foot, reaching the bridge ... and in the exchange of gunfire ... receiv[ed] ... a wound in the leg."[5] The Americans soon realized they were greatly outgunned. Then, just as the Bolsheviks were beginning to press forward and outflank Hicks' sailors, a group of French soldiers arrived to bolster their defense.[6] This combined French-American force stalled the Bolshevik assault. Ensign Hicks, knowing their puny flatcar with its piles of sandbags offered little protection from the heavier Russian weapons, ordered the Americans to retreat. They traveled back to Tundra, arriving that evening. From there, Hicks sent off a telegraph message, stating, "Arrival of railway detachment at Tundra Station at 10:45 P.M. ... [bridge] destroyed ... 30 versts south of that point." (Russians measured distances in a unit called *verst* equal to six-tenths of a mile.)

Over the next few days Ensign Hicks, along with the detachment of French soldiers supporting his sailors, rounded up Bolsheviks, and on August 10, 1918, he delivered over fifty prisoners to the British troops occupying Archangel. Following this, Ensign Hicks was informed by Ambassador David Francis that "American troops [were] to obey the commands of [British] General Poole."[7] Hicks also learned General Poole had formulated a plan to drive the Bolsheviks from their positions near the town of Obozerskaya, sixty miles (95 versts) south of Tundra, on the Archangel-Vologda Railroad. One group, Force A, would push its way south along the railway, toward Obozerskaya, while another, Force B, would take boats and travel on the Dvina River southward until reaching the settlement of Tiogra. Then, Force B would march westward and flank the Bolsheviks. Ensign Hicks and his sailors were slotted into Force B, along with "100 French ... 35 Russian S.B.A. [Slavo-British Allied Legion], and 27 Poles."[8]

Force B left Archangel on August 13, 1918, the Allied group riding in barges towed by motorboats. They chugged southward on the Dvina River for two days before arriving at Tiogra. An officer recorded, "At 5:30 A.M. they entered Tiogra and learned that a [Bolshevik] force was in the next town, Seletskoe nine versts away." He continued, "At 5:00 P.M. Force 'B' found itself facing 250 Soviets with machine guns and an armored car. By 7:30 P.M. the Allies had bombed the car, blown up one of the Red machine guns, and taken [Seletskoe]." The Americans took an active part in this fight, with Seaman Dewey Perschke taking a bullet in his arm.[9]

Meanwhile Force A shoved its way southward, along the tracks, pushing the Bolsheviks backward, before eventually reaching the outskirts to the town of Obozerskaya. Here, the Bolshevik resistance stiffened and the Allied troops were not able to advance any further. It was now up to Force B to attack from their flanking position, some 35 miles (55 versts) away. On August 31, 1918, Ensign Hicks and nearly 200 Allied troops moved forward from Seletskoe. Their leading elements encountered a Russian sign reading, "You are the destroyers of humanity. It will go hard with you if you attack Obozerskaya. You had better go back. We have you surrounded."[10] Soon after this, Force B collided with the Bolsheviks, who had been bolstered by nearly 300 Baltic sailors. Ensign Hicks reported, "The fighting was intense that day and that night ... [and we] were forced to ground due to heavy resistance ... two sailors were wounded, one in the arm, the other in the ankle."[11]

The fighting continued the next day, but by then a force of Bolsheviks had slipped behind the Allies and recaptured Seletskoe. This news, along with a message warning of a Bolshevik force that was marching from Obozerskaya, gave Force B's leaders great concern. They called off their attack and set up defenses, blocking the road from Tiogra to Obozerskaya. Then, the Allied force broke up into separate groups, each aiming to join Force A, located north of Obozerskaya. Ensign Hicks and his sailors were ordered to remain behind to protect this movement's rear. The Americans held their position that night, having been told they would be reinforced by a detachment of Russian soldiers.

On September 2, 1918, Hicks and his sailors marched westward, toward the Archangel-Vologda railroad. They had been frustrated because the Russians who were supposed to reinforce them had never arrived. Instead, the Russians had plundered the Allied supplies, stealing the food and ammunition Hicks' sailors would need in their trek to join Force A. The Americans, abandoned and without supplies, struggled westward, as good as lost. Nonetheless, much of Force B reached the safety of the Archangel-Vologda tracks the next day. Unfortunately, no one knew what had happened to Ensign Hicks and his sailors. Captain Joel Moore wrote, "It was this episode in the early fighting that caused the frantic radiogram to reach us on the Arctic Ocean urging the ships to speed on to Archangel to save the handful of Allied men threatened with annihilation on the railroad ... and we were to go into it wholeheartedly to save them."[12]

The men of the 339th got their first impressions of the world they would soon occupy as the *Somali* steamed past Archangel and headed across Dvina Bay to Bakharitza, the city's port. Private Godfrey Anderson wrote, "The entire vista was dreary and desolate, the sky being heavily overcast and the vast swamps stretching interminably."[13] Then, once the *Somali* was tied up, the unloading process began. Anderson noted, "The *Somali* was eased over to a dock at Bakharitza, and the winches and derricks began unloading the cargo, which was transported to one of the warehouses along shore, and the sick were moved to a rather primitive Russian hospital not far away."[14]

Captain Joel Moore, suffering from the effects of the Spanish flu, also had to deal with the effects of influenza on his company. First Sergeant Walter Dundon's muster rolls revealed at least one-third of Company M had been hospitalized—a severe loss. The 1918 U.S. Army Company Organization Table was built around a configuration of four platoons, with each 53-man platoon to be commanded by a lieutenant. Thus, each captain, along with his company headquarters squad, had at his command 256 soldiers.[15] But now, with so many men incapacitated by the Spanish flu, Moore and his lieutenants would have to improvise. They derived an organization of four much smaller platoons, each composed of two half-platoons, built around a machine gun team, with the company's enlisted men to be evenly divided among the formations.

Captain Moore had received intelligence describing the Bolsheviks' activities and what needed to be done; they were to rescue the American sailors and to retrieve the stolen war materials. Lieutenant Harry Costello (MG Co.) recorded, "The Bolsheviks ... had seized the huge stores of supplies and.... All serviceable boats, railway rolling stock, hospital equipment and medical supplies, ammunition, [and] guns."[16] Lieutenant Primm added, "It was reported that the retiring Bolsheviks had taken to Vologda millions of dollars' worth of these stores we were supposed to guard."[17]

The 339th's Third Battalion, led by Maj. Charles Young, was the first to disembark. The battalion's four companies clambered down gangplanks. Major Young loaded his battalion onto two trains, Companies I and L on the first and Companies K and M in the second. Private Cleo Colburn noted, "We were taken off the boat and shoved right to the front. We boarded the trains about the size of dry goods boxes at noon and rode all afternoon and most of the night."[18] The Russian boxcars were nothing like what the doughboys had ridden in before; called *taplooshas*, they were eight feet wide and twenty-two feet long.[19] One of the Third Battalion's rifleman groused, "We were cooped up in those filthy, smelly railroad cars for hours."[20]

Russian locomotive engineers worked the old engines. These machines were obsolete in the United States and barely functioning here in northern Russia. They pulled the soldier-packed boxcars at hardly more than ten miles per hour. Lieutenant John Cudahy (Co. B) wrote, "[They were] wood-burning locomotives of a type used in our country 50 years ago ... [and the] rolling stock [was], rickety ... [and] tumbled down."[21] But regardless of their condition, the trains chugged southward, out of Bakharitza and into the impenetrable and gloomy Russian forest.

The Archangel-Vologda railway was standard five-foot gauge, though with but a single set of tracks. The ride was jolting, as the rails had been nailed to railroad ties already well into stages of rot that had been set upon a thin layer of gravel. The soldiers peered out the boxcars' open doors and watched as the endless Russian forest pressed against them. They noticed striped posts—verst markers—showing the distance they traveled. Bakharitza's location was at verst 598, and the trains were headed to verst 475. The troops noticed occasional sidings, attended to by small settlements, nestled in the cleared areas. These villages contained a few buildings, a water tank for the locomotives, and, as Private Cleo Colburn (Co. I) remarked, "[the Russians] burnt wood in their locomotives, about 4 foot cord wood. And about every ten versts ... there'd be a little stream of water, and right alongside that little stream ... would be a little village. And alongside that little village would be piles of cord-wood for these [trains] that come along there."[22]

The sun dipped below the western horizon and the shadowy Russian forest turned foreboding. The Yanks noticed how early the evening sky had darkened and were reminded just how far north they were. The September date meant an ever-shortening length of daylight as this near-Arctic area moved toward winter. The soldiers, who had been ordered to leave their heavy packs at the docks, suffered from the chilled night air. Lieutenant Charles Ryan (Co. K) wrote, "The battalion ... was ordered to leave immediately for the south with just the clothes on our backs and a single blanket."[23] Later that night, the trains stopped at a station to take on wood and water. Lieutenant John Cudahy described the scene: "The decrepit Russian locomotive gasped convulsively and stood still by an old station of huge logs." Cudahy continued, "Under the lurid light of a flaming torch, was revealed a trainload of prisoners, passing north from the scene of hostilities somewhere below. They made an un-heroic spectacle, with their shrinking countenances and un-soldierly, nondescript uniforms, so that some American wag, in a spirit of bantering patronage, called them 'Bolo wild men.'" From that moment on the American soldiers referred to the Bolsheviks as "Bolos." Lieutenant Cudahy added, "The shabby prisoners, [the] first living sign of a real battle, sent a thrill up and down the spines of these young men, who were so ardent for war and knew so little about it."[24]

Very few of the greenhorn American soldiers got much sleep that night. Instead, most just endured the jolting ride, staring out into the sinister-looking forest, smoking, and joking with their comrades. Private Cleo Colburn (Co. I) recalled, "We were transported up there in boxcars—and all our rifles were up against the wall, and of course there was a lot of hilarity and fooling around in the boxcars. And the car door was open and my rifle was kicked out—lost." Colburn continued, "And of course we couldn't go back and get it." The young soldier, now being ribbed by his comrades, worried about what would happen when the company formed in the morning and he did not possess his rifle. Later, Pvt. Colburn's train came to a stop just north of Obozerskaya. The men from Companies I and L unloaded from their boxcars and were ordered to form up. Colburn's lost rifle quickly came to the attention of his company commander, Cpt. Horatio Winslow. The weaponless soldier remembered, "When we unloaded for inspection, I didn't have a gun. Captain Winslow said to me, 'You're in an awful predicament to go into battle.' He gave me [his] sidearm."[25]

Major Young led his two companies forward, following the railroad tracks, passing through Obozerskaya, now abandoned by the Bolsheviks, who had retreated when they learned the American trains were approaching. Once beyond the town's limits Maj. Young called his officers together, leaving his nearly four hundred men to remain standing in close marching order. The doughboys glanced about and noticed a number of holes in the ground, some with smoke coming from them. A few soldiers quietly joked the holes looked like bomb craters. Not long after this a French officer appeared and began to shout at Maj. Young. The exchange told the inexperienced Yanks something about their battalion commander. One wrote, "Morning found [us] ... not far from the important village of Obozerskaya ... [the] two companies of Americans, 'I' and 'L' ... [were] halted in ranks before [a] tall station building, with [Maj. Young] ... holding officer's call at command of a bugle. An excited little French officer popped out of his dugout and pointed at the shell holes in the ground ... and told Major Young [he] feared the Bolos any minute would reopen artillery fire."[26] Major Young, now realizing he had his men standing in formation within a combat zone, quickly shouted for his men to take cover in the nearby forest. The men scurried away from their exposed position, taking refuge among nearby trees, but not before some took issue with their commander. One remembered, "Maj. Charles Young was not one of the favorites of the regiment."[27]

Meanwhile, the second train, loaded with Companies K and M, had been stopped on a siding dozens of versts north of Obozerskaya. The men waited expectantly, wanting to catch up with their comrades. The doughboys asked why they were doing nothing, but their officers had no answer, leaving the impatient men to sit around, listlessly, staring at the sinister-looking forest. One wrote, "The railroad [on] ... which we were operating [went] ... right through the forest. It was virgin timber, perhaps 50–60 feet high and real thick."[28] Hours later, an armored train rumbled past. Lieutenant John Cudahy (Co. B) recorded, "[It was a] captivating spectacle ... a ferocious war monster with massive plates of steel like dragon's scales, [and] huge funneled naval guns." He continued, "The locomotive set in rear of [flatcars] which were piled with sandbag barricades where Lewis automatics poked out murderously."[29]

Meanwhile, while the second train's men did nothing, Companies I and K had work to do. Major Young sent his two companies forward, the platoons spread out in skirmish order. The untested Yanks moved cautiously, gawking at what they saw. Private Cleo Colburn (Co. I) wrote, "On our march we saw rifles, belts, caps, ammunition and everything along the tracks where the [Bolos] had been pushed so fast that they were forced to leave them. In one pile beside the tracks we found about 75 or 100 rifles." The young soldier admitted, "On our march forward I found a rifle in the woods that was usable—the same type we were using and it used the same ammunition. So then I had a rifle again."[30]

French soldiers met the Americans and guided them into positions overlooking a deep ravine separating them from the Bolsheviks. The French pulled out as a cold rain began to fall. This, as evening descended upon the doughboys, was going to be their first night on the battle line. The Americans soon found themselves soaked, hungry, cold, and not knowing what they were supposed to do. One rifleman grumbled, "One blanket, a poncho, and sleeping in 28 inches of oozy mud ... we wondered what we had done to deserve this."[31] Some built fires to warm themselves, but word quickly was passed: Maj. Young had given orders, "No fires on the outpost." This made no sense to the shivering soldiers, as they could see numerous campfires among the Bolshevik positions. Later, a nervous American, anxious in his rookie vigilance, accidently shot one of his comrades. Joel Moore (Co. M) recorded, "That first night we had a casualty, a painful wound in a doughboy's leg from the rifle of a sentry who cried 'halt' and fired at the same time."[32]

Companies K and M arrived onsite the next afternoon. Captain Joel Moore's Company M was detailed to relieve I and L. His four platoons were guided into position while the tired troops pulled out, to head back to Obozerskaya. Moore's formation was understrength, 1st Sgt. Walter Dundon reporting, "Company weak owing to a large number of men left at Bakharitza sick with Influenza—178 men ... [it] took all officers and men for the outpost." Dundon, after he and Cpt. Moore inspected their positions on an outpost line that was four and a half miles long, also noted, "No shelters on outpost except at three posts."[33] Once Moore's men were settled, he received word from Maj. Young that he had to send three of his lieutenants back to battalion headquarters. Young had new duties for lieutenants Milton Carpenter, George Stoner, and Clarence Primm. Captain Moore now had to operate with just three—James Donovan, Wesley Wright, and Robert Wieczorek. Moore's first sergeant recorded, "Lt. Carpenter detailed for special duty with Bn. Hq. as Bn. Supply Officer.... Lts. Stoner and Primm [put] on special duty at machine gun schools at Bakharitza."[34] Captain Moore's riflemen gazed out at the Bolshevik positions as more rain dampened their world. The sun set and vision was reduced to little more than frightening shadows. One of his officers wrote, "[There was a] stillness, heavy almost to the point of suffocation." He added, "the shroud of skies that hover [above] the trees, and the shadow of ... gloom that reaches out from the forest ... bears down upon the spirit with deep intangible melancholy."[35]

Back in Obozerskaya, the men of Companies I and L spread out and took possession of any structure that provided protection from the rain. They warmed themselves by fires, scarfed down army rations, and bedded down for the night. Maj. Young was busy, having set up his HQ in the town's best building. He had received orders to send a unit eastward, toward Seletskoe and Tiogra, in search of Ensign Hicks and his sailors. He also was told to send troops to guard a railroad siding north of Obozerskaya. Major Young put Cpt. Michael Donoghue in action. The captain of Company K detached two platoons and sent them north to protect that railroad siding, with its train repair shop and a wireless station. He also sent two platoons, 1st Lt. Charles Ryan in command, in search of the missing men. Lieutenant Ryan, along with his little force of about 120 troops, hiked east, struggling through "[a track] that proved impassable." He added, "The men turned around, having waded three miles up to their knees." Ryan's men did not find any sign of Hicks and his boys, but they did discover "carts, supplies, weapons and even fresh graves, [all] evidences of Force B." Lieutenant Ryan also remarked, "[We] bivouacked for the night somewhere on the trail in a cold drizzle.... The mosquitoes [were] awful ... [and] they have eaten me alive."[36]

In Obozerskaya, Maj. Young, who was a stickler for regulations, admonished his troops, denying them permission to fraternize with the local Russians. The young Americans, though, had been stunned by the locals' poverty, often seeing the locals dig into their mess halls' refuse cans for leftover food. Communication with the locals was not that difficult because there were soldiers in Companies I and L who were Russian or Polish immigrants. Major Young's orders made little sense to them, and they ignored Young's orders when he was not around.

Captain Joel Moore's riflemen survived their first night out on the picket line, though it proved to be a long, wet, and cold night. First Sergeant Dundon wrote, "[It] was pretty tough, that cold drizzly night."[37] The next morning, September 8, 1918, a squad from Company I brought rations but declined offers to stay. Captain Moore and his first sergeant inspected the outposts and relieved thirteen men who were too ill to remain on the line. Moore sent them back to Bakharitza. The hours went by slowly, the doughboys working to improve their outposts by cutting down branches and fashioning makeshift shelters. Meanwhile, the Bolsheviks remained hidden among the thick stand of trees just beyond the ravine separating the two forces. That afternoon, engineers arrived and, accompanied by a group of Russian laborers, began work on repairing the damaged railroad bridge. Surprisingly, the Bolsheviks did nothing to impede this activity.

In Obozerskaya, Companies I and L were busy, the soldiers making themselves comfortable. The town's extensive railroad yard contained dozens of unused boxcars. Captain Grant Cherry turned his Company L men loose among the boxcars, allowing them to create living quarters out of these vehicles. Meanwhile, Horatio Winslow's men took possession of the town's structures, though many of the men were aghast at the buildings' odor. Joel Moore wrote, "Obozerskaya village was home.... Here in the peasant homes ... we came to tolerate the ... nauseating smell of their rooms ... it was because of the lack of real soap and their use of a combination of fish oil and crude oil in a substitute for soap that made their clothes smell so [bad]."[38]

On the front line, Cpt. Moore's men greeted a second night of outpost duty with more confidence than their first night. Their posts were better constructed, and many had hidden little stoves and fireplaces within them. Pine and spruce limbs roofed over parts of the line, giving the enterprising Yanks protection from enemy bullets and from the September chill. Even though 1st Sgt. Dundon did not lose more men to sick call the next morning, he noted, "Ice on ground this morning. Men on outpost wet and cold."[39] September 9, 1918, proved to be just as quiet as the day before. Captain Moore received word that there might be Bolo movement along his company's right flank. He ordered one of his lieutenants to take a patrol and investigate. This was the first time any of Moore's soldiers ventured out from their defensive positions searching for the enemy. Dundon recorded, "Patrol sent in afternoon to investigate reported operation of enemy patrol on right flank south. No enemy found."[40]

Back in Obozerskaya, word was passed to the Americans that Ensign Hicks and his sailors had safely reached a post along the Archangel-Vologda railway. The naval officer and his entire crew were quickly transported to Archangel. Ensign Donald M. Hicks was then awarded the Navy Cross for his efforts. Captain Horatio Winslow's Company I relieved Moore's men the next day. Major Young ordered Moore to house his men in a little village just west of Obozerskaya. Captain Moore wrote, "Co. found quarters in village on Onega Road. Officers given front room of fine house."[41] He was also impressed by the improvements that had

Obozerskaya's train yard contained massive amounts of firewood (U.S. Army Signal Corps).

been made to Obozerskaya. Trains made daily runs between Obozerskaya and Bakharitza, bringing in building materials, supplies, and additional allied soldiers—Poles, French, British, and Russians. Workers, wielding axes and shovels, were hacking out a runway from a nearby field, while crews were assembling airplanes. And no one could ignore the armored train that towered over the Russian boxcars. It was described as "ferocious-looking ... bristling with machine guns and naval artillery pieces."[42] The Allies were in Obozerskaya to stay. The question now for the Americans—what would they now be doing? Lieutenant Clarence Primm wrote, "We had had no orders from our own headquarters [at] this point."[43]

Chapter 5

The Americans Settle In

September 11, 1918: First Sergeant Walter Dundon studied Company M's roster; so many men were out because of sickness. The Spanish flu and the effects of inclement weather had so reduced the company that Dundon's final tally for the company's morning report was 104 able-bodied riflemen.[1] Walter Dundon was born November 22, 1890, in Elk Rapids, Illinois. Not long after this, his parents, Tom and Margaret, moved to Chicago. There, Tom secured a good paying job at an iron works. Meanwhile, Margaret's responsibilities as a housewife increased over the next few years as their family grew.

Life went well for the Dundon family until Tom Dundon died suddenly, leaving Margaret to fend for herself and support five children. She moved her family to Elberta, Michigan, a small lakeside town serving as the link between the Ann Arbor Railroad and ferry companies transporting goods and people across Lake Michigan. Margaret opened a business that became well known and provided enough income to support her family. A local historian noted, "[Walter Dundon's] mother ran a bakery and restaurant across the street from the water front.... The backroom of Dundon's Bakery was a place [where] the river drivers would sleep after driving logs down the river."[2] Her son Walter, showing a good sense for numbers, worked as a bookkeeper. He also attended high school and graduated in 1907. Dundon joined the army four years later. Private Dundon was sent to Alaska, where he took part in the military's duties of providing security, law enforcement, and infrastructure construction for that remote region. He served his three-year enlistment, then mustered out in 1914. Dundon returned to Elberta and got a job working as a brakeman for the Ann Arbor Railroad. He stayed with the railroad for a short time before moving to Detroit and taking on a job at an auto body factory.

The United States entered the Great War in 1917 and not long afterward draft notices went out to America's young men. Walter Dundon completed his draft registration on June 7, 1917, the form noting he stood five feet, 10½ inches tall and had blue eyes and light brown hair. Once at Camp Custer, Dundon was immediately promoted, since he had three years of previous military service.[3] Sergeant Dundon was tasked with drilling the new recruits. Whenever he had time off, the young NCO went into nearby Battle Creek and there he met 18-year-old Cecile Hager, the daughter of a local carpenter. Their relationship blossomed and they married. Sadly, when Walter Dundon left for Europe, he never again saw his wife.

Cecile's obituary would record, "[They] married in June [1918] ... and three weeks later her husband left for overseas duty."[4] Dundon would never know Cecile had died until he returned home from Russia. In fact, he would list her as his emergency contact in June 1919 as he filled out his ship-transport forms, not knowing she had died in May 1919.

But today, in Russia, as Company M's senior NCO, 1st Sgt. Dundon went about the business of running Cpt. Joel Moore's combat unit. First Sergeant Dundon's immediate responsibilities revolved around keeping his troops healthy and fed. Strangely, food was becoming an issue. It was not a problem of insufficient amounts; the dispute was quality. The men did not like what they were eating. One of Dundon's sergeants, Matthew Grahek (Co. M), speaking for many of the men, stated, "The British were dishing out the food. We were supposed to get American Swift & Armour bully beef; [but] they were giving that cheap stuff from Argentina." He continued, "I didn't like that a bit. They were ... pawning off their stuff to us."[5] A rifleman added, "There was a lot of mutton and there was also tin beef.... The trouble was that there was a lot of M & V. They called it Meat and vegetables."[6] For Dundon, though, besides the M and V issue, what really rubbed him wrong was there was no coffee. And what frosted Dundon even more was their battalion commander, Maj. Charles Young, refused to confront the British supply officers about this problem. The complaint of Pvt. James Siplon (Co. I) was a common one, when he railed, "When we had Maj. Young, we never could get any coffee. They were just feeding us this British tea."[7] Dundon completely agreed with his troops; how could Maj. Young expect his American soldiers to fight a war without coffee?

First Sergeant Dundon knew the rations problem was just a sideshow to the real complication; the British were running everything. Even though Dundon was unhappy with Maj. Young's performance, what made everything worse was the fact the American officers were always outranked by the British. Private Russell Hershberger (MG Co.) summed up this situation, writing, "We were under English command.... If we got a commander ... that was higher-ranked than theirs, they would right away get a man in that was higher-ranked than [ours]."[8] Dundon watched his captain being forced to submit to Maj. Young's orders, knowing the actual directives had come from British mouths.

Captain Joel Moore approached 1st Sgt. Dundon and told him to form the company; the boys were going into action. First Lieutenant Gerald Danley (Co. I) had reported seeing a Bolo railroad gun on the tracks three miles south of Obozerskaya. When he reported this to Col. Guard, the commanding British officer disagreed, saying, "The gun in question was in fact the smoke pipe at a sawmill." Danley persisted, pressuring the colonel to allow the Americans to dispatch a patrol. Once obtaining permission, Danley's small force moved southward and "the smokestack suddenly belched fire, and a shell twisted and turned over the patrol and landed on the reserve trenches they had just passed through."[9] Moments later, while near the verst 468 signpost, Danley's men came under fire. They took cover and sent out a call for reinforcements.

Company M soon had 104 men and three lieutenants standing before Cpt.

Company M moving southward from verst 468 on September 11, 1918, just moments before coming under artillery fire (U.S. Army Signal Corps).

Moore, ready for action. First Sergeant Dundon recorded, "[The company] arrived ... at [a] house near 468, [and] passed through Danley's [men] ... with orders to move south [to] clear up the situation as to the advance of the enemy armored train, and as to the presence of enemy infantry which was reported in strength 1500 yards to the south."[10] A rifleman added, "[Then] we were formed in ... [marching] order and marched along in the edge of the woods for about a half mile."[11] The Allied artillery onboard the armored train opened up, firing over the Yanks' heads, causing one Yank to remark, "I shall never forget how the fellow ahead of me jumped when our old 3-point-seven made its first bark."[12] A Bolshevik cannon returned fire. Captain Joel Moore reminisced, "Remember that first Bolo shell ... that thing far down the straight track three miles away.... There came the distant boom. Came then the whining, twisting, whistling shell that passed over us and showered shrapnel near the trenches where lay our reserves. He shortened his range and we hurried on."[13] Private Cleo Colburn (Co. I) recalled, "They began shelling [us] but we were stretched out in a skirmish line and advanced faster than they thought we would, so we kept ahead of their fire. Some of it was close enough. They cut off trees the size of your head and larger, just above us as [the shells] came sizzling through the air."[14] Moore added, "[We] learned that it takes many shrapnel shells ... to hit one man."[15]

Captain Moore's doughboys pushed toward verst 466, still under sporadic artillery fire. Then, when they were several hundred yards from a large clearing surrounding the railroad siding at verst 466, Bolshevik machine gun fire began to search for American flesh. Cleo Colburn recalled, "One of the lieutenants said to us, 'give 'em hell boys.' It was right then that I knew what we were up against."[16] Captain Moore gave orders, deploying the formation; Lt. George Stoner's platoon would straddle the railroad tracks and hold the center, Lt. Robert Wieczorek was to take his platoon and cover the left flank, and Lt. James Donovan's men would shift to take the right flank.[17]

The Americans inched forward slowly, firing as they advanced. The range was still long and both sides shot wildly. One Yank complained, "[Our Russian rifles] ... didn't shoot good. Sometimes when we got on the skirmish line why we'd shoot a dozen shots ... before they [Bolos] realized that we were shooting at them."[18] The Bolshevik fire increased as the Americans closed the distance between the two forces. Finally, the Yanks reached the edge of the clearing surrounding verst 466 and halted, having now been under fire for about thirty minutes. Captain Moore detached three squads from Stoner's men and gave them to 1st Sgt. Dundon with instructions to reinforce Lt. Wieczorek's platoon. Wieczorek and Dundon were to lead that battle group in a flanking movement, staying within the tree line, and then strike the Bolsheviks' left flank. Captain Moore recorded, "When the attack had fully developed on the left, Lt. Donovan pushed rapidly forward on the right of the railroad, skirting the clearing and fell on the enemy's flank 500 yards beyond the clearing."[19] The Bolos, being pressed from the right and the left flanks, retreated. Cleo Colburn proudly proclaimed, "We met ... and had it hot and heavy until nearly dark, when we drove them back."[20]

Captain Moore ordered Donovan to pursue the retreating Bolsheviks while Wieczorek and Stoner mopped up at verst 466's siding. Donovan's force chased the Bolsheviks to a recently repaired bridge near verst 464. The Bolos put up a short fight to hold the bridge but fled, leaving the position in American hands. Moore sent word back to Obozerskaya of their success, and not long after that the British commanders arrived. Captain Moore wrote, "The position was ours with the loss of a [single] man....We liked the place ... we never did intend to give it back to the Bolo."[21] Lieutenant George Stoner added, "Baptism of fire ... very successful, interesting, and exciting."[22] The British officers commended the Yanks, with one stating, "One good Allied soldier can outfight twenty Bolsheviks." Afterward, though, Col. Guard accused Lt. Gerald Danley (Co. I) of insubordination. Danley, knowing he had been right in arguing against the Brit earlier in the day, refused to accept this rebuke and the two officers squabbled into the night.

Lieutenant Donovan established posts at the verst 464 bridge and recalled the rest back to verst 466. Cleo Colburn (Co. I) noted, "We laid low until it was real dark and then went back."[23] A small amount of rations were brought to Cpt. Moore's men. Moore wrote, "That first night at 466 ... cold and supper-less ... we did get our overcoats and blankets apiece and some bully beef and hardtack."[24] The next morning, September 12, 1918, found the Americans secure in their defensive positions at verst 466. A team of U.S. Army Signal Corps engineers established phone communications between verst 466 and battalion headquarters at Obozerskaya. The Allied armored train parked itself at verst 466's siding, its men loitering near their vehicle, ready to respond at a moment's notice. Captain Joel

Moore met with verst 466's siding manager, and using Sgt. Jacob Kantrowitz (Co. M), a Russian immigrant drafted out of the Bronx as an interpreter, learned the area had been controlled until the day before by about two hundred Bolsheviks. Not much else happened during the daylight hours, though a report came from the outposts at verst 464 that the Bolos had damaged the bridge during the night. Later, the British commander Col. Guard was replaced by another British colonel, this one called Sutherland.

Colonel Sutherland proved to be more accepting of the Americans, though his views on tactical positioning of troops had been molded by his experiences in the trenches in France. First Sergeant Dundon, who escorted the colonel around the area's defensive positions, wrote, "The new O.C. [is] peculiar in views on entrenchments. The Old man cannot see that bush warfare should be different from No Man's Land on the Western Front."[25] Captain Horatio Winslow's Company I arrived at the siding, along with Cpt. Grant Cherry (Co. L) and troops. Both units bolstered the Allies' strength. They brought with them British rations and tea, alleviating the shortage of food. The rest of the day went smoothly, and though it was chilly for the men out on the front line, nothing happened. The next day was no different, with but one change: a reporter from the United States arrived, bringing with him bags of mail. This was the first time the doughboys had received any word from home.

The Third Battalion's commander Maj. Charles Young arrived that afternoon, now saying he had recovered from an ailment that had left him incapacitated for several days. Captains Moore, Winslow, and Cherry reported to Young their situations. Strangely, that evening, Maj. Young chose Cpt. Cherry as a lodging partner. Walter Dundon recorded this fact, writing, "Maj. Young still on sick list, but better. He went to 466 to stay out all night with Capt. Cherry."[26]

The next morning, September 15, 1918, proved to be pivotal for Maj. Young. A Bolshevik airplane buzzed the Allied positions at verst 466 before flying north to verst 474, where it dropped three bombs. No one was injured, though a number of trees were blasted into pieces. The plane returned for another pass over verst 466, but this time the Americans were ready. Rifles and machine guns opened fire at the aircraft, hitting it enough times to knock out the engine. Major Young yelled at the men to cease fire, convinced the plane belonged to the Allies. Lieutenant Albert May (Co. I) recorded the incident: "When this plane appeared I ordered the men to fire.... Young flew into a rage and ordered my men to cease firing. I told them to keep shooting. We knocked the plane down. Young... ordered me to assemble a squad and begin hiking down the railroad tracks to where the plane had crashed in an open field. This was 200 yards beyond the wire." Albert May continued, "Major Young took [this] patrol out, hollering, 'don't fire, we're an American patrol.'"[27] Captain Joel Moore added, "But the Bolo ... answered with his own Lewis gun sending the American officer to cover where he lay even after the Bolo had darted into the woods."[28] Once the Bolshevik pilot had escaped, Maj. Young emerged from his hiding place, covered with mud. The doughboys found Young's appearance amusing. Moore recalled, "Here comes a Russian plane over. It comes down, lands on the track, and the guy gets out with a machine-gun. [Maj.] Young says, 'Don't shoot. We are Americans.' This guy, 'rat-a-tat-a-tat.'"²⁹

This incident damaged the soldiers' remaining respect for the major. Lieutenant May wrote, "Several days later we were coming in off a patrol and one of my men, while passing Maj. Young, said, 'don't fire, we're an American patrol.' Young again flew into a rage and ordered the man to step forward. When no one did, he ordered me to tell the culprit to speak up…. No luck. I told the major I couldn't make men talk if they did not want to."³⁰ The hostility toward Charles Young grew even worse once this news circulated among the Third Battalion's troops. Captains Moore, Winslow, and Cherry met to discuss sending a note to Col. George Stewart, asking to have their battalion commander replaced. Albert May recorded, "The situation got so bad [we] finally sent a telegram to Col. Stewart asking him to relieve the major." May continued, explaining his men feared they "wouldn't get home alive" with Young as their commander and admitted, "my men [have] threatened to kill [him] if he was not relieved."³¹

September 16, 1918, dawned gray and spitting rain and sleet. Some of Co. M's men guarded the siding at verst 466 while the rest worked on improving defenses. Company L's platoon manned the front line at verst 464, along with two platoons from Company I.³² The morning hours went by quietly, though the rain and sleet continued to plague the soldiers. This inactivity ended not long after noon when the pickets at verst 464 noticed activity to their front. Then Bolshevik artillery fire swept the Yank outposts. The Americans hunkered down. The artillery fire lasted for some time, pounding the American positions with blasts of flame and concussion. These shells impacted among the trees, turning limbs into lethal splinters, which spewed in all directions. Eventually, the barrage ceased. The pummeled doughboys peered from their hideouts and saw commotion among the trees, advancing Bolos. The Americans waited until the Bolsheviks were about two hundred yards away and then swept the attackers with machine gun and rifle fire. The Russians fired back, commencing a hot exchange. Most of the Bolo bullets thudded into the tree trunks above the Americans' helmets. Others, though, did not miss; Pvt. Philip Sokol (Co. L) had a chunk of lead rip through his body. He became Company L's first man to die in combat.

The Reds greatly outnumbered the Americans and they slowly pushed forward. In one area of the battlefront the Bolsheviks worked a machine gun team into a position that enfiladed an American position. The machine gun raked the Yanks, its bullets slicing into Pvt. Ignacy Kwasniewski (Co. I), killing him. More machine gun fire pinned down Kwasniewski's comrades, enabling the Bolsheviks to close in on the Yanks. Seeing his comrades' plight, Pvt. Robert Day (Co. I) crept forward from his position and reached a spot where he was able to kill the gunner and destroy the machine gun. This allowed the riflemen around Kwasniewski to drive the Bolos backward. Robert Day would be awarded the Silver Star for his actions.³³ As the fight continued, it became obvious the Bolo battle line extended beyond the Yanks' left. The Bolsheviks soon realized this and rushed more men to crowd past the Americans' unprotected flank. First Lieutenant Gerald Danley (Co. I) sent a runner with a message requesting reinforcements, but the man could not get through the Bolos' torrid fire. Danley sent a second and then a third, but they also were pinned down by the Bolsheviks' shooting. Finally, Lieutenant Danley turned to Company I's bugler, 26-year-old James F. Revels, challenging him to get the message back to headquarters. James Revel succeeded in getting through and later would be awarded the Distinguished Service Cross.

Captain Horatio Winslow, now aware of the critical situation at verst 464, sent 1st Lt. Gordon Reese (Co. I) with the company's remaining two platoons to help. Lieutenant Reese, knowing from the message he had received the Bolsheviks were working around the American left flank, aimed his men toward that location. Reese's force collided with the Bolos and the two groups raked each other with rifle fire. Bullets slapped into the trees as well as human flesh. Twenty-seven-year-old Pvt. Anthony Soczkoski (Co. I) dropped, killed by the Russian fire. The Americans stopped the Russian enveloping movement and forced the Bolos to seek cover. The fighting continued for the next hour. More men fell but neither side gained any ground. Unfortunately, by this time the Americans had shot up most of their ammunition and, because of their isolated position on the Allied left flank, were out of communication with the main battle line. Lieutenant Reese faced a pivotal moment; his men would soon have no means by which to continue the fight. He gave orders to "fix bayonets" and then led a charge. The audacity of this assault shocked the Bolsheviks, who broke and ran.

First Lieutenant Gordon Reese's bayonet charge rolled the stunned Bolsheviks backward, smashing into their main line's position, which slowly crumbled. Pockets of Russians began to creep away from the fight, until the entire Bolo line collapsed and the remaining Bolsheviks fled. Lieutenant Reese linked up with Lt. Danley's main line. The Yanks consolidated their position, and now that the fight was over, sent out patrols to determine how far away the enemy had retreated. Private Cleo Colburn (Co. I), now a veteran of his first battle, wrote, "First skirmish with Bolsheviks ... amid rain and hail. Two men [killed] in Company I, one in Company L."

Major Young sent Cpt. Joel Moore and Company M to relieve the "battle veterans" of Companies I and L. Moore's men settled into the outposts and then sent out patrols to scour the battlefield for bodies. They located a dozen dead Russians.[34] Captain Horatio Winslow welcomed his veterans back at verst 466. The men were tired and "wired" from their experience. These doughboys were civilian soldiers no more. Their elation, though, was tempered when they gazed at the bodies of three Americans. Suddenly, these boys from America understood war's lethality.[35] Major Charles Young had his adjutant, Lt. Lewis Jahns, send a message to Cpt. Winslow and Cpt. Cherry: "The Battalion Commander ... wishes ... to express his high appreciation of the gallant work done by.... Lieut. Gordon B. Reese, Sgt. Carl W. Venable, Co. L, and Pvt. Edward Kurklewicz, Co. I ... [as] conspicuously gallant and worthy of special mention."[36]

Sunrise on September 17, 1918, found Cpt. Joel Moore's soldiers manning the outposts and trenches near verst 464. The Bolsheviks remained quiet, but Moore could not trust them to remain that way. He recorded, "Our patrols ... kept in contact with Red Guard outposts ... occasionally bringing in wounded Bolos or deserters, who informed us of entrenchments and armored trains and augmenting Bolshevik regiments."[37] The next day, a few hours after noon, Cpt. Cherry and his single platoon relieved Company M, though because of Cherry's small numbers, several squads of Moore's men were forced to remain on the line. Company M returned to verst 466 in time to learn Col. Stewart was present, having ventured out of Archangel. First Sergeant Walter Dundon wrote, "Col. Stewart visited camp but did not visit 'M' Co."[38]

The Yanks solemnly laid their brothers to rest that evening. Joel Moore described the affair: "The first three Americans killed in action in North Russia were buried." He continued, "It was impossible to get one of our chaplains from Archangel to come to Obozerskaya to bury them. The American officer in command engaged the local Russian priest to perform the religious service." Moore noted, "By some trick of fate it had happened that these first Americans who fell in action were of Slavic blood, so the strange funeral which the doughboys witnessed was not so incongruous after all." He added, "With the long-haired, wonderfully-robed priest came his choir and many villagers, who occupied one side of the square made by the soldiers standing there in the dusk to do last honors to their dead comrades. With chantings and doleful chorus the choir answered his solemn oratory and devotional intercessions. He swung his sacred censor pot over each body and though we understood no word we knew he was doing reverence to the spirit of sacrifice shown by our fallen comrades. There in the darkness by the edge of the forest, the priest and his ceremony, the firing squad's volley, and the bugler's last call, all united to make an allied funeral."[39]

The men came away from the ceremony saddened by their comrades' deaths but also feeling relief to be alive. That feeling gave way to anger when they realized their commanding officer, Col. George Stewart, who was present at verst 466, did not attend the ceremony. They did not understand how the man who had ordered these men to carry out his bidding, and in doing so were killed, did not have the courtesy to honor them with his presence. The men searched for reasons why Stewart had not appeared and came away with two possibilities for his behavior: "He was at the site, but read a magazine during the service; [second] he hurriedly left before the service began." They all suspected, though, "it appear[ed] he could have attended, but chose not to."[40] This caused resentment among the Third Battalion soldiers.

Three platoons of Company M went back to the outposts at verst 464 on September 19, 1918, and remained there for the next three days. Major Young, after listening to the after-action reports from his captains, realized the Bolsheviks were always outgunning his soldiers. Everyone expected the Bolos to always outnumber the Yanks; that was not the issue. The real problem revolved around the fact the Reds had more machine guns. Charles Young relayed this message to Col. Stewart, who had returned to Archangel. The 339th's colonel ordered Lt. Clarence Primm (Co. M), who had been in Archangel instructing soldiers in the use of the Lewis machine gun, back to Third Battalion headquarters. Lieutenant Primm was to commence Lewis gun instruction at verst 466.⁴¹ Primm soon began teaching the doughboys at verst 466 how to use the Lewis gun. However, for the Americans to be able to employ their newly acquired knowledge, they would need those machine guns. It would be up to Col. Stewart and Maj. Young to wrangle the crucial weapons from British storehouses in Archangel.

CHAPTER 6

A Muddled Assault

September 27, 1918: Major Jesse Brooks Nichols looked at the note handed to him by an aide; he was to report to Col. George Stewart. The 33-year-old officer had just returned to the Second Brigade's headquarters in Archangel, having come from inspecting one of his companies. The frustrated battalion commander wondered what his colonel wanted. Nichols, a man of action, did not like the fact his four rifle formations—Companies E, F, G, and H—were stationed in and around Archangel, while the First Battalion was battling its way up the Dvina River and the Third Battalion was fighting its way southward on the Archangel-Vologda railway. Major Nichols would soon learn he was to assume a new responsibility.

Jesse Brooks Nichols was born July 11, 1885, in Dunkirk, New York, to Edward and Posey Brooks Nichols. His mother died soon after his

Major J. Brooks Nichols was the wealthiest man in the 339th Infantry Regiment (National Archives).

birth, forcing his father, who was both financially astute and socially respected in the community, to hire nannies to help guide the young boy.[1] But then, in 1892, when Jesse was five, his father died, leaving the orphan to be raised by his grandmother, Julia A. Brooks. Four years later, in November 1896, his grandmother passed away. Julia Brooks, a widow, had been the sole owner of the Brooks Locomotive Works, a massive firm dominating the economy of Dunkirk, New York. Her company built locomotives, sometimes as many as eighty to a hundred each year.[2] She named her grandson Jesse Brooks Nichols, as well as another grandson and three granddaughters, as beneficiaries to nearly one-half of the Brooks Locomotive Works' capital shares.[3] Each child's inheritance was bound up in a trust that would become available to them when they reached the age of thirty. The value of each trust was estimated to be nearly $125,000 ($3.9 million in 2020).[4] His grandmother's will stated, "Clare A. Pickard [was to be] special guardian for Jesse."[5] Clare Pickard, a respected attorney who handled much of the company's legal matters, was tasked with managing Jesse's trust, seeing that the boy was properly raised and allocating a sufficient allowance to pay for all child rearing and education costs. Pickard performed his responsibilities admirably; by the time Jesse graduated from the elite boarding school Hill School in Pottstown, Pennsylvania, the value of the youth's trust was even more than when he first received it.[6]

J. Brooks Nichols (he chose to go by his middle name) went to Yale and graduated in 1908 with a degree in science. He went to work for an oil and coal company headquartered in Lexington, Kentucky, and there he met 19-year-old Rosa Sparks Dunlap. They married later that year and the first of their three sons was born in 1909. The Nichols family moved to Detroit in 1910 when J. Brooks took a job as the purchasing agent at the U.S. Radiator Corporation. He became the company's director three years later as well as the director and treasurer of Detroit Princess Manufacturing. In 1914, J. Brooks and Rosa began construction of a 20,000 square foot mansion on Detroit's famed Lake Shore Road that included a "large center hall, drawing room, music room, library [and] a ballroom ... [as well as] a garden, a cottage, and stables."[7]

Nichols, however, in the spring of 1917, took the examination to become an officer, passed, and then attended Officer Candidate School at Ft. Sheridan, Illinois. He was commissioned as a first lieutenant in May 1917 and as a captain two months later. The newly minted captain was sent to Camp Custer, and in early 1918 he was assigned as adjutant to Col. John Craig, the 339th Infantry's commander. Nichols was promoted to major in May 1918 and given command of the regiment's Second Battalion.[8] He proved to be efficient and well respected; as a fellow officer recorded, "every army man you speak with ... say Major Nichols is a fine officer."[9]

As the leader in charge of protecting Archangel, Maj. Brooks immediately began "crossing swords" with the British leadership, who insisted upon making sure the Americans and Russians were directly under British control. This did not set well with the Americans nor with the Russian people. Sadly, most of Archangel's citizens could not tell the Brits from the Americans, and because they did not trust the British, they also did not have much faith in the Yanks. It became Maj. Nichols' responsibility to change this situation. His first test came quickly; Archangel's streetcar drivers went on strike, paralyzing the city. Major Nichols sent out a call to the men of his battalion, seeking soldiers with streetcar experience. Since so many of his troopers were from Detroit, he soon had a number of men he could send out to take over the driving of the stalled streetcars. Nichols announced to Archangel's citizens there would be no fees charged. Then, "for the next ... thirty hours, Americans were conducting the streetcars, or acting as motormen, and at every place ... there were two or three American soldiers to keep the crowds from overloading the cars."[10] The strike collapsed, and the Archangel citizens began to recognize the differences between Americans and the British.

On September 27, 1918, Maj. Nichols was summoned to Col. Stewart's office and ordered to take over command of the Third Battalion. The 339th's headquarters in Archangel had excellent communication with this formation, using a telephone, a telegraph, and a small contingent of wireless operators at Obozerskaya to keep in close contact.[11] Major Nichols quickly learned the Third Battalion's companies were spread out. Most of Companies K and L were east of Obozerskaya, while Companies I and M were on the railway, facing the Bolshevik positions a few versts south of the town.

The British high command wanted the Americans to attack. Lieutenant John Cudahy (Co. B) summarized the Brit's philosophy: "All patrols must be aggressive ... and it must be impressed on all ranks that we are fighting an offensive war and not a defensive one."[12] The Third Battalion's commander, Maj. Charles Young, outranked and smothered by British self-importance, could do little to inject American opinions and needs. Meanwhile, Cpt. Joel Moore's men alternated with Cpt. Horatio Winslow's in manning the outposts and trenches near verst 464, each company sending out patrols, searching for the Bolos. Normally little came of these activities; however, on September 24, 1918, 26-year-old Pvt. William Donnor (Co. M) got separated from his patrol. Private Donnor wandered about, lost for several hours. Walter Dundon wrote, "Pvt. William Donnor (Co. M) got lost. Visited enemy camp by mistake, but escaped."[13] Lieutenant George Stoner added, "[Donnor] ... returned at 4:30 PM ... some experience for him."[14]

The next day, September 25, 1918, with Company M on duty at verst 464 and Company I resting in Obozerskaya, Col. Stewart arrived at battalion headquarters. Colonel Stewart and Maj. Young paid a short visit to Cpt. Moore's headquarters at verst 464 but left quickly when the Bolo artillery began shelling the area. The 339th's commander then returned to Archangel. Later that day, Cpt. Moore's patrols discovered the Bolsheviks had pulled back from their positions during the shelling. Moore, on September 26, sent Lt. James Donovan and an oversized patrol to determine how far the Bolos had retreated. Donovan's patrol returned with the news they had explored as far south as verst 458 before detecting Bolshevik presence.[15]

This news excited the British commanders at Obozerskaya. General Robert Gordon-Finlayson immediately ordered a converging assault to be made against the enemy's works at versts 458 and 455. Captain Joel Moore described the British general's plan: "Maj. Young [was] to divide his two American companies into two detachments for making the flank marches and attacks upon the Red positions. The marches were to be made ... in the afternoon and night, and the attacks to be put on at dawn."[16] A third force, composed of thirty French soldiers and two machine gun teams from the 339th Machine Gun Company, were to move straight down the railway to a point 500 yards north of the bridge at verst 458

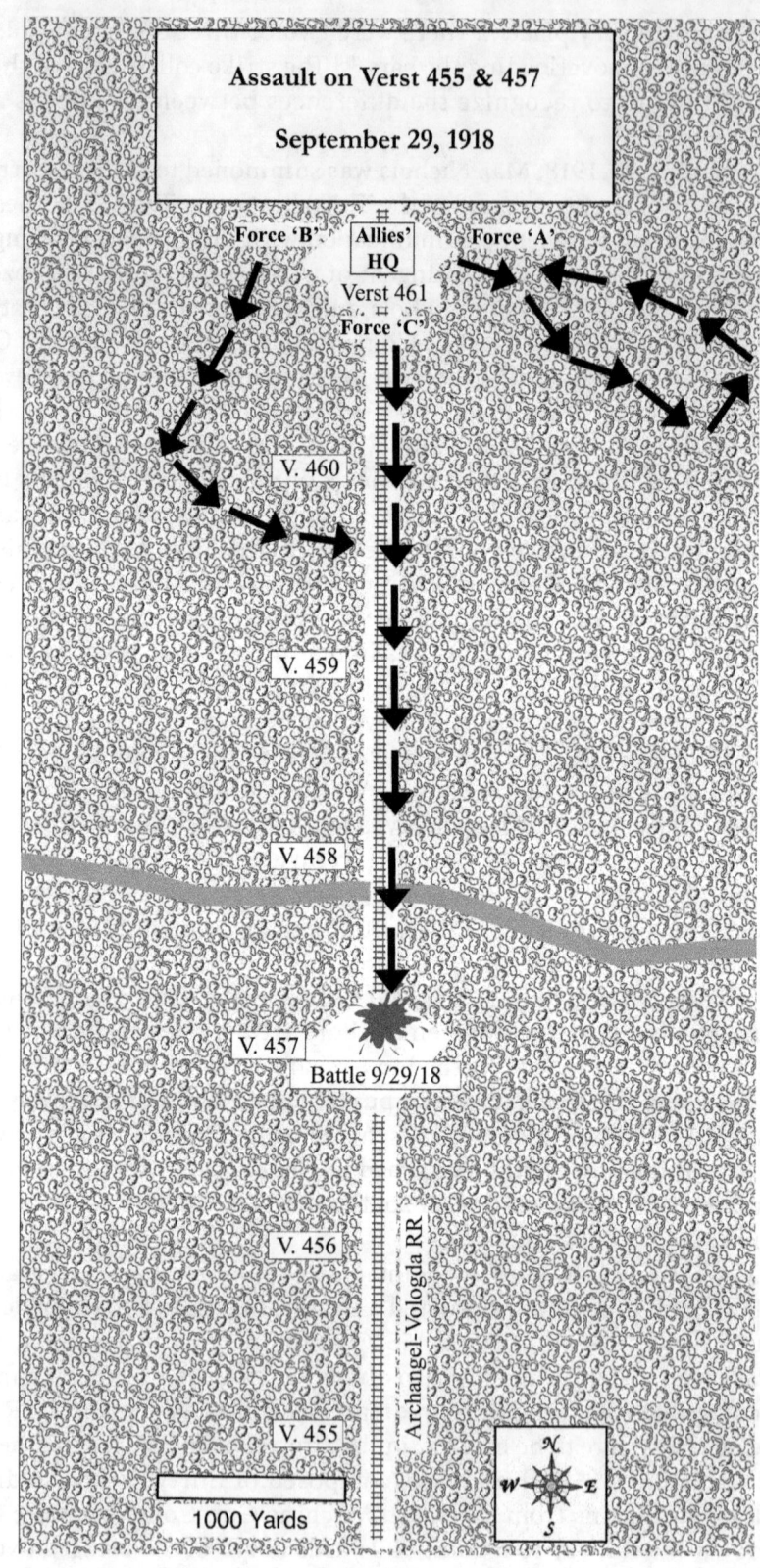

and assault from there. Thus, as planned, the attackers would strike the Bolshevik positions simultaneously from the left flank, the right flank, and the center. The American staff officers shuddered at the plan. One wrote, "This split the three weak columns against a force of Reds variously estimated at from four to ten times as large as the attackers."[17] Captain Joel Moore angrily retorted, "This hurriedly contrived advance was doomed to failure before it started."[18]

The plan went into action just after 1:00 p.m. on September 28, 1918. Captain Joel Moore, leading the left flank formation (Force A), loaded his company of just over one hundred men onto a train with instructions to move southward no later than 2:30 p.m. Company I's two platoons were to join Moore's men as soon as a contingent of French soldiers relieved them from their picket duty. Unfortunately, the French troops could not find Company I's men, preventing Cpt. Moore's force from moving on time. The Company I officer in charge of the two platoons waited as long as he could, but when they did not arrive, requested permission to pull his troops out of their postings. Once these platoons received authorization to abandon the picket duty they hustled to the railway.[19] The train left Obozerskaya at 4:00 p.m.[20]

Force A reached verst 461 and unloaded from its train at 5:00 p.m. The men formed into marching column, ready to head east, into the woods, and then trek south, their goal a location just east of the Bolo positions at verst 455. Meanwhile a second train arrived, this one carrying Force B, two platoons of Company I and the trench mortar section. They unloaded and turned west, also prepared to hike into the Russian forests, their aim verst 457. Major Charles Young established his battalion headquarters at verst 461 and gave the order for the two battle groups to march.[21]

Captain Moore turned to Cpt. Griffen, a British officer armed with a map and the authority to lead the march. Griffen led Force A away from the tracks and into the dense Russian woods, his goal to find an old south-leading road running parallel to the tracks. Joel Moore wrote, "At five o'clock in the afternoon the detachment struck into the woods … [with] a British intelligence officer … guiding us, although he had no familiarity with the swamp-infested forest area."[22] The lateness of their start meant the early Russian night soon overtook the soldiers, stealing their ability to see and forcing the Brit to use his compass. He quickly found himself in trouble. Lieutenant Albert May (Co. I) remarked, "The compass in North Russia, while pointing N is really pointing SW, so you must make delineation, know your pace scale, [and] keep a pad before you and record as you go. Otherwise you are lost."[23] Captain Griffen blundered about for some time before eventually stumbling upon a primitive road. Incredibly, this road was not what the British headquarters had expected it to be when they planned this mission. Captain Moore grumbled, "We came to a certain broad north-south cutting laid out in the days of Peter the Great."[24] Albert May added, "[It was not] a real road—just trails … [with] four feet of quagmire."[25]

Force A moved onto this mud-choked lane and inched southward, the men struggling, each movement a contest with boot-swallowing mud. Their advance became painstakingly slow, the mud forcing the Yanks to struggle for every step.

The British plan had been for Force A to make the four-mile hike to the appointed attack point in an hour or so and then have the men get a full night's rest. Lieutenant John Cudahy (Co. B) remarked, "It seemed to the officer planning this attack a simple thing to follow one of these lanes, and take the course of a north and south aisle until a point was reached opposite the enemy position." Cudahy continued, "He did not know that the forest paths were deep with clinging, slimy morass, and bog that gave no footing."[26]

The hike southward floundered, stuttered, and came to a halt. The darkness was complete; the men could not see what was in front of them nor where they had been. Each soldier had to rely on his hearing, listening for the sounds of the man ahead of him. When a man fell, everyone behind him was forced to stop. Their line began to string out as gaps appeared in the column, and since no one could see for any distance, these spaces grew. Joel Moore recorded, "Ears told you [the man in front of you] was tripping over fallen timber or sloshing in knee-deep bog holes. Hard breathing told the story of [our] exertion."[27]

Captain Griffen, now soaked and mud-splattered, peered at his compass in absolute bewilderment as the instrument argued the road—a trail cut nearly two hundred years ago—was going in the wrong direction. A halt was called but some of the men did not hear the command and continued to wander about. Then, once the marched resumed, the groups became farther separated. John Cudahy wrote, "There is nothing to do but have a go at it, so plowing through waist deep swamp and awful, oozing quagmire, [we] lurch on." He continued, "Struggling forward, still forward, [we] are caught and tripped, and sprawl splashing in the cold water and the bog, but [we] get up and drag on until all are breathing with heavy sobbing gasps."[28] At times an unlucky soldier would wallow into deep, mud-choked holes and flail helplessly until being pulled to safety. Private James Siplon (Co. I) complained, "[Sometimes] the [water] was waist or chest deep to most men ... and the men were all carrying packs on their backs."[29] Joel Moore added, "We struggle on. We lose our direction. The marsh is a bog.... We must flounder on. The column has to spread. Distress comes from every side. Men are down and groggy."[30] Lieutenant Clarence Primm wrote, "There was a short halt for a rest. When we were to start again I went to urge on three men who were standing in a group with their heads together like football players in a huddle. I had to awaken them!"[31]

The road ended, giving way to a large open expanse, barely visible to the exhausted soldiers. The leading troopers ventured out into the clearing, only to discover they had worked their way into a thigh-deep swampland. Private Siplon noted, "When we got up there in about the middle of the night ... [we] were all soaked ... and the path stopped and [we] got into a deep swamp."[32] Captain Moore wrote, "Damn that unverified old map.... It did not show this lake that baffle[d] our further struggles to advance. Detour of the unknown lake without a guide, especially in our present exhausted conditions [was] impossible."[33]

Captain Joel Moore did not know where they were, did not know which way to go, and could not see in any direction. There was no use in continuing; Moore called for a halt. The exhausted men crowded around, NCOs sorting out the mud-splattered men, determining who was missing. Comrades sought out the lost while everyone remained mired in this mud-choked hell. Private Cleo Colburn (Co. I) grumbled, "When we stopped to rest in the night, of course you couldn't lie down, so I took my belt and wrapped it around a tree and around myself and slung in that for probably a half-hour's sleep."[34] There was nothing they could do until morning. Private Jay Bonnell added, "Slept in a swamp all night and it was raining so we had no place to lay so we did not do any sleeping but walked back and forth all night to keep from freezing."[35]

Meanwhile, Lieutenant Albert May's Force B was not doing much better. Though May's men had less distance to cover, they encountered the same appalling marching conditions. Albert May recorded, "The British colonel ... advised me ... that he would detail two British officers who had made [a] reconnaissance of the positions to go with me and place me in position." May continued, "We started out about dusk and marched through the dense forest. Darkness came quickly. There was no trail and progress was slow. We had no way of knowing where we were or what progress we were making." He added, "About 2:00 AM the two British officers left us out in the woods, stating they had to get back, and handed me [a poorly drawn map].... We ended up in a swamp, knee-deep in water."[36] Lieutenant Albert May ordered his men to halt. They would spend the rest of the night right where they were. Lieutenant Lawrence Keith, commanding the trench mortars, discovered his men suffered even worse than Lt. May's riflemen. His artillerymen, burdened with having to carry their heavy weapons, quickly fell behind and lost contact with the infantrymen. Lieutenant Keith recorded, "We ... attempted to follow Lieut. May through an almost impassible swampy bog.... The men and their equipment were often waist deep in the mire." Lawrence Keith noted, "I turned back to the [railroad tracks] ... where we camped until daylight."[37]

Allied artillery opened fire upon the Bolshevik positions at 6:00 a.m., blasting the verst 457 area for fifteen minutes. Force C, composed of French infantry and a machine gun detachment, had not had any problem hiking down the railway to the bridge at verst 458 the night before. They easily moved into position to attack and immediately let loose several volleys. Their French commander, Cpt. Alliez, knew the Americans were supposed to strike the Reds' positions from both east and west. He then would send his men forward. But the Yanks did not attack. Captain Alliez spread out his small force into a skirmish order covering a front of about one hundred yards but did not advance. Instead, the captain sent out runners to determine why the Americans were not attacking.

Captain Joel Moore's men were not close to their assaulting position. In fact, by 8:00 a.m., Force A was nearing verst 461, as Moore had decided "judgment now dictates that it is best to retrace our steps and cut in at 461 to be in position to be of use in the reserve."[38] Lieutenant Cudahy wrote of this retro movement, "At dawn, two soldiers, who in days of peace, had been timber cruisers in the pine woods of the Michigan Peninsula, led their comrades to ground firm enough for footing, and half dead from fatigue, brought them back to the railway."[39] In effect, Moore's battle group had returned to the starting point, his men frustrated and exhausted.

Lieutenant Albert May's Force B, once daylight provided vision, moved toward the sounds coming from the Archangel-Vologda railway. Lieutenant Keith, along with his mortars, had been able to link up with May's riflemen. He reported, "The enemy could not be seen nor could the emplacements be found as we were too far west of our objective." The sounds of artillery, followed by machine gun and rifle fire, told Lt. May where he needed to go. Force B worked its way toward its objective, but again, as Lt. Keith noted, "we were unable to follow."[40] Albert May's men reached the railway at verst 458 and cautiously advanced toward the Bolshevik trenches. Major Charles Young recorded, "The attack was made at 6:30. Few of the enemy were met and they immediately retired."[41] Lieutenant May, not knowing what had happened to Force A, halted his riflemen and had them take cover in the Bolsheviks' abandoned defenses; he was soon joined by Lt. Keith and the trench mortar teams. Albert May made contact with Cpt. Alliez, who brought his Frenchmen forward and passed through the Americans, advancing to just north of verst 457. Major J. Brooks Nichols reported, "The French party ... entered the enemy's first line positions at 457½ without opposition. They then came under heavy machine gun fire."[42] Captain Alliez, knowing his force was quite small, had his men dig in. Both May and Alliez sent runners back to headquarters, seeking instructions.

Meanwhile, back at battalion headquarters at verst 461, Maj. Charles Young struggled to find out what was going on. He sent out a number of runners, but they never reached Lt. May's position and eventually returned empty-handed, meaning Young only knew of Force A's location; Cpt. Moore's weary men rested beside the railroad tracks. Charles Young told Cpt. Moore, "To [have his men] get as much rest as possible, dry their clothing, and get some breakfast."[43] Major Young knew Forces B and C were somewhere south but not where they were. The battlefield had grown silent, indicating nothing was happening, but he had lost control of his forces, and the Allies' push southward had gone nowhere.

An Allied train chugged into the siding at verst 461 to disgorge a pile of supplies and a small number of soldiers. One of these men, Maj. J. Brooks Nichols, immediately marched to battalion headquarters and presented Maj. Young with a message. Major Charles Young wrote, "Major J.B. Nichols 339th Infantry, handed me a copy of S.C. No. 9 ... dated Sept. 27th 1918, by which I was superseded as Co. O. 3rd Battalion by Major Nichols." Young continued, "I explained the situation to him and told him it was my intention to delay turning the battalion over to him until after the operation ... was finished. He suggested ... that as he was to take over sometime he might as well do it [now]."[44] Charles Young gathered his things together and left the headquarters. Captain Moore reported to Nichols, who ordered "every man at once to be made as comfortable as possible ... [and] to build fires and warm and dry their clammy water-soaked feet ... [plus] Bully and tea and hardtack [to] revive a good many."[45]

The quiet did not last. The Bolsheviks, realizing the Allied advance against their positions had been carried out by a very small force, massed their infantry for a counterattack. The Reds struck the French right flank and rolled them backward. The Bolo infantry pressed northward, supported by artillery and machine gun fire, pushing up against Lt. May's two platoons. Lieutenant Lawrence Keith wrote, "Fire was opened upon us from our front ... [and] we were being attacked on the flank. Firing became very heavy." He added, "Heavy fire was also opened on our right flank, slightly to the rear." Keith noted, "[My] platoon was then caught in this heavy crossfire and ... [as] I endeavored to withdraw my men to a new strongpoint.... I was wounded." The lieutenant also admitted, "Three trench mortar barrels, three base plates and one elevating stand, and about six trench mortar shells were left behind."[46] The doughboys scuttled backward. Private James Siplon (Co. I) recalled, "The only thing we could do was retreat."[47]

Major Nichols, hearing the sounds of combat, ordered Force A to mobilize. Captain Moore's men were slow to respond; however, 1st Lt. Dwight Fistler (Co. I) and the Company I troops that were with Cpt. Moore immediately moved southward along the railroad tracks. Fistler and his men raced down the tracks and arrived in time to help the combined French-American force check the Russian counter attack. Nichols, again, ordered Cpt. Moore to march to the sound of the guns. Joel Moore wrote, "No one platoon can do it. Too many men are [exhausted] from the night march. A volunteer platoon is organized." Moore continued, "[1st Sgt. Dundon] picks out 58 who are most willing and in the best shape."[48]

A lull in the fight occurred as Cpt. Moore's improvised company hustled southward. Bodies dotted the area, mostly Russian, but here and there were American and French casualties, abandoned when the Allies fell back. Attempts to rescue the wounded comrades were driven off by intense Bolshevik machine gun fire. The Allies could see the Bolos reinforcing their lines with more troops; it became obvious another Russian attack would soon be coming. The American and French soldiers checked their ammunition and realized they were running low. They knew a second Bolo attack would be fatal. Moore recorded, "The second attack of the Reds was waited with anxiety."[49]

The Bolsheviks arose from their trenches, pressed toward the Allies, and slowly began to overpower the doughboys and Frenchmen's abilities to resist. Captain Moore wrote, "The Reds were in great force and well led. They came at a new angle and divided the Americans and French, [and] completely overwhelming the trench mortar men's rifle fire."[50] Captain Moore's improvised combat unit crossed the bridge at verst 458 and hurried southward just as the Allied line collapsed. Moore recorded, "The Bolos charged with their devilish yell and won back their trenches and we saw the French and the Americans come running back along the railroad side."[51] Company M pushed forward, its two Lewis gun teams anchoring its flanks. The Bolsheviks opened fire upon the Yanks once they were fifty yards south of the bridge, spraying the doughboys with intense machine gun fire. Joel Moore recorded, "It was a machine gun bullet that hit Lt. Donovan in the left side, following a rib around to the backbone, just missing the vertebra and clipped through the thick muscles below the right shoulder ... no one else was hit."[52] Lieutenant Fistler's platoon arrived, bolstering Captain Moore's men, and they were followed by a handful of mortar men from Lt. Keith's platoon, all ready for more fighting. These soldiers, along with Company M's Lewis gun teams, one led by Sgt. Mathew Grahek and the other by Cpl. Frank Rahn, created a lethal wall of steel that "inflicted such losses upon the enemy ... he did not attempt to retake the bridge in force that day."[53] The Bolo attack was shot to pieces. Charles Young recorded, "The enemy attack was repulsed by 3:00 P.M. and our troops consolidated [the position]."[54]

The Bolshevik infantry fell back to their trenches, putting several hundred yards between the two forces. The shooting quieted down, though never went silent. The men on both sides hunkered down, resting though vigilant, ready to repel any movements by their foe. The Americans scanned the deadly space separating the two sides, studying the fallen in search of missing comrades. It did not take long before they could see a wounded American lying exposed, pleading for help. Sergeant Mathew Grahek (Co. M) crawled out of the Allies' trenches and inched his way nearly 150 yards to his comrade. The Bolsheviks saw the 22-year-old sergeant creeping toward the wounded man and immediately opened fire. Machine guns stitched the ground all around Grahek, and Russian mortar fire blasted near him, but the resolute NCO closed the distance on the American, reached him, and hauled him back to safely. He was awarded the Distinguished Service Cross for this action.

The field remained relatively quiet until 6:30 p.m., when the Bolshevik artillery opened fire. The sun set and vision was limited, preventing the British officers at headquarters from seeing what was occurring. They decided the Russians were preparing for a night attack aimed at retaking the verst 458 bridge. Joel Moore wrote, "The British officer ... [had] heard that the enemy was at the bridge and issued an order to his artillery to fire at the bridge."[55] The barrage landed directly upon Cpt. Moore's volunteers. Private Schlioma Dyment (Co. M) was the first to suffer blast and shrapnel wounds; his injuries proved fatal. More shells rained down to explode among the Company M positions, the blast, flame, concussion, and shrapnel injuring Pvt. Matti Niemi and Cpl. Frank Rahn. Private William Drews went down, as did Pvt. John Jerrain and Pvt. Joseph Karapuz. The Yanks huddled in the shallow trenches, terrorized by the bombardment, finding no way to escape the deadly shells. Private Andrew Yasas and Pvt. Paul Smaglick were mangled by shrapnel, while Cpl. Charles Riha received a minor wound. More shells descended upon the Americans, pounding their senses and spewing them with flame, steel, and dirt. A blast detonated near Pvt. Clarence Miller, stunning him badly. Later, Miller would be found "crying beside his comrade [Cpl.] Frank Rahn."[56]

Back at headquarters, the French officer, Cpt. Alliez, who knew where Moore's soldiers were, raced to Col. Sutherland and let him know about this serious mistake. Colonel Sutherland ordered the deadly fire to lengthen range. The shelling shifted, but the damage had been done; Cpt. Moore's men had suffered terribly. Medical personnel rushed in to attend to the wounded, carrying the injured men away from the battered trenches and loading them onto a train, prepared to rush them to the hospital in Archangel. The train arrived at Bakharitza in the early hours of September 30, 1918; however, by then, the 32-year-old Matthei Neimi had succumbed to his wounds. Later a Yank would complain, "Time after time ... the infantry, after gallant success, was shelled out of position." He added, "The effect on the morale was most disastrous."[57]

Captain Moore's men dug in, restored their ammunition supplies, and established lethal fields of fire. Nevertheless, during the night Col. Sutherland ordered them to retreat north of the bridge at verst 458. Major Nichols refused, causing the two officers to clash. Joel Moore recorded this encounter, writing, "Major Nichols ... when the order came over the wire for [the] Americans to withdraw ... from the bridge ... [he] shoved the order to one side till he heard from the officer at the front and then requested a countermanding order."[58] Colonel Sutherland backed down, and Moore's doughboys spent the night reinforcing their position. The French contingent augmented the defenses, along with men from Company I. Thus, when the sun came up, the Allies were well prepared for a Bolo assault.

Rations arrived just after 10:00 a.m., along with kettles of hot tea, but the men did not get to drink the body-warming liquid. A mass of Bolsheviks emerged from their positions and advanced. The Allies held their fire until the Bolos came within range and then canvassed the attackers with devastating machine gun, rifle, and mortar fire. The Bolsheviks took cover immediately, and for the next three hours, an exchange of fire rattled across the Russian countryside. The Reds gave up and withdrew, leaving the Allies holding their ground. The Bolsheviks then began a disheartened artillery barrage. Captain Moore wrote, "The enemy made it warm for us but only one man was wounded."[59]

The Allied force held its position south of the verst 458 bridge for the rest of the day, sometimes receiving Bolshevik artillery fire and other times hearing Allied shells scream overhead. Night came and went, with the Yanks and French grimly holding their position. One soldier wrote, "Both forces now dug in to await developments. Positions were consolidated, and affairs settled down to a daily routine of artillery actions and minor raids."[60] The Yanks in Companies I and L, now veterans of being under fire, had a new appreciation for their foe. Moore wrote, "The Bolsheviks had earned our respect as a fighter."[61] They also had a growing resentment for the British. One doughboy remarked, "All they can do is issue orders to us, but insofar as fighting is concerned, I have not seen one near the front lines since I've been here."[62]

Chapter 7

Assault on Verst 455

Herman Yopp was one of nearly 500 soldiers reassigned to the 339th Infantry as replacements (Library of Congress).

October 1, 1918: Private Herman Yopp followed a slow-moving line of soldiers, shuffling off the transport ship *Caesarea* and onto a wharf at Bakharitza. The 22-year-old soldier, like nearly every other fellow in this queue, had no idea why he was here in Russia. All he understood was he had been reassigned. Herman Yopp was born July 2, 1894, in Paducah, Kentucky, the eighth child of Andrew and Agnes Yopp. Herman's father, the son of a German immigrant, ran a grocery store, assisted by his eldest son. The Yopps lived in town, where Herman and his siblings attended the local grade school. Herman, once he finished eighth grade, got a job at a feed store, selling seeds, alongside one of his older brothers. Herman did so well as a seed salesman that when he reached the age of eighteen he was given the responsibilities as the store's manager.

America's entry into the Great War forced the young feed store manager into the military. His June 1917 draft registration card listed him as being tall, with brown eyes and brown hair though partially bald.[1] He entered Camp Custer, along with about a hundred other Kentucky draftees in April 1918 where he undertook basic training and was assigned to Company L, 337th Infantry. Private Yopp's battalion boarded the transport ship *Nevasa* on July 22, 1918, and traveled by convoy to France. He stepped onto French soil two weeks later.

Private Yopp's 337th Regiment was transported to Nièvre, France, in the Loire Valley, but did not move to the trenches. Instead, the regiment's men were separated into small groups and dispersed among American units that had suffered serious losses.[2] Then, in September 1918, Yopp along with 161 other 337th comrades was designated as replacements for the 339th Infantry.[3] Private Yopp boarded the *Caesarea* and two weeks later found himself marching down the ship's gangplank and onto Russian soil.[4] He had no clue why he was there, as "he had been drafted with the idea that [he was] going to France, and then, all of a sudden, wound up in Russia."[5]

The 339th Infantry during its first month had suffered so many losses due to the Spanish flu, injuries, sickness, and combat casualties that Col. George Stewart was forced to plead for reinforcements. In October 1918, the 339th received ten officers and 479 enlisted men.[6] Twenty-seven riflemen were sent to Company I, and forty-three, including Pvt. Herman Yopp, ended up being added to Company M. Herman Yopp recalled, "After a week's stay in Archangel and eating battalion mess, which consisted of 'grass stew' and hardtack three times a day, and tea for breakfast only, I was transferred to 'M' Company." Yopp continued, "[I] will never forget the first meal. A whole mess kit full of oat meal, dried apple sauce, bread and coffee.... When we were about half way through eating, Captain Moore made a little speech. He said that if anyone wanted seconds he could have them. I was so full that I hardly had room for all the applesauce."[7]

The company Pvt. Yopp joined was composed of a group of men more experienced than the novices who had stepped ashore a month earlier. Captain Joel Moore's riflemen, NCOs, and lieutenants had endured cool and rainy weather, incomprehensible British leadership, and horrible food. They also were missing comrades, victims of the Spanish flu, exposure to bad weather, and Bolshevik bullets. Joel Moore's troops felt like veterans now, most having adjusted to this strange and lethal situation. They accepted the replacements, knowing more riflemen on the line meant less work for everyone. One "old hand" remarked, "We did get replacements from France, from another unit that trained at Camp Custer. [They] went overseas the same time we did, but they went to France and we went to Russia."[8]

As Herman Yopp relished the last of his applesauce and coffee, he learned just how much of a luxury those items were to the veterans around him. The Third Battalion's first commander, Maj. Young, had not battled against the British directives, forcing old English rations upon the Americans. Eating greasy mutton and drinking English tea did not set well with the Third Battalion's doughboys, and this situation did nothing for their morale. Fortunately, when Maj. J. Brooks Nichols took over command of the battalion, he immediately recognized his troops' fragile morale. The major called a meeting of his company officers and senior NCOs, asking them what needed to be done. One of the sergeants, speaking point blank, said, "We want coffee," and from that moment on, Nichols was lectured on the faults of British rations. Private James Siplon (Co. I) declared, "After Major Nichols got in there.... He got us coffee ... and American rations." Siplon added, "Quite often we had beef stew and potatoes. In the field, bully beef and hardtack.... We began to get oatmeal for breakfast, and even once in a while we'd get pancakes."[9]

By October 6, 1918, Company M's platoons were deployed near verst 458 and 461, having just taken over for Company I's men.[10] American rations, gallons of strong coffee, and a large shipment of mail from home had raised the Yanks' morale. Lieutenant Primm remarked, "The men lined up and received ... mail ... from the States.... We have just had a big supper. The men are singing—the first I have heard since crossing the Arctic Circle."[11] Private Clement Grobbel (Co. I) agreed, writing to his parents, "I am well, and am in good health, under the conditions of this country." He continued, "You only see the sun for a few hours a day, and the rest of the time it is raining. We have fair time, while off duty ... the life is not bad, if a fellow could get some plug chew."[12]

The British high command wanted another push against the Bolsheviks, but this time Maj. Nichols refused to allow the Brits to create a plan without American input. First Sergeant Walter Dundon noted this difference: "October 7— Amalgamation of French and Americans for attack on 455 and 457½ ... Stoner and Wiesczorek's platoons with Cpt. Boyer's sections. Lt. Primm's platoon with Lt. Soyer's sections." He added, "Drill on woods; marching and approach."[13] Captain Moore's men practiced alongside their French allies for the next several days, perfecting movement through the Russian woods and swamps and attacking against prepared defensive positions. Lieutenant Primm remarked, "My men have been all this morning in the woods practicing with a French platoon, the men mingled, alternating one French and one American.... I can only say that French and American soldiers are training together in a kind of warfare known in Africa but not in France, and the only thing that remains of the drill-field formation is the [term] bush fighting."[14] And his doughboys enjoyed being shoulder to shoulder with the French veterans. Private Siplon (Co. I) explained, "We were great friends with the French.... We knew what day they got their wine ration. We'd go over and visit them at night. We couldn't talk French and they couldn't talk American, but we got along all right."[15]

The planned assault was set for October 14, 1918. By this time, more convalescing men returned to Company M, bringing the unit up to nearly two hundred fifty men.[16] Captain Moore wrote, "We are ready for the operation. Every man has had a chance at the *bahyna* [baths] and has on clean underclothing.... Each carries in his pocket three or four 'V.B's [rifle-fired grenades] for the French riflemen who will shoot the grenades." Moore also added, "Each man has gone with his French comrade to the big barrel and carries a pleasant canteen on his hip."[17]

The Allies' plan of attack appeared simple on paper, but the Americans had learned nothing was easy in Russia. Allied reconnaissance determined the Bolos had a forward defensive position at verst 457, supported by a well-placed machine gun. There also were detached posts extending to the east of the Archangel-Vologda tracks for some 800 yards and to the west about 400 yards. Major Nichols wrote, "The enemy had a good position and an excellent field of fire.... The M.G. posts on the west of the track were situated high enough to fire across the railway to the east." Nichols commented further, "At verst 455½ there was a reserve line ... [but most importantly] at siding verst 455 there was an armored train, including their batteries, field and machine guns."[18] Captain Joel Moore's goals were the destruction of the Bolshevik force at verst 457, as well as at verst 455, and the capture of both railroad positions.

The British high command wanted more—they desired the capture of the Bolo armored train. This feat would be accomplished by the inclusion of a detachment of American combat engineers. This force's responsibilities were to slip past the Russian positions at verst 455 and place charges on a bridge just south of verst 455, and, by destroying it, trapping the Bolo armored train. If all went well, this assault would be far more successful than what had taken place in the September attack. For the American riflemen, though, they had their doubts, as Pvt. Charles Stringham (Co. M) retorted, "It looked like such an impossible feat to us before we started."[19]

On October 12, 1918, assault assignments were designated: Lt. Clarence Primm, along with French lieutenant Soyer, were to lead their men in a march that placed them just southwest of verst 457; Lt. Robert Wieczorek's platoon and a French detachment under Cpt. Boyer, along with Lt. George Stoner's platoon and another Boyer detachment, would march farther south and strike verst 455 from the west. This formation would also include the engineers, who would continue on to their planned location not far from the bridge they were to destroy.

The next morning at 8:30, Cpt. Moore led his three platoons, along with their French comrades, away from verst 466 and traveled to verst 461. They crossed the bridge south of verst 458 and entered the woods. Bolo observers in an observation tower at verst 457 noticed the Allies' movements and moments later opened fire with artillery. Captain Moore recorded, "Lt. Stoner's Russian guide and point entered the woods ... on the long march to gain the rear of 455 ... Inside fifteen minutes the ... column ... [came] under the shrapnel fire of the enemy guns." Fortunately, though, the Bolshevik artillery was ineffective. Moore continued, "We pass[ed] untouched."[20]

The French and Americans began their trek through the Russian forest. This time, though, their march was different; it was daylight, they had maps, and there were guides who knew the area. Lieutenant George Stoner, who along with his French counterpart led the column southward, recorded, "[My] Russian guide and point enter the wood[s] ... on the long march to gain the rear of 455 ... The long thin column of blue and olive drab threaded its way through the forest by way of the blazed trees."[21] The attack force hiked all day, quietly making its way around the Bolshevik defenses at verst 457 and southward, steadily working to reach a location just west of verst 455. Years later Joel Moore would recall, "Remember how those helmets of ours would ring loudly in our ears when a branch came swinging back? Remember the dead silence and absolute motionless of our column when [an] airplane passed over us twice in the woods that afternoon?"[22]

Captain Moore, knowing his men were making good time, halted the column in the early afternoon. He wrote, "Remember the pleasant hour of rest for lunch? As you ate and drank with the Frenchies and tried to talk parleyvoo ... with them?"[23] Then the Yanks and Frenchmen continued their march. Darkness

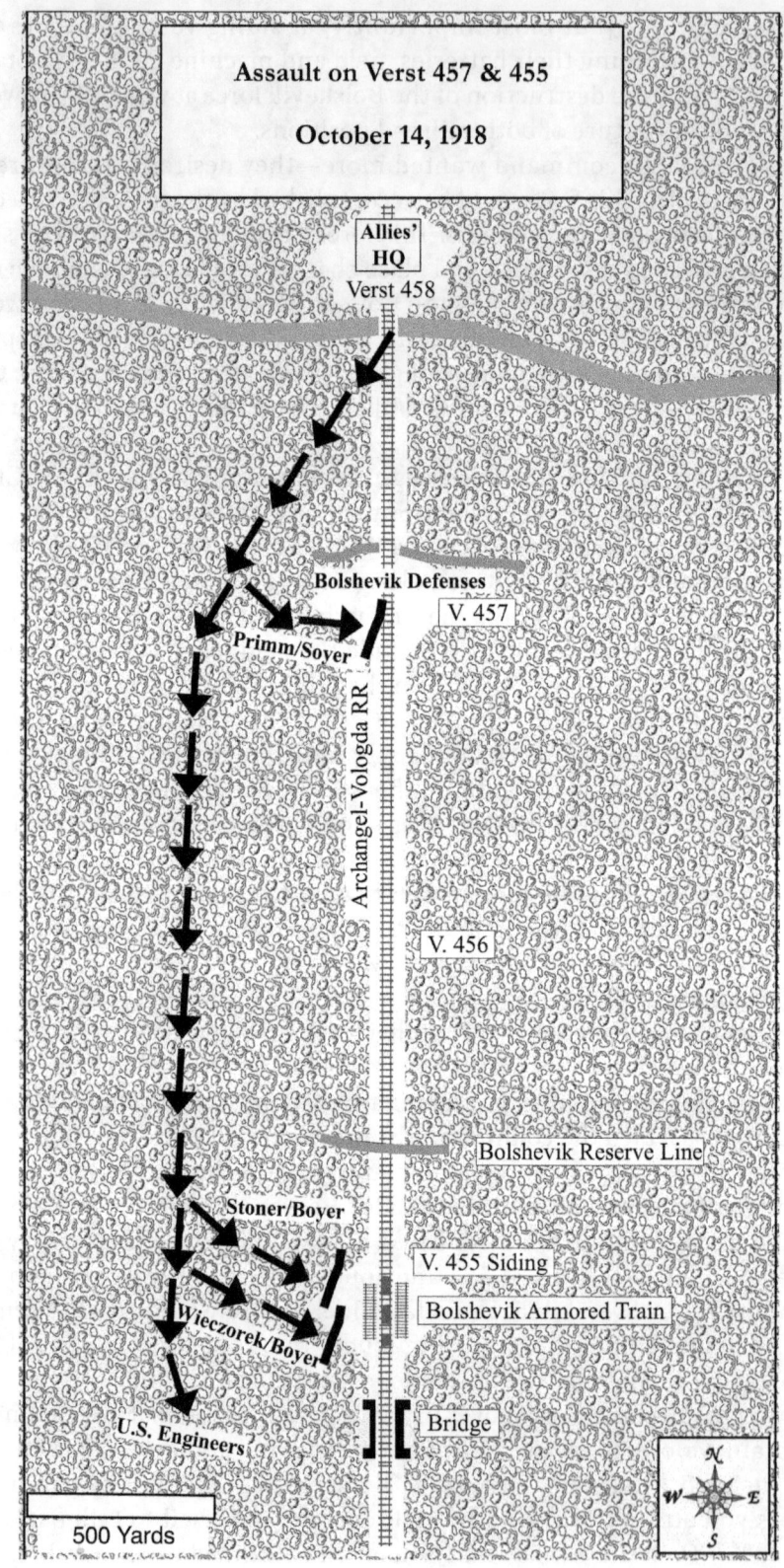

overtook the troops as they neared their hike's destination. The force's platoons were each assigned a position, facing outward, creating a hollow square.²⁴ The men, knowing silence was necessary to maintain surprise, moved quietly to their posts, aware they were now within a half mile of the Bolshevik positions at verst 455. Rain began to fall, tormenting the soldiers who were not allowed to build fires. The men munched on hardtack and shivered. Private Steven Starr (Co. M) grumbled, "[My] teeth chattered in the cold, rainy night [as] we slept within sound of the enemy's noisy camp."²⁵ Lieutenant Primm added, "All night under the sky in the rain, no blankets."²⁶

Those few men who did sleep were rousted at 5:15 a.m., and within a quarter of an hour everyone had quietly lined up to move out. The men were ready to march—movement meant the possibility of getting warm. Captain Moore recorded, "It is ... dark and foggy. Men are stretching their cold and cramped frames. The rainy night has been interminable. Trying to lie on a log or recline against the side of a tree has been weary business. No smokes. No eats."²⁷ At 5:30 a.m., Lieutenant Robert Wieczorek's platoon led the way toward the Bolshevik positions. The soldiers moved slowly and quietly, the point men creeping forward cautiously. The pre-dawn darkness limited vision and Lt. Stoner's platoon drifted southward, eventually losing contact with Wieczorek's men. Captain Moore halted the advance until contact was made between the two units and Stoner's force could reassemble in their proper position. By now, the sun had risen, the fog had begun to thin, and Moore's men were behind schedule. The plan had been for them to reach their assault point before 6:40 so they would be ready when Allied artillery began shelling the Reds' defenses.

A volley from Russian rifles smacked into the trees around Lt. Wieczorek's men. The Yanks sought cover, dismayed to know their surprise was gone. Joel Moore reported, "The Bolos' listening post and his big tower on his left flank now stand him in good stead. He sees the little platoon creeping in and sends a force out to attack."²⁸ The Americans and French quickly responded, moving forward, shooting as they advanced. Lieutenant Stoner rushed his men forward to come up beside their comrades, and the two units pushed against the Bolos. Then, Bolshevik artillery began pounding the area, but the shells were aimed too high.

The veteran French officers proved critical in supporting the rookie Americans. Captain Alfred Hasselvender and Lt. Conrad Dequerte both put themselves out in front, ignoring Bolo fire, and led the Allies forward. Both men would later be awarded the Distinguished Service Cross. The Yanks and French crashed into the Bolshevik position and in ten minutes of fierce fighting drove the defenders backward. Allied artillery then began pounding the Reds, both at verst 457 and 455½.

The two American-French platoons pushed out of the woods and onto the cleared ground west of verst 455's railroad siding. The Allies could now see where they had to go; the siding at verst 455 was built on a clearing about a half mile across. Lieutenant John Cudahy (Co. B) described the siding, writing, "[There was a] log station [house], several woodchoppers' houses in the center, and near them piles of corded pine to feed the wood burning locomotives."²⁹ Hundreds of

Bolshevik soldiers milled about, many scrambling to take cover from the Allied artillery.

The French and Americans rushed forward. Captain Moore wrote, "Firing and shouting, and yelling the ... platoons press on. The enemy opens fire in our direction with machine guns and with pointblank artillery fire. But he is rattled. His fire is high."[30] The attackers surged forward as Bolshevik bullets sliced into them. Corporal Homer Steinhauer (Co. M) was wounded and Pvt. Benjamin Jondro (Co. M) was struck in the arm by a bullet. The Americans and French pressed further, eliminating points of resistance one by one. Soon, only a handful of defenders clustered around two machine guns, but this machine gun's fire was lethal. Private Walter Merrick (Co. M), "Wallie," as his comrades called him, a 28-year-old farm worker from near Sandusky, Michigan, was "in front of one gun ... [when] a ball [went] through his head."[31] Later, a Bolshevik round shattered the knee of Pvt. John Keller (Co. M). Not long after this, though, the fight ended. The last of the Bolo defenders fled, leaving behind two Hotchkiss machines and a number of wounded and dead.

Lieutenant George Stoner recorded what occurred next: "The enemy in panic leaps on his troop train and dashes away to the south."[32] Joel Moore wrote, "The engineer detachment ... [did] not get up in time to blow the track." Private Ray Lawrence (Co. M) raced after the train, only to be wounded in the wrist by shrapnel from a grenade. Captain Joel Moore surveyed the area, studying the Bolshevik positions and machine gun emplacements, shaking his head. He wrote, "[I] tremble to think what they could have done to us had they held [to] their machine guns."[33]

Captain Boyer took command of his French veterans and created a defensive position at the south end of the verst 455 clearing. Meanwhile, Cpt. Moore gave orders to mop up the locality. Moore's first sergeant determined the blood payment the Americans had paid for this railroad siding. Walter Dundon recorded, "Our casualties—1 killed and 4 wounded in 'M' Co. French casualties—2 wounded."[34] A messenger was sent northward to inform headquarters the position had been taken, and not long after this a U.S. signals team arrived to start laying telephone wire. Back at headquarters, Maj. Nichols wrote, "At 9:15 A.M. Capt. Moore reported that he had taken the siding at v-455." The battalion commander also noted, "the enemy's armored train and troop train had escaped south, the Engineers not being able to get in back of the trains in time to destroy the rails."[35] Captain Moore, his objective secured, wrote, "Before noon the French and Americans have arranged defenses for any possibly counter-attack and fires are burning cozily at each post where [the men] are drying socks and waiting for the chow sergeants to get up the rations." Moore added, "[Unfortunately] the chow train [was] ... pulled hastily back by order of the British commanding officer because the Bolos chose to do a little long distance shelling ... it was four o'clock when the men finally got their hot mess."[36]

Meanwhile, Lt. Primm and Lt. Soyer's combined platoon had struck the Bolshevik defenses at verst 457 precisely as planned—hitting the Bolos' exposed left flank. This fight had been quick, with Maj. Nichols writing, "The enemy had run away." Primm consolidated the position and waited for new orders, and once Nichols learned that verst 455 had been taken, ordered him to reinforce Cpt. Moore. Nichols wrote, "At 11:00 A.M. the engagement was over.... Two heavy Hotchkiss M.G.'s and 2 telephones with paraphernalia were captured."[37]

Major Nichols gave the command for Company I to advance. Captain Horatio Winslow's four platoons, two hundred men in all, led by lieutenants Albert May, Gordon Reese, Forest McKee, and Gerald Danley, along with a French company led by Cpt. Apsche, marched southward along the tracks. Winslow's platoons passed through Moore's men, crossed the bridge that had not been blown, and pushed their way to verst 454. They ran into a scattering of Red riflemen but easily brushed them aside. The Yanks and French forced their way farther south, crushing any form of defense the Bolsheviks tried to put against them. Finally, the Bolos fled in disorder. One doughboy remarked, "The enemy was on the run."[38] It became a race between the French-Americans' advance southward against the sun's movement toward the horizon. The sun set with the southward march nearing verst 450.[39] Here, the Bolshevik armored train sat, its artillery lobbing occasional shells at the advancing soldiers. When Winslow and Apsche's men approached the armored train, it retreated farther south.[40] A jubilant Pvt. Clement Grobbel (Co. I) admitted, "The life is not bad, it is like hunting rabbits, only on a bigger scale."[41] Grobbel's thoughts were seconded by Pvt. James Siplon (Co. I), who, reflecting upon the day's success, exclaimed, "[The Bolos] didn't have any [discipline]... They would fight as long as they had the advantage, and when they didn't have the advantage, why they'd run away."[42] Captain Joel Moore, though, contemplated what could have happened that day and murmured, "We have monkeyed with a buzz saw and suffered only slight[ly]."[43]

The Allies improved their defenses at verst 455 that night. The British command staff moved its headquarters to the verst 455 siding. Their communication with Archangel was quickly established by a U.S. Army Signal Corps detachment, which soon was able to brag, "The switchboard at verst 455 was able to give thirty different connections at once at any time of day or night."[44] The senior British officers were pleased, and they immediately began preparations to take more ground from the Bolsheviks. Strangely, though, later that night Maj. Nichols received a message he was not quite sure how to interpret: "Gen. Poole ... had left for England."[45] General Frederick Poole had been the senior British officer in Archangel, in charge of the entire North Russia Expeditionary Force. He had been the architect of all their activities on the Railroad front. Nichols wondered, with Gen. Poole gone, who was in charge?

Regardless of who sat at the senior chief's desk in Archangel, dawn on October 15, 1918, saw more Allied activity. Captains Winslow and Apsche were ordered to keep advancing southward. Company I's riflemen, along with the French, pushed against light opposition, gaining two more versts to 448, but then things began to go sour. An Allied battery of Canadian guns, tasked with softening up the Bolo positions, did not get the word from their British superiors that Cpt. Winslow's men had reached verst 448. Their bombardment fell among the Yanks, causing an angry Lt. Albert May to write, "One of our men was killed by a Canadian shell ... [a] three-inch shell hit him in the back and exploded. There wasn't anything left to bury."[46] Private Frank McLaughlin, a 27-year-old railroad clerk from Elk Rapids, Michigan, was interred near where he had been killed.

Then, Cpt. Horatio Winslow was blindsided by an unexpected problem; his French allies received word an armistice was being proposed on the Western Front. Joel Moore wrote, "The *Poilus* had heard of the proposed armistice on the Western Front. '*La guerre finis*,' they declared and refused to remain with 'I' Company."[47] Winslow's lieutenants were dumbfounded as they watched the French soldiers turn their backs and walk away. The senior French commander, Cpt. Boyer, rushed to the scene and broke up the scheming Frenchmen, but the damage was done; the *Poilus* were finished fighting. Captain Winslow found himself in a dicey situation; half of his combat strength was no longer reliable. He ordered his lieutenants to stop advancing and to establish a defensive perimeter. His riflemen hunkered down for the night, a night in which the temperature dropped well below freezing. This was the coldest night since the Americans had arrived in Russia. A deeply chilled Pvt. Roy Rasmussen (Co. I) noted it was a "very heavy frost."[48]

On October 16, 1918, Maj. J. Brooks Nichols knew he had serious organizational issues needing immediate attention. The French troops had marched northward, leaving Cpt. Winslow's unsupported men by themselves. Nichols ordered Joel Moore to relieve Winslow's soldiers. But Cpt. Moore's platoon commanders were also dealing with the French departure. Moore's first sergeant recorded, "[We] dissolved [the] French-American combination and reorganized Co. into four platoons. Moved forward at 3:00 P.M. to support Co. 'I.'"[49] That evening Lt. George Stoner noted in his journal, "Reorganized platoons. Moved up to 448."[50] Captain Winslow's weary troops trudged back to verst 455, battered by the needless death of Pvt. Frank McLaughlin, as well as the loss of another four comrades who had been wounded.

Joel Moore's platoons moved into Company I's recently dug trenches. Joel Moore observed his troops and wrote, "The men ... around their campfires sat and talked of the strange campaign, talked of the rumors of German collapse, and speculated on the effect on their war. All night they sat with rifles in hand, for the Bolos and 'M' Co. had several exchanges during the night." The British high command, though, safe and secure at headquarters at verst 455, did not find the loss of the French infantry to be a serious problem. They pressed Maj. Nichols to send his men further south. Thus, later that evening, Cpt. Moore received orders to continue the push. This time, though, rather than sweep around the Bolshevik flanks, Nichols demanded the attack to march straight down the railroad tracks, right into the Reds' faces. Joel Moore explained his commander's logic, writing, "We determined to push a frontal attack straight down the track.... If we stuck close to the railroad we could keep our lines in [contact] and ... the Bolos we had passed would be in worse fix than we would be, as they would be cut off from the main body."[51]

Company M's sergeants had their squads up by 4:00 a.m. on October 17, 1918. Captain Moore, having learned there might be a sizeable Bolshevik force out in the woods west of the railway, put Stoner's larger platoon on the west side of the tracks and Wieczorek's platoon to the east. Lieutenant Primm's platoon, which had been deployed out in front of the company during the night hours, was moved so they could follow behind Stoner's people and protect his flank and rear. Then the doughboys hunkered down to await an expected artillery barrage, scheduled for 6:30 a.m. The Yanks worried about the artillery, as they had little trust in the British leadership. However, this time the artillery fire was accurate. Captain Moore remarked, "And with the first shell thrown over by our artillery, the advance began in squad columns."[52] His men cautiously approached the Bolo defensive line. They slowly advanced through the woods on each side of the railroad tracks, the platoons in skirmish order, spread out nearly a hundred yards wide on each side. Lieutenant Stoner's platoon rushed the enemy's works and, after a short burst of fighting, drove the Reds backward. Joel Moore noted, "Luck was with us. Not a man was hit."[53]

Lieutenant Robert Wieczorek's platoon, moving forward east of the tracks, did not find any Bolo defenses. They continued to cautiously creep forward. Just after 7:00, with the rising sun burning away the mists, Wieczorek's riflemen were halted by a sluggish stream. They could see a large area of cleared ground beyond the water. Soon, Lt. Stoner's men reached the water barrier and also stopped. Captain Moore described the verst 445 location: "[The company's] advance was finally halted at the edge of a broad stream that flowed beside a big clearing about half a mile square and filled with wood piles and occupied by about a dozen houses.... Careful reconnaissance ... disclosed the fact that the clearing was occupied by the enemy in considerable strength. We afterward found it to have been between 500 and 600."[54] Captain Moore brought up Lt. Primm's platoon to reinforce Stoner and Wieczorek.

Joel Moore gave the command and the three platoons splashed across the stream, yelling and hollering. Again, for the second time that morning, the Yanks had caught the Reds unaware. Moore's men charged across the clearing, rolling over the Bolshevik riflemen. The fighting was sporadic, though fierce; in one location a well-protected Bolo machine gun position sprayed a line of doughboys with dangerous fire, forcing the doughboys to seek cover. They could not move, the Reds' fire pinning them in place. Corporal Robert Pratt (Co. M), a 24-year-old from Ashton, Michigan, wielding his Lewis machine gun, led a squad of comrades forward, working to flank the machine gun nest. His bravery earned him a Distinguished Service Cross. The Bolshevik opposition collapsed once this position fell. Captain Moore wrote, "The scrapping was hot enough on both sides of the clearing. But we had the enemy's goat. The attack was so impetuous that the enemy's fire was wild and his lines broke from cover to cover frantically."[55]

The Americans took possession of the verst 445 station but did not stop. Moore sent Stoner's and Wieczorek's platoons forward, trailing after the fleeing Russians. He recorded, "There [followed] a vigorous chase ... [as the] first and second platoons [pursued] the enemy through the woods, while the third platoon was consolidating the ground." The Bolsheviks disappeared in the distance, racing away from the Americans. Lieutenant George Stoner's and Robert

Wieczorek's men moved steadily southward, their skirmish line moving down the tracks. Their energy seemed relentless, and the men knew they had been fortunate. Joel Moore noted, "Not a man was wounded although several had their clothing and equipment riddled."[56]

Back at verst 445, Cpt. Moore was surprised to see Cpt. Apsche arrive, leading a contingent of French soldiers. The French captain informed Moore the siding was to be consolidated and prepared for defensive operations. His Frenchmen were to help mop up the battlefield. Apsche's *Poilus* fanned out, searching for dead bodies. A horrified Yank recalled, "The French fighting on our side ... took the gold teeth out of the [Bolo dead]. Took the butt of a pistol and knocked their teeth out."[57] Captain Apsche also notified Joel Moore that he must halt his advance. Moore sent a runner to Lt. Stoner, who sent back word that his point men had reached verst 444. Moore ordered Lt. Primm to advance to that location and dig in. First Sergeant Dundon wrote, "Objective reached and enemy defeated before 9:15. French Co. under Apsche came on to support and help consolidate position. Lt. Primm's platoon consolidated the advance outpost line at curve 444.... No casualties. Enemy dead 9; prisoners 4."[58] The day went by quickly, the Yanks and French digging trenches, reinforcing machine gun positions. Darkness soon fell over the area and the temperature plunged below freezing again. Those riflemen in Company M who could took shelter in the peasants' houses built along the tracks.

October 18, 1918, went by quietly. Captain Moore's men worked to improve their defenses, while a signals team extended the telephone line, connecting verst 444 with headquarters. Then, that afternoon, a company of Royal Scots arrived to reinforce the position. Their commander brought word the Allies were not going to give up this position; however, by evening, patrols and forward posts were bringing in reports of a new Bolshevik force moving through the forest, pushing northward, and preparing for a counter attack. Contact came at 4 o'clock the next morning when the Royal Scot pickets opened fire and the two sides battled each other for a few minutes, shooting blindly in the dark, before the Bolsheviks withdrew.

The quiet lasted briefly, only to be blasted apart by a heavy artillery barrage, the Reds' shells pounding the American positions, catching many unprepared. Corporal Simon Bogacheff (Co. M), a 26-year-old Russian immigrant who had settled in Detroit before the war, was knocked to the ground, shredded by shrapnel. Private Ray Vickary (Co. M), a 28-year-old from Saginaw, Michigan, was also severely injured. More explosions pulverized the Americans, seriously wounding 25-year-old Pvt. David Oslund (Co. M), a Swedish immigrant from Princeton, Michigan, and 24-year-old Pvt. Ora Dusseau (Co. M), one of the replacements from the 338th Infantry who had only been on Company M's muster rolls for a few days. Joel Moore recorded these casualties, writing, "They were hard hit by shrapnel burst ... they were standing outside during the furious bombardment."[59]

The Americans and Scots reappeared from the shelters once the barrage ended, expecting a Bolshevik assault. An hour went by, and then another, but the Bolos did not attack. NCOs ordered some of their riflemen off the line and told them to improve their defenses. First Sergeant Walter Dundon recorded, "Bomb-proofs constructed in afternoon."[60] The rest of the day went by without any Bolo aggressive movements. Night came, and along with darkness, a thick snow blanketed the landscape.[61] Company I's Clement Grobbel wrote his parents, "It is getting colder every day, and it is starting to snow now, but we should [not] worry, we have good heavy sheep's lined coats." Grobbel also stated, "I was promoted from Private to Corporal of a Lewis Auto gun crew."[62]

October 20, 1918, dawned cold and snowy, but this new condition did not prevent the Bolsheviks from firing their cannons. An early morning barrage raked the Allies' newly constructed shelters, blasting tree limbs and branches and ejecting deadly shrapnel in ever-widening circles. Other shells dropped among verst 444's railway station buildings, punching holes in walls and roofs and shattering windows. Twenty-three-year-old Pvt. John Boysen (Co. M), another "just-in" replacement, was in one of these buildings when a blast erupted nearby. He was cut in the forehead by flying glass.[63] The barrage ended and the riflemen tended to the destruction, thankful for not being hurt. Outposts were relieved, coffee consumed, meals eaten, and socks dried over campfires. Meanwhile, everyone waited, expecting a Russian attack.

But no attack came. Instead, Cpt. Moore received word his company was to be relieved, and that noon, Cpt. Horatio Winslow and his riflemen filed into the clearing at verst 444. Winslow's platoons replaced Moore's men, who then hiked northward, away from the front line. First Sergeant Walter Dundon recorded, "Co. moved to 466 for rest and outpost duty."[64]

Chapter 8

A Change in Strategy

October 20, 1918: Brigadier General William Edmund Ironside, having settled into his new office in Archangel, met with Gen. Robert Finlayson, the Railroad front's commander. The newly-appointed senior British officer and Finlayson discussed the situation south of Obozerskaya, with Finlayson explaining, "He had disposed the troops in his command as far forward as he could, thereby making 'elbow room' for [Archangel]."[1] General Ironside, the 38-year-old Scotsman from Edinburgh, was born May 6, 1880. His parents, Surgeon-Major William Ironside and Emma Richards Ironside, lived the life accorded to a British senior officer. Sadly, the surgeon-major died in 1881, leaving his wife with two children—a daughter, Mary, and William. The widow, her income now much less as a pensioner, moved her little family to St. Andrews, Scotland, and went about the business of raising her children.[2]

William attended St. Salvator's School until the age of thirteen, when he went to the Tonbridge School. Then, at age sixteen, he was enrolled at the Royal Military Academy. During these years William's mother loved to travel, and she took her children with her, introducing them to worlds much different than the quaint one at St. Andrews. The young boy was fascinated by foreign language, and with assistance from his mother, he learned to speak German, French, and Flemish. He also, while traveling with his mother in Russia, decided "to learn to speak Russia on his own."[3] William was also a rough and tumble fellow,

Brigadier General William E. Ironside took over command of the Allies in North Russia in late September 1918 (*The War Illustrated*, 1918).

excelling at boxing, soccer, and rugby. He received considerable recognition in rugby—so much so he was nicknamed "Sapper-Ironside." Though William did well in all subjects except higher math, he surpassed all of his classmates in foreign language, a situation causing occasional difficulties. In one instance, when his ability to speak flawless German was better than his instructor's, his peers took offense at the fact he was raising the grading bar. This problem resulted in a fistfight (he won) and his transfer to a French class, where he also outdid his instructor.

William graduated from the Royal Military Academy in July 1899 and received a second lieutenant's commission in the 44th Field Artillery. His unit was sent to South Africa, where, because of his language abilities, he quickly learned to speak Afrikaans. Lieutenant Ironside recalled, "I had sworn to myself that I would learn the language properly. I was already supplied with an extensive vocabulary and all I had to do was listen to the pronunciation and learn which words were current in Afrikaans."[4] Ironside began wearing Boer clothing and living among the enemy, all the while collecting intelligence. By the time the war ended, Lt. Ironside had been wounded three times and earned recognition as an officer with a great future. And William Ironside by now had grown quite large, standing nearly six feet, five inches tall and weighing around 250 pounds. Of course, his peers tagged him with a nickname—"Tiny."

Ironside was promoted to captain in 1908, to major in 1914, and with the increasing demands of the Great War on Great Britain, he was commissioned lieutenant colonel in early 1916. Two years later, in January 1918, and now as a full colonel, he assumed command of a brigade and, with that, the temporary rank of brigadier general. Then, in early September 1918, Brig. Gen. Ironside's world was shattered; he was summoned to headquarters and notified he had been removed from his position as brigade commander. Ironside remarked, "It was a bad blow. I felt it in my bones that the Germans were beaten at last, and I wanted to be in at the death." Ironside continued, "The worst had happened.... I had been selected to go to North Russia."[5] Soon, though, Brig. Gen. Ironside was on his way to Archangel, saddled with the instructions "to hold the fort until the local Russians can take the field ... [and] to prepare for a winter campaign."[6]

Once William Ironside stepped into Archangel's British headquarters, he instituted a different mentality than what had been customary for the British staff. Before, under Gen. Poole, Russians were treated as colonials to be exploited, and Allied troops (also regarded as colonials) were thought to be vastly superior to the Bolsheviks. The British senior staff immediately saw Ironside's different approach; after all, their new commander thought enough of the Russians to be able to speak their language. Ironside gathered his staff together and began mining them for information. He went out and about in the city of Archangel, spending time with the local leaders, businessmen, Russian soldiers, and everyday citizens. He even interviewed Bolo prisoners. Ironside also met with Col. Stewart and Ambassador David Francis. The ambassador came away from the meeting impressed but also unhappy. He wrote Washington, "General Ironside is in command. Can not we arrange that an American general command Allied forces here?"[7]

General Ironside concluded that there had to be a change in emphasis of

Blockhouse near verst 445 (U.S. Army Signal Corps).

action. One of his senior officers recorded Ironside's decision, writing, "The expedition had thus far been operating offensively ... [but it now] became a question of holding to the ground already gained, with the forces already in place, until such time as the Allied Commanders saw fit to abandon the entire undertaking."[8] The general sent out orders, instructing the troops in each sector to halt their offensive movements and to immediately commence constructing defenses.[9] Captain Joel Moore recorded this transformation, writing, "We were only a few verst north of Emtsa, but many versts distant from Vologda, the objective picked by General Poole ... [but] we dug in."[10]

The riflemen in Companies I and M saw immediate evidence Ironside saw things differently from his predecessor. One doughboy, surprised and pleased by the change, wrote, "The Lewis gun ... it was air-cooled. In Russia it got [very cold] ... the ... Vickers machine gun [was water cooled], and ... had to have anti-freeze in [it]." Another Yank agreed, stating, "Can you imagine using a water-cooled gun up in that climate?"[11]

The temperatures continued to plunge and on October 22, 1918, a heavy snowfall covered the ground. The next morning Lieutenant Primm wrote, "Just now we have ... snow on the ground. Instead of rain, from now on we shall have snow whenever the load in the clouds gets too heavy."[12] At that time Cpt. Winslow's platoons defended positions near verst 448, while Cpt. Moore's men were housed in Russian houses and box cars at verst 466. A supply train arrived, bringing with it winter clothing. The men of both companies donned this new attire. Private James Siplon (Co. I) exclaimed, "We had big fur coats that were mixed wool. It would go down to almost your ankles." He continued, "We [got] sleeping bags. We always carried our sleeping bags—heavy wool sleeping bags.

We'd take our coats off and take our shoes off, crawl into them and use our coat for a pillow."[13] Lieutenant Primm added, "Yesterday some weird garments were issued to us. Great black fur turndown caps, white on the outside when turned down. Long canvas overcoats, lined with sheepskin. Leather vests, felt lined. Mufflers, mittens with one finger, [and] socks."[14]

Company M moved southward on October 24, 1918, and relieved Cpt. Winslow's platoons. First Sergeant Walter Dundon recorded, "Co. moved back to front. One squad left at 466, one at 452. Remainder of [company] at 448." He added, "Enemy machine gun fire at 9:15 P.M."[15] Meanwhile, once Company I settled into their quarters, Cpt. Winslow's men received the news they were to begin fortifying their defensive positions with blockhouses, barbed wire, and firing lanes. Soldiers from the 310th U.S. Engineers arrived, armed with construction tools, building supplies, and blueprints. They organized the riflemen into work teams, and assisted by local Russian workers, they began building blockhouses. Major Nichols secured funds to pay the Russians, and by using the many Russian- and Polish-speaking soldiers in Companies I and M, the Americans were able to get them working. James Siplon, toiling beside the locals, remarked, "The Russian men, all they were good for was to build [things]. They were good carpenters. You'd give them an ax and a saw, and they could go to work. They could do anything with an ax and a saw. But outside of that, they wouldn't do any work."[16] The results had to come quickly, as the blockhouses, barracks, support structures, and defensive positions had to be built before the ground froze. Corporal Cleo Colburn noted, "The piles of wood that were along the railroad front were used as our blockhouses. There'd be a pile of logs the size of a house and inside there would only be room for a squad because we had all of this extra protection."[17] Captain Moore wrote, "All of our barracks, washhouses, latrines, blockhouses, and stables were designed to use available timber stocks. For a form of rapid construction we used double walls six inches apart and filled the spaces with sawdust."[18] Private James Siplon (Co. I) added, "We'd build those blockhouses and put machine guns in them, and then put in fire lanes so that the Bolsheviks couldn't cross without being seen."[19] Private Russell Hershberger (MG Co.) reminisced, "The blockhouse was an eight-sided building, and in each one of their sides, there was a loophole there to fire out with machine guns. That's what we had to sleep in. We had pretty good sleeping quarters."[20]

The Yanks, along with the French and Royal Scots, were settled in by the end of October 1918. Of course their officers continued to work the soldiers, but because they were no longer preparing for the next assault, the men had more time off. They were completely isolated, deep in the Russian wilderness, and as the weather chilled even more, the riflemen preferred to stay inside, spending more time with the locals. This brought about personal exchanges between the doughboys and the Russian civilians. Corporal Clement Grobbel (Co. I) wrote, "We have great sport with the Russians ... learning them to speak English. They are the greatest fellows you ever seen for tobacco. If they see you clean out your pipe or drop a cigarette butt, they [go] after it like a flock of geese. For a cigarette or a little tobacco they will do most anything for you."[21] Private John Toornman

(Co. G) recalled an older woman's actions: "We used to give her sugar if we had it. She put it in the oven, and the sugar would melt and turn brown. It got hard, she would take it out and break it, put it on a dish, and pass that around. Everybody'd take a piece of that hard sugar, stick it in [their] jaw, and drink tea."[22]

Company I arrived at the front lines on October 30, 1918, and replaced Cpt. Moore's doughboys. Company M's riflemen hiked away; they were cold, hungry, and tired as they climbed into the boxcars set to take them to verst 466. Captain Moore received an order to let his men rest in the boxcars, which had been furnished with wood-burning stoves. His doughboys clustered around the stoves, enjoying the warmth and not caring that their train was not moving. Soon most were asleep. Then, once darkness came, the train chugged north. Captain Moore described what happened next: "The train was sent northward, expecting to be shunted off at [the] siding at Obozerskaya. Instead, during the night, the train was sent on northwards. The Co. awoke in the morning to find itself at Isaka Gorka [a couple miles south of Bakharitza]."[23] Lieutenant Stoner laughed, "[It was a] wild Ride to Isaka Gorka."[24] The "lost" company was returned to Obozerskaya that evening and the men allotted to their quarters. First Sergeant Walter Dundon recorded on November 1, 1918, "One platoon on outpost duty at 466 ... Remainder of Co. very much occupied in outpost duty at Obozerskaya." He added, "Glad to get back to a bathhouse."[25]

While Moore's men were on their wild ride Company I manned the front lines near verst 445. Captain Horatio Winslow's platoons were spread out along a defensive perimeter covering at least a mile, east-west. The outposts were established in such a manner that the posts were in contact with each other during the daylight hours. At night, though, darkness hampered communication, but this situation was not considered serious, especially now that winter was setting in and the Bolos appeared reluctant to strike. However, on the night of November 2, 1918, they did. James Siplon recorded what happened: "[Pvt. George Albers, Co. I] was on outpost that night ... probably about 50 yards ahead of the reserve lines. He was surprised at that time [and] ... he was captured. These fellows crawled up on him, and they had white sheets over them, and in the snow he didn't see them. They cracked him over the head and grabbed a hold of him." Siplon continued, "We attempted a patrol action to try to see where he went. There was no chance to get those fellows.... We didn't think we'd ever see him again.... We just figured they would torture him to get any information, and probably mistreat him. We had misgivings about the whole thing, and we were pretty down hearted about it at the time."[26]

Private George Albers (Co. I) was a 27-year-old wholesale meat salesman from Muskegon, Michigan. His draft registration card described him as tall and slender with blue eyes and brown hair.[27] He recalled, "A guy crawled up on me in the snow while I was on sentry duty.... The Bolo knocked [me] senseless with the butt of his rifle, then took [my] fur coat, [my] shoes, and even ... uniform." Albers continued, "When I came to I was being carried away on a stretcher.... We hiked 200 miles toward Vologda with the temperature 40 below. It was pure hell. We got black bread and fish soup—once in a while." Later, Albers would claim to be the first American soldier brought to Moscow.[28]

Chapter 9

The Great War Ends

November 3, 1918: Corporal Clement Grobbel looked up at the early morning sky, thick with clouds promising snow. The 23-year-old had grown up enjoying Michigan's outdoors and was accustomed to this kind of weather. To this young soldier, northern Russia's environs seemed similar to Michigan's wilds. Clement Anthony Grobbel was born November 2, 1895, to Anthony and Mary (Minick) Grobbel. Clement's father operated a saloon and pool hall in the village of Warren, Michigan, while Clement and his siblings received their primary education in a nearby one-room schoolhouse. Clement relished being outdoors and was prone to an occasional bit of mischief. In 1903, at age eight, he probably was the culprit in a fire that burned a neighbor's barn and icehouse. Of course, he claimed complete innocence. The local newspaper reported, "Those buildings were a total loss and the rest of the village was saved from the spreading fire only because the wind shifted direction." The news report "attributed the cause of the fire to little boys making and smoking cornstalk cigarettes."[1] Grobbel family history blamed Eddie, one of Clement's younger brothers, for starting the fire, but the facts do not add up to support this belief. Eddie Grobbel was three years old at the time. Clement's grandson, Mike Grobbel, believes "Clem may have been the instigator and fled the scene when the fire got out of control, leaving the two younger ones behind to take the blame!"[2]

Corporal Clement Grobbel (Co. I) was 22 years old when he was sent to Russia (courtesy Mike Grobbel).

Two years later, in 1905, Clement's father turned from saloon keeper to farmer. Clement toiled on his father's farm, though in his free time he roamed Michigan's woods, armed with a small-caliber hunting rifle. The young man finished high school, helped his father on the farm, and developed an interest in all things mechanical. Later, while in Russia, he would write his family, "It is so long since I tinker[ed] around a[n] auto or gas engine that I almost forgot how they work."[3] Clement's farming days ended on May 26, 1918, when he was drafted and found himself headed to Camp Custer. Grobbel was assigned to Company I and, within a few months, like every other soldier in the 339th Infantry, found himself in northern Russia.

On November 3, 1918, Company I's four platoons were spread out along the Archangel-Vologda railway. Captain Horatio Winslow had Lt. Gordon Reese and his platoon working on blockhouses near verst 446, and another platoon, Lt. Forest McKee's, stationed back at verst 448. Company I's main strength was at verst 445, with its platoons led by Lt. Albert May and Dwight Fistler, supported by six French machine gun crews. These two platoons routinely rotated men to forward posts at versts 444 and 443½.[4] In all, Cpt. Winslow had just eighty-seven Americans and fifty-three Allies under his command at verst 445.[5] He also had artillery forward observers who were linked to an Allied battery by telephone line, ready to call in support. Horatio Winslow's doughboys had been on the front line for several days, and though little had happened, they were tired and ready to be relieved by Company M.

The Allied artillery let loose a short barrage directed at a Bolshevik outpost south of verst 443. The Bolos did not respond, though a little while later a Russian airplane buzzed Captain Winslow's positions. The Yanks and French opened fire on the plane but it was not affected. The plane completed its observation and disappeared to the south. Quiet filled the rest of the afternoon and evening. Darkness smothered the area.

November 4, 1918, began much as the past evening ended quietly. Captain Winslow, though, warned his lieutenants and sergeants to keep their squads vigilant, as he had received word the Bolos were planning to attack.[6] His forward observers at verst 443½ confirmed his suspicions around 1:30 p.m. when they heard Russian voices. Soon, the Yanks spotted a Bolo patrol and opened fire. The Reds fired back, but with no real intensity, and this skirmish soon petered out. Then, a heavy Bolshevik artillery barrage pounded the area at verst 446, scattering Lt. Reese's construction crews. Captain Winslow, believing this to be the beginning of the Bolshevik assault, sent word to Lt. Reese to bring his men to verst 445, and this was done once this artillery fusillade ended.

Captain Winslow sent forward patrols to search out the enemy's presence, and word filtered back to the main line—the Bolsheviks were massed and primed to attack. Winslow's men prepared for the expected assault. At 2:15 p.m. the Red infantry crept forward, the Bolos working to keep hidden among the trees and ground cover.[7] Eventually, though, their approach could be heard. The Americans opened fire, rifles and machine guns ripping through the cold air. The Russians fired back, their shots sailing above the entrenched doughboys, but they continued to push forward, closing within fifty yards. Company I's lieutenants were soon able to determine the main Bolshevik force was aimed toward the American left. Captain Winslow ordered Lt. Fistler, whose men manned the left flank's forward positions, to withdraw 300 yards. Winslow also ordered Lt. Gordon Reese to reinforce the company's left flank. Reese sent two squads from his platoon to accomplish this task.[8]

Bolshevik artillery commenced pounding the Americans at verst 445, forcing everyone to take cover. This barrage lasted until about 3:00 p.m., when the cannonade shifted to strike verst 448. The American riflemen at verst 445 arose to their positions as the Russians surged forward, howling and shooting. The Americans increased their fire, their bullets slicing into the Bolsheviks. Though the American fire was heavy and Russian infantrymen were falling, the Bolos continued to close the distance between the two forces. These Bolsheviks (between 800 and 1,000) appeared more experienced and able than those the Yanks had fought against before, as this was not just a clumsy, straightforward rush.[9] Their leaders moved men about, seeking out weak spots in the American defenses, and, even more critically, the doughboys' vulnerable flanks. They approached the Yank lines so closely they "were near enough to hurl grenades."[10]

Lieutenant Gordon Reese, commanding the Yanks' left, moved his squads, shifting riflemen to fill holes and ward off the advancing Reds. One of these soldiers, 26-year-old Pvt. Leo Ellis, was acting as an ammunition carrier. He hurried from position to position, making sure everyone had sufficient ammunition. At one point a squad needed to move to a new location. Private Ellis pitched in and hauled the squad's Lewis machine gun for them. Lieutenant Reese's platoon, aided by soldiers like Pvt. Ellis, stopped the Bolsheviks. Unfortunately, though, they were unable to prevent other Reds from slipping around their flank. Lieutenant Reese rushed to that position, only to be shot down, wounded seriously.[11] Private Leo Ellis also fell, riddled by Bolshevik fire. He died, his body surrounded by the ammunition he was carrying.[12] More Bolos edged around the flank.

Corporal Theodore Sieloff, a 29-year-old from Detroit, saw what had happened to his platoon commander and, realizing the danger facing his company, rose from his safe position and moved to a location where he was able to fire upon the flanking Bolsheviks with his Lewis machine gun. The Bolos scattered, punished by his withering fire. Later, Sieloff's award citation read, "Cpl. Sieloff … delivered effective fire on the enemy. Although exposed to enemy fire from two directions, he held the enemy in check until his gun had become disabled, when he dismantled it, replaced the broken parts and renewed his fire, repulsing a strong force of the enemy."[13] Corporal Sieloff's effective fire broke the Bolshevik's flanking movement. The Bolos could not get around Sieloff's blistering gunnery, so they withdrew.

Meanwhile, another force of Bolsheviks had massed along the Archangel-Vologda tracks and pushed heavily against the 40-man platoon of Lt. Albert May, which straddled the tracks. The Yanks delivered an intense fire upon the attackers, but the Bolos pressed forward, protected by woodpiles, trees, and debris beside the rail line. Soon, their fire pinned down many of Lt. May's squads.

Albert May shifted other riflemen, trying to free the pinned men, but a Bolo bullet sliced through him, rendering him helpless.[14] The Russians pressed closer, their shooting debilitating. Private Martin Zawacki, a 25-year-old rifleman from Detroit, fell, severely wounded. Soon the leaderless platoon began to crumble. The Bolos sensed this weakening and pressed forward, buoyed by the notion they could break through the American center.

Corporal Clement Grobbel understood what needed to be done; a more effective fire must be placed upon the Bolsheviks, otherwise they would crack the American line. The 23-year-old moved from his safe position and scrambled up onto the railroad tracks, completely exposed to the Russians' fire. He opened fire with his Lewis machine gun, spraying the Bolsheviks. The resolute NCO consumed magazine after magazine, the empty brass shells piling up at his feet as he pulverized the Bolos' aspirations. The Russians cowered before his devastating fire, their assault broken. Corporal Clement Grobbel would be awarded the Distinguished Service Cross for his actions, his citation reading, "When attack[ed] by a largely superior force, in order to deliver a more effective fire, Cpl. Grobbel voluntarily left his trench and took up a position on top of the railroad bank. Although exposed to heavy machine gun fire, he held his position and fired his Lewis gun until the enemy was repulsed."[15]

Captain Horatio Winslow, his left flank surviving due to Cpl. Sieloff's presence and his center bolstered by Cpl. Grobbel's bravery, could see that his American line was just hanging on. He turned to the forward observers, faced with making a risky decision, calling in close artillery support. Winslow knew from experience that Allied artillery fire was unreliable; to call for close support might result in disaster. But something had to be done to break the Bolshevik attack. Winslow ordered the artillery support. Joel Moore reported, "The Americans were helped by the accurate fire of the ... artillery, and the Reds lost heavily." He added, "Company 'I' ... sustained a terrific attack by the Reds in powerful force [and] repulsed them finally after several hours."[16] The Bolsheviks fell back, taking their wounded with them. Their losses had been heavy. Cpt. Winslow reported them as "including 28 prisoners, 200 dead ... and 150 wounded."[17]

The afternoon grew quiet after 4:00 p.m. Captain Winslow's company, though severely tested, had held. But the cost had been steep; one American was dead, three were wounded, and another was missing. Fortunately, the missing soldier made his way back to the American lines. Later, headquarters sent an ambulance car, rifle grenades, and machine gun ammunition, along with two platoons of French troops, to support Winslow's force.[18] Darkness overtook the battlefield, ending the fight. Captain Moore wrote, "After the big attack the enemy left us in possession [of verst 445] and we began to fear winter as much as we did the enemy."[19]

On November 5, 1918, three platoons from Cpt. Moore's company moved into Company I's positions and relieved the weary men. The leadership of Cpt. Winslow's company was down to just two lieutenants, and his men filed out of their defenses and returned to verst 455. They boarded a train and were taken to Obozerskaya.[20] Here they would rest and carry out work details, as well as help construct winter defenses. There was work to do at each of the railway stations. Walter Dundon (Co. M) noted, "[One] Platoon cut fire lanes for blockhouses at 458 ... Balance of men working on blockhouses ... [others] to guard engineer crews cleaning wreck on front line sector of railroad."[21] The wreckage had been caused when "[a] Russian engine crew was drunk and went up under full steam ... [and] had run into the sleeping cars, and killed one man."[22]

Construction continued on the blockhouses. Private Alfred Lewis (Co. M) described their work: "We cut down the tall spruce and pine trees, trimmed them, sawed them into sections, and carried them onto the site, where we would build a blockhouse." He continued, "[We] played the logs together for the four walls—an estimated four-foot (bullet-proof) thickness, strapped together by posts that were wired between the logs. And then, more of a carpenter's job—building the roof, and fixing the doors and windows, [plus] there were horizontal slots in the wall left for the machine guns." Alfred Lewis added, "They provided quarters for living for a squad to take over and defend the area." He also noted, "Block houses were spaced down both sides of the railroad probably a block or more apart."[23]

Company I returned to the front line a few days later, relieving Cpt. Moore's men. Company M boarded a train and was transported to Bakharitza for some R and R. Captain Horatio Winslow's hundred men, along with some Scotsmen and a French contingent of soldiers, were now all that manned the front. This changed, though, on November 11, 1918, when news reached the Railroad front's outposts that the Armistice was completed, and at 11:00 a.m., the Great War was over. Private James Siplon (Co. I) wrote, "That's when the French quit. The first inkling that we got of it was the Frenchmen coming out with their jugs of wine." He continued, "That morning there was something different. Not only did they come out with their flasks of wine, they came out with jugs of everything else. They were dancing around and hollering and whooping, *'Finé la guerre!'* And we said, 'what's the matter with you guys?' 'Armistice!'" They were all done.[24] The shocked doughboys in Company I watched as their French allies loaded their gear onto a train and headed north to Archangel.

The American riflemen, giddy with the thought the war had ended, and with hopes of following the French back to Archangel, turned to their officers, their hearts in their hands. Sadly, the doughboys' dreams were crushed. Private Albert Slaught (Co. D) grumbled, "Everybody wanted to go home once they knew the war was over ... but they kept us there."[25] Ambassador David Francis immediately marched into Gen. Ironside's office and demanded to know when the Americans would be sent home. He came away from his meeting seething. Francis wrote, "[The] signing of the armistice has created some uncertainty among the American and French troops. The reasons heretofore assigned for their presence in north Russia no longer seem valid to them.... Officers and men inquire why military operations are necessary against the Bolsheviki.... The situation is aggravated by the British." He added caustically, "There is ... a suspicion that the British may be 'imperialistic' and that American forces are possibly being used towards ends which do not accord with our ideas."[26]

Private James Siplon (Co. I) grumbled, "We didn't want to fight any more, either. Our officers [were told], 'It [the Armistice] don't mean the end of it for us.'" He continued, "The Armistice's impact on the soldiers was bad. [We] thought we were through. Everybody thought they were going back to Archangel."[27] Not getting answers from their own brass, the frustrated Yanks turned to the nearby Scotsmen, seeking answers. Private Sam Safer (Co. E) noted, "One night shortly after we learned the war had ended we asked a [Royal Scots] sergeant major why we were in Russia.... He said, 'I wish I could tell you but I really don't know.'"[28]

Finally, though, Cpt. Winslow received word why the Americans would not be leaving Russia. He passed the news on to his troops. James Siplon recorded, "The White Sea was frozen over, and ... we were stuck here for the winter. There was no way of getting out."[29] Captain Winslow's squads gathered together, the men trying to fathom this unsettling news—they were trapped in Russia with no way out until spring. They would have to protect themselves from the winter and defend themselves when the Bolsheviks attacked. Private Alfred Larsen (Co. D) railed, "After [the Armistice] there was a different kind of morale.... They [Bolos] didn't mean anything to us. We wanted to stay alive and get the hell out of there ... [we] knew [we] were fighting for self-preservation."[30] James Siplon summed up the American's situation: "They left us alone there with the.... Russians. So there we were."[31]

Chapter 10

Archangel

November 11, 1918: An excited 25-year-old James Maitland clambered onto the train, lugging his barracks bag. He and his fellow comrades in Company M were headed to Archangel for a couple weeks of R and R. Private Maitland was from Sandusky, Michigan, born January 23, 1893. His parents, John and Mary Maitland, were both Scottish immigrants who had moved to America a few years before James, their fourth child, was born.[1] James' father was a carpenter, and his income was enough to sustain the family, which eventually included five youngsters. Their town, Sandusky, was a small community, numbering less than a thousand people. James attended elementary classes at a local school, completing through the sixth grade before quitting and going to work as a farm hand.

The young man continued to live at home, though he never took up his father's carpentry business. Instead, he remained a field hand, working as a paid farm laborer on his neighbors' farms. Then, soon after the United States entered the Great War, he received orders to register for the draft. James Maitland, in June 1917, listed his occupation as "farmer" and was described as of medium height, with dark brown hair and dark blue eyes.[2] A year later he found himself assigned to Company M, 339th Infantry, and soon, in Russia, battling the Bolsheviks. But now that the Great War had ended, he wondered why he could not go home. Maitland, like many of his comrades, believed, "This is a hell of a place, and the U.S. can't get [us] out of here any too soon."[3]

Private Maitland and nearly two hundred other riflemen in Cpt. Joel Moore's company looked forward to some time off in Archangel. He soon realized, though, the company was not going to the city. Instead, he was informed the company was headed to a place called Smolny, separated from Archangel by a mile of water.[4] A light snow fell as James Maitland's company arrived at the Smolny barracks and was herded into newly-constructed wooden, warehouse-like barracks. The men spread out their sleeping bags while NCOs scrambled to find firewood for the buildings' empty stoves. Captain Joel Moore wrote, "A desperate sergeant took a detail of men and salvaged a lot of logs lying near the river's edge, borrowed some Russki saws with a few cigarettes, commandeered some carts and brought ... in a fine supply of wood." Joel Moore's men quickly learned "as far as proper heating of quarters was concerned, men at the front provided better for themselves than did the commander at Smolny, Major Young, provided for those fighters in from the fighting front."[5]

The next morning, November 12, 1918, Company M's men awoke in a heated building, the stoves tended by fire-watch teams, to find ample supplies of hot coffee and breakfast waiting for them. Then they were marched to a bathhouse, and for the first time since leaving England, they treated to unlimited soap and hot water. This glorious experience was followed by a "cootie" inspection.[6] Now washed, rid of lice, and wearing clean uniforms, the men were marched back to their barracks and assigned work details. One rifleman noted, "Of course you're never idle in the army. You've always got something to do. It was either guard duty, or training, or issuing [or loading] something."[7]

Captain Joel Moore and 1st Lt. Clarence Primm reported to Col. George Stewart's headquarters in Archangel, located in the city's Technical Institute. Clarence Primm described the building: "[It was] located in the northern part of the city ... a four story solid looking building ... of brick and stone ... around 150 feet square and 80 feet high, with a small court in the center."[8] Captain Moore observed his commander and commented, "Colonel Stewart was given quarters in a steam heated building, modern and roomy, where he enjoyed considerable comfort, but no authority."[9] Moore added, "Colonel Stewart ... [had] lost touch with his battalion and company commanders.... The doughboy[s] ... knew that the strategy was all planned at British G.H.Q."[10] Following a brief meeting, Moore and Primm returned to Smolny, directed by Col. Stewart, "to do close order drill." Moore noted, "It was not a bad place to drill. Just right for a platoon at a time."[11]

Company M's activities did not change for the next forty-eight hours: fatigue duties, firewood details, KP drudgery, and close order drill. Then, Cpt. Moore received word that Col. Stewart was arriving to inspect the men. A doughboy recorded what happened next: "[The captain] ordered every man to have his hair cut an inch and a half long."[12] The next day, November 16, 1918, Col. Stewart arrived. Captain Moore had the company arraigned by platoons, with each unit's NCOs having readied their men for inspection. Stewart's visit was short and without note. Joel Moore recorded, "Col. Stewart [did not] say a word of encouragement about the work of the company."[13] The company was dismissed, and passes to visit Archangel were handed out to the first batch of lucky riflemen—the ones whose appearance had most pleased their NCOs.

Archangel, normally a city of approximately 50,000 residents, had swollen to nearly twice that number as refugees from all across Russia had fled to the city. Lieutenant Primm described the city: "[Archangel is] built on a low bluff jutting into the Dvina River, the city appears to be mostly waterfront. In fact, it is only a few blocks wide. It is crescent-shaped, with one horn in Smolny—a southern suburb having dock and warehouse areas—and the other in Solombola on the north, which is half as large as Archangel, and possesses sawmills, shipyards, hospitals, a seminary, and a hard reputation." He continued, "The main street of Archangel is Troitsky Prospect.... Here runs a two-track trolley line connecting Smolny and Solombola. The cars are light and run very smoothly. During wartime chiefly women operated them.... Between the main street and riverfront, near the center of the city, is the market place, which covers several blocks. It is full of dingy stalls and alleys occupied by nondescript traders and dingy stocks for sale."[14] A rifleman added, "It was far from being a modern city. The streets were very poor. Housing was very poor." He also noted, "Of course there were some nice places."[15]

The Yanks explored the city and found parts of it similar to the rural villages they had seen for the past two months. One American recorded, "[The] streets were unpaved and always churned into foot-sucking mud; sidewalks were planks laid endwise and constantly in need of repair; sanitation was almost nonexistent ... and a distressing poverty was everywhere."[16] Another doughboy added, "There [was] the poor class, and they were really poor. Women doing chores like brushing and greasing the tracks where the streetcar switched, and brushing the street with their round style brooms."[17] Of course, others saw things quite differently. Private Joseph Sauter (Co. K) remarked, "The gals out in the country, they're all big, husky girls ... but, you get into Archangel, [it's] just like a different race. The girls are dressed like Americans."[18] Lieutenant Primm observed, "The churches are of interest ... the larger ones were all erected for 'Orthodox Russian' worship." He also noted, "Each bell has a clang all its own.... When all the church bells in Archangel start calling at a given hour ... [it is an] utmost confusion of tone and ... tempo."[19] And Cpt. Moore, also impressed by what he saw, wrote, "You heard the chimes of many cathedrals. It was so different from the Russia [we] had seen at the Obozerskaya front."[20]

James Maitland worked as a farmhand before the war (Library of Congress).

Most of the young men were not interested in Archangel's churches and

Troitsky Prospect was Archangel's main street (U.S. Army Signal Corps).

cathedrals; they were more preoccupied with acquiring food and drink and spending time with the local ladies. Private Alfred Lewis (Co. M) recalled, "Our uniforms marked us ... as foreigners.... After some serious study of the translation handbooks, there was real incentive ... in going out and ... trying a few words. Sometimes it brought an eager smile of appreciation, or a baffling response ... [and] from the girls, more likely a snicker or laugh, but in most cases, warm respect for a soldier's try."[21] Captain Joel Moore recorded, "You learned that all girls in Russia did not wear boots, and many of them were pretty and dressed daintily, and [they] coyly attracted the attention of American doughboys."[22] One of his riflemen reminisced, "I especially remember the park right downtown, in which people in the evening would promenade around this circular walkway and always counter-clockwise.... The boys ... like to catch on with the girls, and, if she was friendly, they'd promenade and carry on conversation as best they could with the language barrier."[23] Another added, "We'd go downtown and dance with the girls and everything else. They were happy-go-lucky. They loved to see a good American boy coming." He then hinted at what happened next: "There [was] one pretty girl up there. I don't want to tell you my history with her."[24]

The amorous young Yanks soon learned about a "special" establishment that was easily identifiable. One of the locals wrote, "There [was] unusual activity involving a house with a green roof. Although I had some knowledge of the facts of life, I didn't know the purpose of that house and imagined it was some kind of club where there was dancing and perhaps special entertainment."[25] There was another "hot spot"—the Paris Café. This site for entertainment became so popular "the British closed [it] down ... because, [as] the proclamation [read], 'Women of easy virtue habitually visit the café for purposes of their profession.'"[26]

Of course the enterprise soon reopened, but only for a select clientele. A rifleman complained, "We went to the Paris Café. An M.P. met us at the door and told us that those rooms were only for the officers and their girls, so we had to hunt another place to spend our time."[27] Needless to say, the Yanks' pursuit of "horizontal refreshment" came with costs; the beds at the American-run Archangel hospital eventually became a third filled with gonorrhea and syphilis cases.[28] The situation became so bad that even the families back home became aware of what was going on. One concerned wife wrote her sergeant-husband, "Dearie, don't fall in love with a Russian girl … that would never do.… Sweetie, be careful—Everything is not fair in love and war."[29]

But not every doughboy succumbed to the siren's call. Many just wanted something to drink, a meal different than what they got in their company mess, and maybe something to buy at a store or in the market. One Yank remarked, "It was a lively town.… At a restaurant I ordered what I thought were veal cutlets and they were delicious.… Later I found I had eaten horse."[30] Oddly for the Americans, purchasing items proved to be more difficult than expected. Lieutenant Clarence Primm wrote, "[In] the interior of one of the large dry goods stores—Shelves and counters were arranged in conventional fashion, but there were no display counters of goods to attract the eye and invite sales." "These merchants had never heard of the American adage, 'What you show, you sell.' Shoppers asked for what they needed. If the articles were in stock they were placed on a counter for inspection."[31]

The soldiers found themselves turning to the American-run YMCA for small things. Private Alfred Larsen (Co. D) recalled, "[At the YMCA] you could get a cup of cocoa or buy some cigarettes.… Cigarettes were fifty cents a package. And I think there was only ten cigarettes in each package—Ruby Queens—English, made in England.… They never gave us anything."[32] Private James Siplon (Co. I) recalled, "We had a Y.M.C.A. in Archangel. If you were lucky enough … you could buy tobacco, some cigarettes, maybe some candy bars before they ran out." He also noted, "Everybody had these paper rubles. You might pay ten or twenty rubles for a chocolate bar."[33] The Americans soon discovered the Red Cross was more generous. Private Alfred Larsen (Co. D) added, "[At the Red Cross] they came and dished out peaches and some Pet milk, or milk of that kind.… Open that can, pour it in your mess kit, put the condensed milk in it, and you've got peaches and cream."[34]

All in all, the young American men enjoyed their visits to the city. An officer wrote, "[It was a] happy city, parties were held with sparkling jollity, and entertainments, and dances, and jingling sleigh rides." He also mentioned a special attraction that fascinated everyone, writing, "[We enjoyed] the long toboggan run near the … cathedral, roistering fun-makers with screaming laughter would glide through the exhilarating Arctic air."[35] Clarence Primm was impressed by the toboggan run, recording, "[It was] built by the American Engineers, its starting point was a high tower on a corner of the main street.… The slide began with almost a sheer drop on an iced surface. Then it ran on a lane of ice, banked with snow, extending … to the bank of the Dvina River … and far out on the river ice

The toboggan run attracted thrill seekers (U.S. Army Signal Corps).

to a huge stack of feathery snow into which the toboggan plunged, burying the passengers."[36] Private James Siplon (Co. I) recalled this attraction, "We'd get all the Russian girls up there. We'd all have partners and all get on that toboggan. And we'd go down those slides and go down the banks of the river and we'd almost go across the river." And, he added with a wink, "the Russian girls, they really had a great time of it with the American soldiers. Flocks of them would come out there to go on the toboggan slides, and [we] had a lot of fun."[37] The Yanks had so much fun the English-language newspaper published in Archangel, *The American Sentinel,* reported, "Five sledders wound up in the hospital after the slide's first day in operation."[38]

The Americans, though, were not the only young men filling Archangel's streets; there were soldiers from other counties as well. Lieutenant John Cudahy (Co. B) observed, "Large numbers of unemployed officers strolled the Troitsky Prospect, very merry and bright, an array of bright, varicolored ribbons, like flower gardens, flourishing on their well-arched chests." He added, "Russian soldiery was everywhere, Russian officers with gaudy uniform and restored Imperialistic hauteur; and Russian soldiers drilling on the parade grounds, with a snap and a smartness that was oddly British."[39] But the Yanks were not impressed by the British; Cpt. Moore's men knew the British were running every aspect of the military planning and thus were annoyed as they watched these Allies strut down the street. Private Russell Hershberger (MG Co.) remembered, "If two or three British soldiers [were] walking down the sidewalk and met some Russians the Russians had to get off and walk out in the street. They couldn't walk on the sidewalk with the British."[40]

The Yanks disliked this British attitude and railed against it. One Yank rifleman remarked, "We got in more fights with the British than we did with the [Bolsheviks].... The British never took the front line. We always had to do all the fighting and they stayed in back of us." He added, "[A British sergeant] swore at me, he said, 'You bloody Yanks, you can't do anything with them.' I heaved off at him, and I hit him in the jaw ... he went to his superior officer ... [soon] there come two or three officers with their drawn revolvers, and they put me under arrest."[41] Another recalled, "A captain ... with the 310th Engineers ... was dancing with a girl [who turned out to be] a British colonel's girlfriend. The colonel didn't like it and ordered him to leave the dance. The American captain refused to do as the colonel ordered, and told him to step out into the hall. The colonel did this and they fought. The captain knocked the colonel down. The next day two British orderlies arrested the captain."[42] Ultimately, with experiences like these, a good number of Americans came away from their time in Archangel feeling poorly about their ally. Private Levi Bartels (Co. I) stated, "Talk about England! I've always said that if we start a war with England tomorrow morning I'll be there."[43] Another grumbled, "All I can say for those poor simps is that they want to step high, wide and handsome out of my way because if I ever happen to meet one I sure will step on his heels. That's just how [us] Americans feel about those runts."[44]

Once the Yanks were back in the barracks at Smolny, their daily routines were maintained. Close order drill continued, as did fatigue duties, K.P. labor, and a plethora of work details designed to keep the "resting-from-the-front" riflemen busy. At night, though, once the work was finished, the young men relaxed, and, thinking about home, wrote letters to their families. Corporal Clement Grobbel (Co. I), like so many of the lonesome doughboys, wrote to his parents, "I am well and enjoying life at present in the city of Archangel.... Don't worry about me for I am safe and sound.... Archangel is some place, it has some fine buildings and fur stores, some of the finest furs you ever seen. I would like to send you a set of furs but it costs too much." He continued, "We all have hopes to arrive [home] soon, but you never can tell." His next sentence, though, expressed a frustration nearly all his fellow soldiers experienced: "A fellow can't write much [on] account of censorship."[45] Mail censorship irritated everyone. One rifleman, his complaint suffered by so many, grumbled, "All the mail ... was strictly censored.... When I returned home, my father showed me [a] letter. Everything had been cut out except, 'Love, your son, Sam.'"[46] A few sharp-thinking Yanks, though, did find a way around censorship's confines. One of these fellows bragged, "[When] I wrote home to my folks, I would use the Dutch language so our captain couldn't read it."[47]

Company M's platoons drilled, motivated by the knowledge Gen. Ironside was going to review the unit.[48] The general arrived on November 20, 1918, at 11:00 a.m. He inspected the men, handed out some medals, and made a short talk. Captain Joel Moore, unhappy with the general's speech, wrote, "Gen. Ironside reviewed us. [He] told us of the fine work done by Company 'I' on November 4th in defense of 445, but he did not seem to remember that the company he was reviewing had done anything worthy of note."[49] Company M's first sergeant, Walter Dundon, also was not impressed. He recorded, "Co. paraded for Gen. Ironside, and to witness the bestowal of decorations on several British officers, French, and American soldiers."[50]

General Ironside inspects Company M on November 20, 1918 (U.S. Army Signal Corps).

One rifleman, though, had a much different reaction to the inspection. Private Alfred Lewis (Co. M) remembered, "I picked up a [souvenir] out of the snow beside the dead body of a Bolo ... 'twas a bayonet from his rifle.... An inspection ... [was] coming up, [I'd] better be right and ready.... Suddenly I realized my bayonet was missing ... in desperation, I dug out the Bolo souvenir; it fit on my rifle well enough, but had rust spots that would not wipe off. I hurried out, entered the ranks ... and found my place in the lineup ... and the inspection 'crowd,' sure enough headed by the General, was making its way along the line." Lewis continued, "The only sound as they approached was the slight rattle of the equipment of the soldier, as he whisked up his rifle to 'Present Arms,' and the click as he yanked the bolt to expose the cartridge chamber. Then all is quiet while the General inspects.... I was at rigid attention as they moved before me, my eyes were drilled straight ahead.... I 'Presented Arms' as sharply as I knew how, the General seized the rifle, and I snapped to 'Attention.' There seemed to be a pause.... Soon the gun was thrust back to my chest." He added, "The procession moved along ... [the general was] hardly out of hearing range when a bit of chatter sprung up. The boys about [me] were chuckling and said, 'Did the General EVER give you the STARE!'"[51]

Company M had a second "cootie" inspection on November 21, 1918. They bathed again and had all their clothing washed. Then, the next day at 1:00 p.m., the unit left Smolny barracks by ferry and arrived at the Archangel railroad station three hours later.[52] The company's rest was over; they were headed south, back to the front. Lieutenant George Stoner noted in his journal, "[November 23, 1918]—At 2:30 A.M. at Obozerskaya.... Arrived at verst 455 at 11:30 A.M ... relieved [Company I] ... my platoon took over outpost."[53] Captain Joel Moore and his two hundred riflemen were now back at the business of war.

Chapter 11

On the Front Lines

November 24, 1918: Twenty-nine-year-old Floyd A. Sickles entered a blockhouse at verst 455 and set his gear on a roughly fashioned shelf. He and the members in his squad would man this post for the next week or until a relief came to take their place. Private Sickles, born March 12, 1890, was from Deckersville, a small village of about 600 people, located in the thumb-portion of Michigan. His father, George, a Canadian immigrant, and mother, Betsy, rented a house in that little settlement. George was the town's barber, and his small shop was the central place for gossip. Floyd, along with his nine brothers and sisters, attended the community's elementary school, but he did not continue on to high school.

Floyd A. Sickles was a barber before the war (Bentley Historical Library).

Instead, Floyd worked in his father's barbershop, and together, the two tended to the community's hair-cutting needs. However, when Floyd reached seventeen, he turned his back on his father's profession and, lured by the promise of good money, moved to Flint, Michigan. There, he got work as a laborer in an auto factory.[1]

The young man discovered being an insignificant cog in a giant auto factory was not worth the extra cash he earned. He also learned how much more expensive it was to live in one of Detroit's suburbs, so he moved back home and went to work for his father. America's entry into the Great War meant Floyd had to register for the draft. His military registration identified him as a barber, standing tall (around six feet), with brown hair and brown eyes.[2]

Floyd was sent to Camp

Custer and assigned to Company M, 339th Infantry. Private Sickles trained alongside the rest of the new recruits in Cpt. Joel Moore's company, and though he was a rifleman, he soon acquired the reputation as the unit's barber. The 339th shipped out to England and from there to Russia, and now, on November 24, 1918, Pvt. Sickles' Company M, having completed its stay in the Smolny barracks, divided its platoons among the various outposts at the farthest southern edge of the American position.

The next three days went by very quietly, enabling Cpt. Joel Moore to write, "Nothing more than an occasional patrol or artillery exchange took place on the railroad [front]." He added, "It was known that the Bolos had begun to augment their forces on our front. Sounds of their axes had been constant on the other side of No Man's Land as it had on our side. They were erecting blockhouses for the winter."[3] The Americans occasionally could see individual Bolshevik soldiers, standing and watching, but neither side chose to shoot. A Canadian artilleryman, also stationed near Cpt. Moore's position, noted, "There are two Bolos who can be seen at some time nearly every day. They are thought to be observers."[4]

Captain Horatio Winslow's platoons replaced Company M on November 27, 1918, enabling Moore's riflemen to return to their boxcars in time to enjoy a Thanksgiving dinner. Lieutenant Clarence Primm recorded, "Thanksgiving Day…. Today we had a big feed of beefsteak, gravy, heavy bread, coffee, jam and pie." He added, "[I] ate too much prior to pie, so left the latter for supper."[5] Not only was there a big meal, but the YMCA also put on an entertaining program, and as one enlisted man recalled, "[An] extra issue of cigarettes [was] greatly appreciated by the men."[6] George Stoner (Co. M) wrote, "Thanksgiving Day in Russia. We are thankful for many, many, things and hopeful too. It could be worse … everyone here is well and everything is quiet. All we are doing is guarding the places we occupy…. The cars we are living in have all been double lined and have electric lights in, so you see we are very comfortable." The officer continued, "We have had a few scrapes … and always came out whole, but our [Bolo] friends have now tamed down and are not giving us any trouble any more." He then groused, "We have not had any mail later than written up to September 30th … the harbor at Archangel is now frozen over."[7]

The next day, November 29, 1918, Cpt. Moore's company moved to the front again, with Lt. George Stoner's platoon relieving the French soldiers manning the blockhouses at verst 445.[8] The Americans were leery of the French, who were now unreliable. One Yank observed, "They [the French] were all tired … they were good soldiers, though … [but] they had had enough of the war."[9] The French were exhausted by four-plus years of war and had no empathy for the Bolsheviks; in fact, these Western Front veterans hated still being in uniform and many blamed the Bolos. The British leadership, knowing the French were ready to quit, continually fed their tired ally with exaggerated stories of Bolshevik atrocities in the hopes of keeping them motivated. Captain Joel Moore, after reading these trumped-up reports and listening to his officers and NCOs on the subject, shook his head in disbelief. Joel Moore, observing the French, realized they believed the nonsense spewed by the British. He wrote, "[We] found the French soldiers wildly

An American soldier stands guard on the Railroad front (U.S. Army Signal Corps).

aflame with the idea that a man captured by the Bolsheviks was bound to suffer torture."[10] Moore wrote, "[I] remember the sense of shame that seized [me] as [I] reluctantly read a general order to [my] troops, a British piece of propaganda that recited gruesome atrocities by the Bolsheviks, a recital that was supposed to make the American soldiers both fear and hate the enemy." Therefore, Company M's commander was greatly relieved when the Third Battalion C.O., Maj. J. Brooks Nichols, "ordered that [this] propaganda should not be further circulated among the American soldiers."[11]

However, out in the blockhouses, the doughboys had little time to ponder the ramifications of British disinformation as they manned their gun posts and struggled to keep warm. The last two days of November 1918 went by without much activity. One soldier recorded on November 29, 1918, "21 single Bolos were seen ... [and] several single rifle shots were heard."[12] Walter Dundon wrote, "[Co. 'M's] Fourth platoon at 446 ... one platoon plus two Lewis guns on outpost ... [and] one platoon on fatigue."[13] Then, the next day, the French briefly pounded the Reds' areas as they registered their repositioned 75 mm guns.[14]

December 1918 started just as the previous month had ended—quietly. There was almost no gunfire to be heard, plus very few Bolo sightings. Vigilant American sentries did notice a small group of Russians working on something near the railway. Their platoon commander sent out a patrol to investigate, but the cautious Yanks did not get close enough to discern what was being constructed.[15] First Sergeant Walter Dundon recorded on the first of December, "One platoon at Verst 446. 1½ platoons plus two L.G. gun teams on outpost duty. Remainder of Co. on fatigue, building flock houses, wire entanglements, etc."[16] Captain Joel Moore wrote about these quiet days: "Those long weeks of patrolling and sentry duty were wearing on the men. Sentinels were continually seeing things at night that were not. Once we were hurried out into the cold darkness by the report of a great multitude of muttering voices approaching from the forest, but not a shot answered our challenge, and the next morning there in the snow were the fresh tracks of timber wolves."[17]

The American soldiers in Company M continued to man their outposts, appreciating the fact their battlefront had gone silent. Though there was little rifle fire, the French 75s bombarded the Bolshevik positions with about twenty shells on December 2, 1918. The Yanks were relieved when the Bolos did not return fire. The one thing that was heard, though, as one Yank recalled, was "[the] expression ... frequently [said], 'it's snowing again boys.'"[18] The weather, as always to individuals who spend a lot of time outdoors, was of the greatest concern, and in northern Russia, as winter's grip squeezed the soldiers, freezing temperatures became the issue. Lieutenant Clarence Primm wrote in a letter, "It is ... cold here ... about 20° to 25° above zero. Snows a little every day. [We] have seen the sun only about twice in the past seven days. We are living by candlelight."[19] Walter Dundon noted on December 4, 1918, "Still on front line. Disposition of Co. same as of [December 2]. Enemy patrol fired on outpost just as Co. was lining up for chow [at] 8:00 A.M."[20]

Boredom, compounded by isolation, began to creep into the soldiers' complaints, a new condition to worry about. One soldier recorded, "Life became a very stale, flat, drab thing in the vast stretches of cheerless snow reaching far across the river to the murky, brooding skies and the encompassing sheeted forests, so ghostly and so still, where death prowled in the shadows and the sinking realization came home of no support or reserves."[21]

The winter temperatures continued to plummet, but the American boys who were mostly from Michigan, Wisconsin, and Indiana did not suffer. They had their secure blockhouses when on guard duty and stove-warmed boxcars when relieved, plus adequate clothing. Clarence Primm wrote with a smile, "When dressed in my heavy socks and overshoes, fur-lined canvas coat and fur cap I have been mistaken by Russians, themselves, for a Russian.... Several times individuals have come to me and started rapid conversation in Russian. It may be that my red mustache and imperial demeanor assisted in the general effect." He added, "I [am] ... writing down Russian words I know, with meanings. I find I have more than fifty ... and some of them are useful in all sorts of connections."[22] George Stoner also liked their winter outfits, writing, "All of our winter equipment has been issued.... We have what [are called] Shackleton boots for our feet and while being big and ungainly, are wonderful for keeping [our feet] warm."[23] These boots, invented by Sir Ernest Shackleton, the British explorer of the Antarctic and the South Pole, kept the soldiers' feet protected but came with problems. One rifleman explained, "The Shackleton boots ... they were warm, but if they'd get wet, they'd ... freeze." He continued, "They were canvas ... and [had] wrap arounds."[24]

Late in the evening of December 4, 1918, Lt. Clarence Primm sent out a patrol. His men floundered about in the snow but did not encounter anything of note. The men returned cold and tired. The officer wrote the next morning, "This snow this morning is about six inches deep.... Daylight does not become real much before 8:30 A.M., and it is practically dark at 3:30 P.M. We have been spitting in the enemy's face, figuratively speaking, for a week now, and both sides [are] apparently satisfied to spit gently."[25] A Bolo patrol discovered the Americans' tracks and reacted. A soldier reported, "During the night an American patrol was sent out along the side of the Rwy. The Bolos ... found the tracks of our patrol and fired about 100 rifle shots."[26] One of the Americans who came under fire exclaimed, "John Bolo didn't send over a bullet with my name, thereon for which I am duly grateful."[27]

Company M members received word that they would be relieved later that afternoon, so the men prepared to leave their blockhouse duties, happy to return to the warm security of their boxcars. Sadly, this did not happen. Walter Dundon recorded this disappointing fact: "Should have been relieved today. Orders changed, disposition of Co. same as of 2nd."[28] The next morning, December 6, 1918, Cpt. Moore's expectant riflemen sighed with relief as Horatio Winslow's men filed into their positions. Company M made ready to move out, but just then an airplane buzzed their positions, strafed the Americans standing out in the open with machine-gun fire, and dropped two 112-pound bombs. One bomb detonated not far from a bridge guarded by the Yanks, while the other destroyed the corner of a building sheltering the First Platoon's headquarters. A Canadian wrote, "About 11:15 A.M. an aero plane passed over 455 towards the front. When it reached our front line it turned and dropped two bombs on our HQ buildings, the second fell just at the corner of one of their huts and killed one and injured two Americans."[29]

One of the wounded doughboys, Pvt. Frank Lachacki, had shrapnel rip through his foot, crippling the 26-year-old wood finisher from Grand Rapids, Michigan. A second casualty, Pvt. Floyd Sickles, was blown to pieces. Captain Joel Moore, in a letter to Floyd Sickles' parents, wrote, "This is the saddest letter which I have had to write.... Your son, Floyd A. Sickles was instantly killed ... by the explosion of a 112-lb bomb.... We buried him in the shell crater made by the bomb, and when the frozen clods of earth were laid tenderly over his remains there was not an officer or man in the company who did not feel that he was putting a good and true brave friend into his final resting place." Moore continued, "You will receive through the proper military channels, notice of his death, and also the personal property which I collected. I am sorry that I could not find it all. The explosion totally destroyed his pack and haversack. His razor was in several pieces. His comb is gone. The stone which I am returning to you I am told he prized very highly because his father had given it to him. I thought also that you would like his shaving brush and mug."[30]

Sickles' comrades were furious. The airplane—a Sopwith Camel, its wings displaying distinctive red, white and blue roundels—was identified as belonging to the British Royal Air Force, its airfield just outside Obozerskaya. Again, American blood had been shed because of British sloppiness. A Canadian artilleryman remarked, "The Americans [were] very much worked up about it and [were]

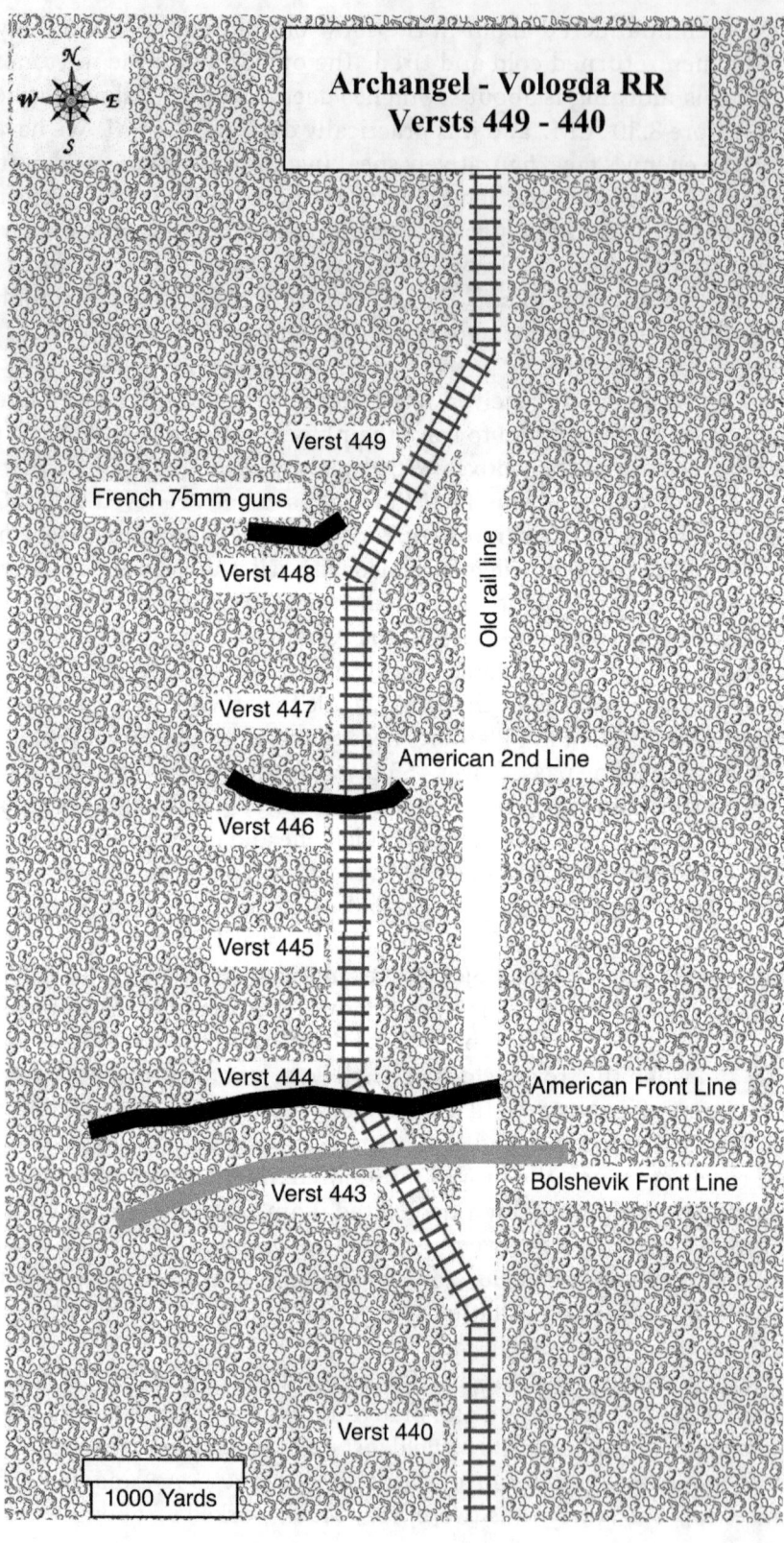

making threats."[31] Captain Moore's enraged men clambered into train cars bound for Obozerskaya at 1:00 p.m., many with hostile intentions; the British were going to pay for Floyd Sickles' death. Captain Moore, though angry himself, knew he must prevent his men from confronting the airmen, as their mood was similar to that of a lynch mob. He found a way to delay the train's departure, forcing his infuriated men to stew in their motionless train cars. Their anger abated somewhat so that by the time the train headed for Obozerskaya, they had calmed down. The despondent men unloaded from the train and headed to their boxcar homes that evening at 7 o'clock. Joel Moore wrote, "[I] consumed the remainder of the day in getting [my] excited and enraged men back to Obozerskaya." He continued, "By [this] time [my] men were cooled off and the nervous Royal Air Force had no occasion to use its rifles in self defense."[32]

On December 7, 1918, the men woke up knowing there would be an investigation of the incident, but there was also work to do; Lt. Primm took twenty-six men and headed west on the Obozerskaya-Onega road. Primm and his troops marched to Bolshie Ozerki, searching for evidence of Bolshevik encroachment. The lieutenant wrote, "[We were sent] to hold a village at a strategic point sixteen miles out on the flank, where the hostile pressure threatened to break the line of communication with the Allied forces in the Onega sector."[33] His men hunkered down in the small village, taking refuge in peasants' homes. Two days later, December 9, 1918, in Obozerskaya, a board of inquiry met and investigated the bombing incident; they found the pilots not to be at fault. Joel Moore wrote in disgust, "A board of officers whitewashed the Canadian flyers ... and the incident was closed."[34] Company M's riflemen, dissatisfied by this pronouncement, could do nothing to change this decision, nor could they forget that another one of their comrades had been killed by British blunders. They went about their tasks bitterly, wishing they were home and knowing that would not happen. Regardless of the Americans' feelings, the strange war's activities did not cease.

A French infantry company arrived in Obozerskaya, unloading a contingent of unhappy soldiers who were soon posted at versts 445, 446, and 447, their task to support the battery of French-crewed 75 mm guns.[35] The French soldiers discovered what the Americans had learned some time earlier; the railway split south of verst 449, with an old line running in one direction and a new line in another. Both lines, though, came back together near verst 442. A Canadian artillery forward observer wrote of this divergence, "There is an old railway line running from 440 to 449 and a new line was built in 1894. The Bolo guns are [behind] 440.... The trees in the old right of way are small and [the Bolos] can see our trains at 449.... We [have] outposts in the trees in the old line old line opposite 446."[36]

Both Cpt. Moore and Winslow's men were always busy, being assigned guard details, fatigue duties involving more construction of defensive works and aggressive patrol routes. One of the riflemen out on patrol, Cleo Colburn (Co. I), added, "[Our three-man patrol] went into [the] woods. We lost out bearing and wandered towards [the] front. We stopped for a minute to rest, and I told [my squad] to make sure that their rifles were in working order. Just then we saw a tree fall, not more than 25 yards from us. We listened for a minute for a [sound] from that direction, but heard none.... We about-faced and double-timed out of there."[37] Later that day Walter Dundon (Co. M) recorded his company's activities, writing, "One-half of 2nd platoon at verst 458, the other half of 2nd platoon and Lt. Wieczorek at 466. Lt. Primm and 26 [enlisted men] of 3rd platoon at Bolshie Ozerki.... [There are] 65 [enlisted men] on outpost at Obozerskaya. Balance of Co. on fatigue."[38]

Company M was supposed to form up and return to the front lines on December 10, 1918, but this did not happen. Instead, Company G, commanded by Cpt. John Conway, arrived. His nearly two hundred men unloaded from the Bakharitza-Obozerskaya train and that afternoon relieved Lt. George Stoner's and Lt. Wesley Wright's platoon from their outpost duties around Obozerskaya. Those two platoons, along with Cpt. Moore and his HQ team, received orders to grab their gear and load onto the train returning to Bakharitza. They left Obozerskaya at 10:00 p.m. The men thought they were going to get some leave time, but this idea was quickly crushed; they were to be given a special duty—they were going to a place called Pinega.

Chapter 12

The March to Pinega

December 18, 1918: First Lieutenant George W. Stoner, Jr., studied the long line of sleighs, all loaded with equipment and supplies. This was the most unusual military convoy he had ever witnessed. George Stoner, born November 15, 1885, was thirty-three years old and the second son of George and Elisa Stoner. He had grown up in Monroe, Michigan, a town of nearly 20,000 citizens located on the western shores of Lake Erie. He was nicknamed "Buz," and he and his five siblings attended local schools in Monroe, supported by their father who captained a fishing boat on Lake Erie. Buz graduated from Monroe's high school and in 1910 acquired a job with the Consolidated Paper Company.[1] He continued to live at home, working at the company's paper mill, until the United States entered the Great War. Then, in early 1917, the 31-year-old passed the examination for officer's school and on August 15, 1917, was commissioned a second lieutenant and ordered to report to Camp Custer, Michigan, where he began drilling new recruits. George Stoner recorded in his journal on September 6, 1917, "First drill of recruits … physical drill, [and] school of the soldier."[2] He continued training soldiers and was eventually assigned to Company M, 339th Infantry. Lieutenant Stoner, on November 20, 1917, wrote, "Received 90 new men, worked until midnight."[3] Stoner was promoted to first lieutenant, becoming Company M's senior lieutenant, and was given command of First Platoon. Now, in the last days of 1918, he was a veteran of several months of combat command.

First Lieutenant George Stoner was the senior lieutenant of Co. M (U.S. Army Signal Corps).

First Lieutenant George Stoner's platoon had been resting at Smolny barracks for the past week, and during that time his men had been able to bathe, wash their clothes, catch up on dental work, and draw equipment. Stoner knew almost nothing about Pinega; in fact, his first comment was similar to many: "Where the hell is Pinega?"[4] The answer looked simple on a map; Pinega was about ninety miles east of Archangel, but the route to that city weaved and bobbed about, making the journey nearly one hundred fifty miles (204 versts).[5]

Captain Joel Moore assembled his force, consisting of Lt. Stoner and his First Platoon, Lt. Wesley Wright and his Fourth Platoon, and a small contingent of headquarters people; in all, just under one hundred men. They were to go to Pinega, tasked with a two-fold mission: "First to reinforce a half of another company which [was] … outnumbered ten to one; Second, to raise a regiment of loyal Russian troops in the great Pinega Valley where half the people [were] loyal and half, Bolo sympathizers."[6] This was to be an overland march; Stoner's platoon would lead, to be followed by sixty-five Russian pony-pulled sleighs and trailed by Lt. Wright's platoon.[7] They were to travel during daylight and at night take shelter among the villages along the way. Joel Moore figured the trek to Pinega would take ten days.

The convoy left Archangel just before noon on December 18, 1918. Captain Moore wrote of their departure: "After the usual delay with sleigh drivers … the convoy was off at 11:55 A.M." He continued, "The trail was an improved government road … the road ran crooked, like the Dvina along whose hilly banks [we follow]."[8] Moore's force traveled without delay. Lt. Stoner's point men moved quickly, his platoon next, followed by the convoy of Russian drivers with their sleighs and finally Lt. Wright's rear guard. Soon, though, the formation began to stretch out. Joel Moore noted, "The point is out of sight in front, the rear party is [now] lost behind [a] curve." The afternoon was clear and cold, but for the warmly dressed soldiers, the expedition seemed exciting. Moore described the scenery they observed, writing, "[It is] a treat to our boys to see rolling, cleared country…. [There are] fish towns and lumber towns on the right … haystacks and fields on the left … [all] backed by forests. Here the trail is bare-swept by the wind … [and there] snow is blown [across the trail]."[9]

They arrived in Uima (Uimaskaya) at 3:15 p.m. after a hike of sixteen versts.[10] Here, chaos reigned for a short while as the Americans and Russian pony-drivers were assigned places to stay. Joel Moore recorded, "Halting is a wonderful performance. The headman—*starosta*—must be hunted up to [find] quarters [for the] officers and men … [but the] American soldiers are quick to pull things [together].… Guard is mounted over the sleighs." He noted, once everyone was secure, "our lowly hosts treat us royally. Tea from the *samovar* steams us a welcome."[11] Captain Moore met with his two lieutenants and his first sergeant; they realized an advance team needed to go ahead of the convoy and organize things before the main body arrived. First Sergeant Walter Dundon wrote, "Arrangements were made for one officer, 1st sergeant and two cooks to leave each station in advance of the sled train each day to have quarters and [a] warm meal ready when the company arrived."[12]

12. The March to Pinega

Russian sleighs were used to transport Company M the final miles to Pinega (U.S. Army Signal Corps).

The next morning, December 19, 1918, Lt. Wright, 1st Sgt. Dundon, and two company cooks—Pvt. Joseph Pavlin and Pvt. Adolph Johnson—left Uima just before 8 o'clock. They were followed by the convoy, which left forty minutes later. Captain Moore recalled, "Second day: Crawled out of our sheepskin sleeping bags about 6:00 [A.M.] well rested. Breakfasted on bacon and bread and coffee. Gave headman ten rubles. Every soldier reported very hospitable treatment." He added, "[The] billeting party [was] given a ... [head] start, traveling ahead of the post to get billets and dinner arranged."[13] The previous day's fine weather was gone, replaced by a bitter wind and freezing precipitation. The marching was hard, as the men and animals were pummeled by sleet and later by thickly falling snow, and within an hour, the convoy stretched out to nearly a mile in length. However, they averaged four versts an hour and by noon their day's destination was in sight. Joel Moore recorded, "[We made] nineteen versts ... [and] halted for the night. No one is sorry. There is the blazing cook's fire, and dinner will be ready soon." He continued, "Men are quickly assigned to quarters by the one-eyed old headman ... who marks [each] building and then goes in to announce to the householder that.... *Amerikanski soldats* will sleep there."[14]

December 20, 1918, was like the previous day's march. The billeting party, this time led by Lt. Stoner, left before the convoy, pulling out of Liabiskaya just after 8:00 a.m. The weather was cold, but the sun was out and the wind less cruel. George Stoner wrote, "Left Liabiskaya at 7:30 A.M., arrived at Kosogorskaya at 10:30 A.M.—19 versts.... Many hills and fine scenery."[15] Joel Moore remarked,

"[The] road is … well beaten by marketing convoys and by Russians bound for church to celebrate Saint Nick's Day…. The fine snow [that] came in the night has ridged each twig [an] inch deep in pearl. What a sight…. Wisconsin, we think … as we traverse the bluffs." Captain Moore, his position toward the front of the column, was quite a distance ahead of the rear guard. Unfortunately for the tail-end troops, the beauty of the wilds lost its allure when the wind increased and falling snow began to blow across their trail. They were still struggling against the elements while Lt. Stoner's platoon and Cpt. Moore's HQ team settled into the comfort of their night's quarters. Joel Moore, befitting his senior status as commander of the formation, was housed in Kosogorskaya's finest home. He remarked, "[I am quartered] in the home of a merchant-peasant…. A fine home [with] house plants and a big clock, and a gramophone."[16]

When Wright's doughboys arrived, word was passed to Cpt. Moore that a squad of rear-guard men had become lost. A team was sent out to find them but returned without the lost squad. First Sergeant Dundon made a note in the roster, listing them as "missing," figuring them to be gone for good. No one could survive in the Arctic cold for long. If they were not able to find cover, they would die from exposure. The missing Americans, Pvt. Herman Yopp and two others, had been at the rear guard's farthest back point. Herman Yopp recalled, "[We were] following the rear guard [and] … got into a blizzard…. The bad weather grew stronger with each passing hour, and soon [we] … stopped noticing the trail." He continued, "Snowfall intensified. After some time [we] … realized that [we] no longer had a road under [our] feet, but a field … [we] were exhausted. [Our] Shackleton boots, lined with leather, slid, [causing us to] continually fall…. [Our] clothing was soaked with sweat and melted snow. It was worth stopping for a breather, [but] the cold instantly made its way under the wet uniform, holding an icy chill. Trying not to think about the closing night, [we] … stubbornly walked, trying to reach the Pinezhskaya road … [but] in vain."[17]

The three lost Americans stumbled forward in the deep snow until they saw a tiny light in the distance. Herman Yopp remarked, "[It was a] light in the window of a hut on the edge of the forest … forgetting all caution, [we] came to the house [and] knocked. The door was opened by a bearded old man, behind whom stood his spouse. The Russians understood everything at a glance and silently let [us] … into the heat." He continued, "[We] warmed up, throwing off [our wet] clothes, [and] were seated at the table and [were] fed with simple peasant food; rye bread, boiled potatoes, meat and a *samovar* of hot tea … [then] were put to sleep on top a hot Russian stove." Yopp added, "The next morning … when [we] left, the peasants brought [us] to the road and showed [us] the right direction…. [We] caught up with the platoon, where [we] were no longer expected, [as we were] considered … dead in the blizzard."[18]

The convoy had pulled out at 8:00 a.m., heading for Kholmogory where the soldiers had been informed they would stay an extra day to rest and recover. The weather was punishing; a severe wind rolled over them, blowing snow into drifts that made walking difficult. Walter Dundon recorded, "[There were] broad areas allow[ing] the biting wind full sweep. Ears are covered and hands are thrashed….

12. The March to Pinega

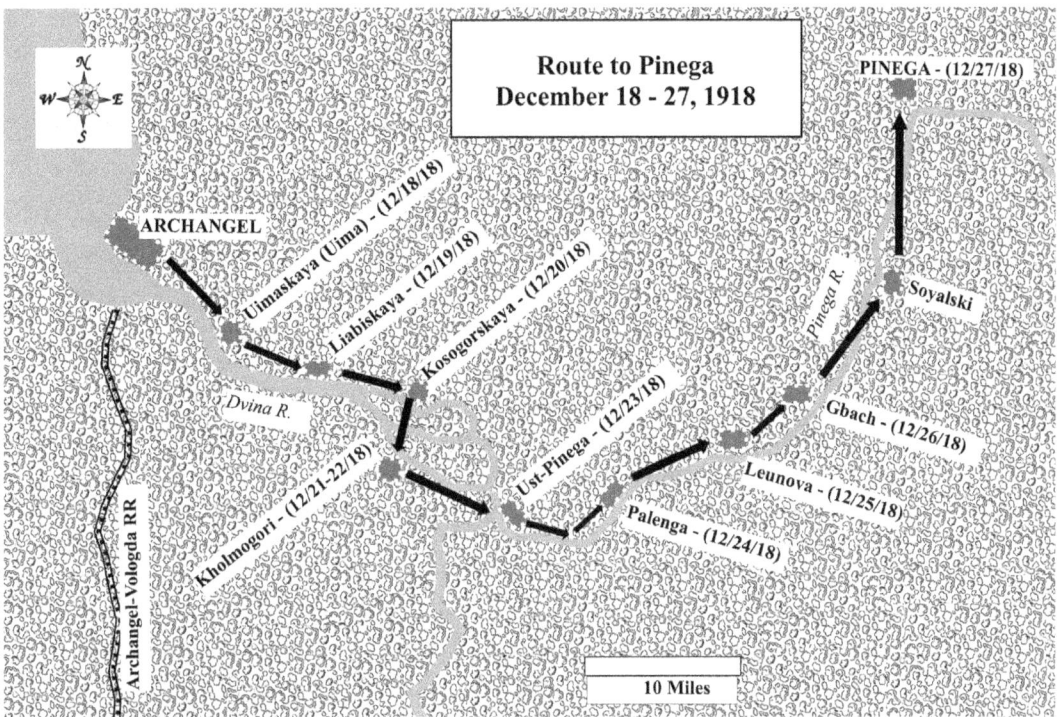

It is desperately cold."[19] The chilled men reached the Dvina River, its waters completely frozen. They made their way across the ice, passing by a steamboat that was trapped and would not be going anywhere until summer's warmth broke up the ice pack. Joel Moore wrote, "The going is ... sternly cold.... The advance guard has out-walked the convoy, and while the ponies toil up the hill [the Americans] seek shelter in the lee of a house to rest and smoke.... It is desperately cold. A driver's ears are tipped in white." He continued, "That barber-[striped] pole [is] a verst post ... it reads 16 ... [we now] look for the barber poles.... We are nearing our objective."[20] The exhausted men reached their destination. Walter Dundon recorded, "We wind into the old river town and pass on for a verst and a half to an old monastery where we find quarters in a subsidiary building which once was an orphans' home. The old women are very kind and hospitable. The rooms are airy and warm."[21] They settled in for the night, with George Stoner writing, "Arrived at Kholmogori at 1:30 P.M. Beautiful scenery, cold wind, poor hiking—21 versts."[22]

The next day, December 22, 1918, went way too quickly for the worn-out Americans. Captain Moore recorded, "Fifth day: We spend the day at rest. Men are contented to lie on the warm floors and ease their feet and ankles. We draw our rations of food, forage and cigarettes."[23] Many of his riflemen, though, while resting, modified their footwear. One doughboy remarked, "We had what they called Shackleton boots. Boy, we had a lot of trouble with them at first! In that snow, they'd slide all over. We put strips of leather on the soles so we could walk on the snow."[24] Other soldiers approached the Shackleton boot problem differently. Lieutenant Primm, observing his men, stated, "They learned faster than

Shackleton did, that the [Russians] had devised footgear a thousand times better for use in that part of the north.... [My men] proceeded to cast aside the 'nose-bags,' as some called them, and don native boots of felt or fur as fast as such boots could be obtained. Some were purchased, some bartered, and some appropriated from dead Bolos."[25]

First Sergeant Walter Dundon examined the men in both platoons and determined a few would not be able to continue. One of the men suffered from frostbite; his comrade noted, "One of the boys, his hand got just a little bit sweaty, and he took off the gloves. And you know, he froze his hands. He lost the whole skin.... The whole hide came off."[26] Other enlisted men, though, suffered from a much more serious condition—pneumonia.

The convoy left the monastery on December 23, 1918, just before 9:00 a.m., about an hour after Lt. Stoner and the billeting crew had departed. Joel Moore wrote, "To Ust Pinega—sixth day: Five sleds and company property are left at the monastery in charge of two privates who are not fit to march."[27] Lieutenant Stoner covered the twenty versts to arrive at Ust-Pinega at 1:45 p.m. The convoy, trudging along, came in just before sunset at 3:30 p.m. The small town had no more than a couple hundred residents, but it possessed a telephone connection to Pinega. Captain Moore put in a long-distance call to Cpt. John Conway, commander of the two G Company platoons stationed at Pinega, letting him know reinforcements were getting close. Moore, also realizing his riflemen were suffering badly, requested additional sleighs, hoping they could be used to carry his men. Moore noted, "Conway ... will try to get sleighs for us to meet us 40 versts away." Later Moore received a more detailed message from Cpt. Conway: "[He was] promising 100 horses and Christmas dinners."[28]

The next morning (and, for the homesick Americans, Christmas Eve), Lt. Wright and the advance group left before sunrise, while the main body pushed out of Ust-Pinega at 8:00 a.m. Their march would be a long one, totaling twenty-three versts. They would have to cross the Dvina River, negotiating both the descent down to it and the climb up and out. The weather had turned quite cold, with both a driving wind and a smattering of snow. Joel Moore wrote, "Up and down the hills our winding, pine-flanked road takes us.... The 14th verst takes us across the river—[we] follow the telephone wires ... the road ... climbs a steep bluff ... what a sight from the top, the whole convoy lies extended from advance guard on the hill, to the rear guard on the river."[29] That evening, the American doughboys settled in with their Russian hosts and, as one soldier reminisced, "hospitality [was] the true word." Joel Moore recorded, "Opened our Red Cross Christmas stockings and the doughboys shared their meager sweets with Russki children."[30]

Captain Joel Moore's riflemen did not rest on Christmas. Lieutenant George Stoner wrote, "Sgt. Dundon, Cooks Pavlin, Johnson & I left ... Palenga at 7:30 A.M.—drove 24 versts to Leonova—11:30 A.M.—Poor billet. Don't look much like Christmas."[31] The sun came out, and for a few hours the bitter cold's grip eased a bit. The Americans, as they shuffled along, saw Russian women washing clothes through holes chopped into the river's ice. Captain Moore's formation crossed the river, an activity requiring the local men to be pressed into manhandling the sleds back up the steep banks. Joel Moore noted, "Good road for 13 versts, to Uzinga. Here we stop and call for the Headman, who gets his men to help us.... Not cold [today]." He then added, "The twenty-fourth verst into Leunovo is a hard drag."[32] The tired soldiers moved into their assigned billets only to find these villagers resented the Americans' presence. Those Yanks who understood the Russian language soon learned "there [were] many Bolsheviki sympathizers in the town."[33]

The Americans were quick to leave Leunovo, pulling out just after sunrise on December 26, 1918. The morning sky, thick with clouds, greeted the men with a heavy, wind-driven snowfall, slowing their march and chilling their bones. Moore wrote, "To Gbach—ninth day: Snow falling as we start on the river road at 8:25 ... We find it level nearly all the way but drifting [snow] makes hard walking.... We arrive at end of our 21verst march at 1:25." He then added, "Met by friendly villagers and [are] well quartered.... The people here view the villages of [Leunovo], Ostov and Kuzomen with distrust."[34] Lieutenant Stoner noted succinctly, "Arrived at Gbach 1:45 P.M. Tough going. Good quarters."[35]

That evening Cpt. Moore received a message from Cpt. Conway that gave the weary officer great joy; there would be a convoy of sleighs arriving next morning—his exhausted and sick men could ride the last miles to Pinega. Unfortunately, when the sun arose on December 27, 1918, Moore got another dispatch, this one explaining the sleighs were waiting at Soyalski, some twenty versts away. Company M's men would have to walk some more. The Americans, though, knowing there was an end to this torturous journey, strapped their gear to their backs and headed northeastward, their last bits of energy propelling them forward. Walter Dundon recorded, "Left Gbach at 8:00 A.M., arriving Soyalski at 11:30 A.M."[36] But now, the situation was different; Cpt. Conway had assembled a convoy of fast-moving sleighs. Each Russian-driven vehicles could hold one American rifleman and his gear and a small amount of company equipment. Joel Moore assigned the first seventeen men to be transported, and this small contingent left Soyalski at 3:00 p.m.

Knowing everybody would eventually get a ride to Pinega, the soldiers found shelter from the bitter cold and biting wind. A couple hours later a second convoy of sleighs arrived, this one totaling twenty-five vehicles. Lieutenant Stoner, assigned a seat on one of these sleighs, wrote, "Left at 3:00, arrived at Pinega at 6:30. Quick trip."[37] His sleigh had covered forty-six versts in three and a half hours! Back at Soyalski, a third collection of sleighs was being assembled with some new drivers as well as a number of Russians who had made the first trip. Captain Moore put the last of his men into this convoy and then climbed into a sleigh of his own. He recorded, "Got away at 9:30 P.M. The Russian sleigh runs smoothly and takes the bumps gracefully.... Light ball-snow falls.... It is desperately cold." He added, "[I] have a good sleigh and can sleep." Moore, though, did not sleep much; instead, he enjoyed northern Russia's atmospheric display. Moore wrote, "[The] Aurora Borealis. It has action, it has color, sheets of light, spires, shafts, beams and broad finger-like spreadings, that come and go, filmy veils of light winding and drifting in, weaving in and out among the beams and shafts, now glowing, now fading."[38] Captain Joel Moore and this final group of Americans arrived in Pinega at 3:00 a.m. Lieutenant Stoner was there to meet Moore, and with the help of an NCO, he directed the soldiers where to bed down. Then, once all the Yanks had been taken care of, the tired lieutenant took to his cot. Stoner concluded the journey, writing, "Up all night quartering men—good sleep after."[39]

Later that day, December 28, 1918, Cpt. Moore and his two lieutenants met with Cpt. John Conway and his senior lieutenant, William Higgins. Conway described the situation in the Pinega area as well as the tough battle that Lt. Higgins and his platoon had fought earlier in December. Conway stressed the point that the Bolsheviks' strength was growing, many of the nearby villages supported the Reds, and most of the local White Russian volunteers were unreliable. He also included the news that the day before a large force of Bolos had defeated a unit of over one hundred White Russians in a fight thirty-five miles south of Pinega. And following this briefing, John Conway turned command of the Pinega area over to Cpt. Joel Moore.

Chapter 13

The Pinega Campaign

Sergeant Matthew Grahek was 27 when he was drafted (Michigan Heroes' Museum).

January 1, 1919: Sergeant Matthew Grahek shook his head in dismay; the platoon of Russian volunteers he was inspecting was absolutely dismal. Grahek smacked his reindeer gloves together in frustration as he watched them stumble about; it was going to take a lot of work before these men could ever go into battle against the Bolos.[1] Matthew Grahek, born July 1, 1890, was from Calumet, Michigan. He was an immigrant, having arrived in the United States from Austria in 1897 when his parents, Joseph and Marie Grahek, made the move to better their lives. The Graheks settled in Michigan's Upper Peninsula when Joseph found work as a copper miner. Joseph's son "Mattie," along with four other brothers and three sisters, grew up in Calumet, all learning to speak English and excelling in the flourishing town's excellent schools. Mattie was a very active youngster who loved the outdoors and excelled in winter sports, especially skiing and ice skating. He reveled in his hometown's sports and hoped to one day become a professional ice skater—a dream sustained by the fact Calumet had its own hockey team, the Calumet Miners, which played in the International Professional Hockey League.

Mattie, unlike his older brother, Joseph Jr., did not follow his father into the mines. Instead, he sought employment in a butcher shop where, using his skills at record keeping, he worked using his brain rather than his brawn.[2] However, the Copper County Strike of 1913 changed things for the 23-year-old, especially when a horrendous fire killed over seventy Italians on Christmas Day, a fire many believed to have been caused by unhappy strikers. Following this, Matthew

Grahek gave up his job at the butcher shop, moving to Detroit and obtaining work as a tire finisher in an auto factory. Grahek was living in Detroit when, in June 1917, he registered for the draft. At that time he was listed as "of medium height, medium build, and with brown eyes and brown hair."[3] Mattie was not happy when he was ordered to report to Camp Custer, and he was further annoyed when he learned he had to pay his own way to the training facility. Nevertheless, once at Camp Custer and assigned to Company M, 339th Infantry, he discovered his skills served him well. Promotions came quickly; Grahek was the company's acting sergeant by the time it reached England.

The acting sergeant also had a rebellious side, a characteristic that did not sit well with his platoon commander, Lt. George Stoner. Grahek remarked, "When we got to England ... another guy and I took a pass and [went] to London. We missed the late midnight train ... [and] couldn't catch a train out of there till about four o'clock the next morning." He continued, "We had to sneak in the back way ... [but] some sucker ... reported us. Lieutenant Stoner, he didn't like me ... [he] busted me down to corporal."[4] Matthew Grahek chuckled, "[Capt. Moore] jumped me right back to sergeant."[5]

Sergeant Grahek proved to be resilient and plucky; in fact, by the time Cpt. Moore's men were given leave in November 1918, Matthew Grahek had already been written up for a Distinguished Service Cross, the British Distinguished Conduct Medal, and the French Croix de Guerre. Grahek remembered, "One time Lieutenant Wright ... says to me, 'Get your men spruced up, we're going to be interviewed by General Ironside.'" He continued, "When [Ironside] got to me ... he noticed ... [my] ribbon ... 'British D.C.M?' [he asked] ... I said, 'yes sir.' He stuck his hand [and] shook my hand."[6] Later, he would recall, "That was water over the dam—a long time ago."[7] Now, he stood watching a gaggle of poorly-trained White Russian soldiers fumble about. Thinking back to that evening with the girls and what might have been, Matthew Grahek remarked, "Water over the dam—a long time ago."[8]

The reason that Company M's two platoons were in Pinega was simple—things had not gone well. Colonel Stewart, acting on British dictates, had ordered Cpt. John Conway (Co. G) to take two of his platoons to Pinega with the mission of raising local volunteers and organizing them for self-defense.[9] Captain Conway and roughly one hundred Yanks moved to Pinega in late October 1918. Once there, Russian volunteers were rounded up, given arms and equipment, and started training. By Thanksgiving Cpt. Conway believed his Russians were ready, and he dispatched seventy doughboys, along with 210 locals, some eighty miles upriver to the village of Karpogora. Here, his force encountered a large number of Bolsheviks. However, once the shooting began, the White Russian troops melted away, leaving only the Americans to face the Bolos. The Reds, on December 4, 1918, struck hard against Lt. William Higgins' platoon. Private Louis Stark (Co. G) recalled, "You could see [the Bolos] were experienced soldiers, for they attacked us from every available point of shelter. They came to within thirty yards of our line. There was no mistaking their nerve."[10] The doughboys, though, were able to stave off several fierce Bolshevik assaults, and by the time the fight ended, a large number of Bolsheviks had been killed or wounded. The Americans had suffered casualties as well; two were killed, Pvt. Clarence Malm and Pvt. Jay Pitts, and four were wounded, including Louis Stark.

The Americans, lacking support from the White Russian volunteers, retreated back to Pinega, arriving on the night of December 6, 1918. Captain John Conway reported to Col. Stewart that the Russian volunteers had been worthless. Conway warned Col. Stewart, writing, "The present situation at Pinega is unsteady. The local volunteers require organizing and those found to be unreliable must be dismissed." Colonel Stewart, unhappy with what had happened, responded, "It is proposed ... to relieve Capt. Conway and the two American platoons now at Pinega by an American Company which will be under the command of a more ... experienced officer who it is hoped will be able to ... stabilize the situation on this front."[11]

And thus Cpt. Joel Moore and his two platoons had come to be added to the American force in Pinega. Joel Moore, now in command of four platoons and what was left of the White Russian volunteer force, assessed the situation. He realized he did not have enough men, so he contacted Col. Stewart, requesting to receive Company M's other two platoons. Once Moore believed dependable reinforcements were on the way, he sent Lt. George Stoner and his platoon some thirty miles south on the Pinega River to Soyala to set up a barrier against any Bolo movements pushing toward Pinega. Lieutenant Stoner, supplied with sleighs piled high with equipment, moved out on December 29, 1918. He noted in his journal, "29 sleighs—45 men. Arrived 7 P.M. Cold trip, up most of the night."[12] Then, Cpt. Moore allocated postings for Conway's men to occupy as well as defensive tasks for Lt. Wright's platoon. First Sergeant Dundon wrote, "Company took over part of guard in village, outpost duty, and building defenses near village."[13]

Joel Moore examined Pinega; the town was the largest in the area, numbering about 6,000 inhabitants. Located on the Pinega River, it was the focal point for marketing and trade throughout this northern area, with the fur trade and lumber industry driving its prosperity. Pinega was linked to Archangel by wireless radio and telegraph as well as the Dvina and Pinega rivers. Travel during the summer was by steamer, usually taking three days, and during the winter by the land route, using sleds and sleighs and taking ten or more days. Many of the community's inhabitants were well educated and prosperous, and the town boasted a fine gathering hall, a good hospital, and a solid set of governmental buildings. Politically, most of the locals had been elated when the czar abdicated, but once they learned of Bolshevik cruelties, many became anxious as to what the future had in store for them. Thus, when Cpt. Conway's force arrived, some of Pinega's citizens took comfort in the Americans' presence, though others did not take kindly to these foreign invaders.[14]

Captain Joel Moore met with the White Russian officer, Cpt. P.T. Akutin, a veteran of the czar's army in the war against the Germans. Captain Akutin had been a graduate student in science at a Russian university before the war began and, though accepting the czar's abdication, he was repulsed by the Bolsheviks' attempts to conquer his nation. Akutin, using the experience he had

Pinega had about 6,000 inhabitants in 1918 (Library of Congress).

gained fighting against the Germans, along with his strong personal strength, held together a small force of White Russian volunteers in Pinega. On December 30, 1918, Cpt. Moore ordered Lt. Wright to send out a combined Yank-White Russian patrol that included Cpt. Akutin. The force came back with four Bolo prisoners.[15] Joel Moore knew Akutin would be the officer key to his building of a fighting force.

On New Year's Day, January 1, 1919, Moore's first sergeant made an assessment of Company M and reported, "1st platoon on line of communications at Soyala … 4th platoon on guard outpost duty and constructing defenses.… Lts. Donovan, Primm and Wieczorek, 2nd and 3rd platoons (117 E.M.) still on designated service [with the] Vologda force … 37 men absent sick [in Archangel], one in confinement, and 2 [sick] at Kholmogori."[16] Captain Moore turned to his riflemen who could speak Russian, writing, "We were fortunate in having with us a great number of Russian born men, who of course were our interpreters."[17] These men interacted with the locals and assisted their own non–Russian speaking comrades into learning basic Russian words. One rifleman recalled, "Our Polish people could [speak] the Russian [language].… We learned their language much quicker than they could learn ours. You know, for eating and eggs, and potatoes, and things like that."[18] In all, the relationship between the Americans and the locals changed, transforming to one of mutual goals and respect. An officer in the 339th wrote of Joel Moore, "[His] life profession was that of college instructor.… [He was] skilled in applied humanity … and possessed of tact and understanding and sympathy, and that indefinable gift of leadership."[19] Another officer recorded, "The situation was handled with such tact and skill that complete confidence in their own ability was not only reinforced but a complete, fully equipped, and well-trained infantry regiment was raised from among the White Guards."[20]

Though the situation was better than before, there still was a long way to go. In the early hours of January 4, 1919, someone set fire to the barracks where Company M's enlisted men were housed. Walter Dundon recorded, "Fire was discovered by [the] fire guard at 3:15 A.M. The 1st Sgt., Supply Sgt., and one Cook, fire guard, and two or three men sick in qtrs., were practically the only men in [the] building when [the] fire was discovered, the balance of the men being on guard. By the time these few men succeeded in saving the ammunition and most of the supplies, there was no chance to save the barrack bags and men's personal equipment."[21] This was a terrible loss of personal items for the doughboys, and most found themselves coming away from the fire having been completely wiped out. When Charles T. Williams, the director for the Red Cross in Archangel, learned of this event, he wrote to Cpt. Moore, "I am very sorry to hear that your barracks were burned just after I left Pinega, and that your men lost considerable of their effects ... we are furnishing [the men of your company] with a complete assortment of comforts.... In the comfort kits will be found many essentials, and in addition, we are including an extra supply of socks, and with the usual supply of cigarettes. I have directed that a case of Ivory soap be included. Soap of the brand I find popular with the men."[22]

Also at this time, Cpt. Moore received word a Bolshevik force was moving northward along the Pinega River and had occupied Trufangora, a village about fifty miles east of Soyala. He sent Cpt. Akutin with his two companies of White Russians, along with a 17-man detachment of American riflemen, to block the Bolo movement. Moore also notified Lt. George Stoner, who was with his platoon at Soyala, to "keep up your own patrolling and stand ready to support the [White Russia] Volunteers."[23] The Bolsheviks responded to this Allied advance by halting their progress and by fortifying Trufangora. Other groups of Reds moved forward on Moore's far right flank, whipping up agitation in the towns of Leunovo, Ostrov, and Kuzomen and thus threatening the Americans' line of communication with Archangel.[24] Joel Moore convinced Col. Stewart to release a platoon from Company F, commanded by Lt. Philip Sheridan. This unit of forty-plus men arrived, and Moore dispatched them to Leunova with the instructions "the people have to be sorted out."[25] Joel Moore knew his troops were stretched dangerously thin. He waited impatiently for his other two platoons to arrive.

The men of Lt. George Stoner's platoon, their right flank now protected by Lt. Sheridan's platoon, remained at their posts around the village of Soyala. Russia's Arctic weather closed down upon them, forcing the Americans to seek shelter with the locals. On January 5, 1919, the temperature was recorded at -15° F, preventing supplies from arriving. Soon, the Americans' rations began to grow thin. One rifleman noted, "About all we had was oatmeal, and some of that was flavored with cockroaches."[26] Another wrote, "[We would] wait until some Russian woman would allow [us] into her kitchen and borrow a kettle from her. I remember one time.... I borrowed a kettle and a stove from [her].... We pooled our rice and I ... put it into the oven, and it began to cook. And it just went over [the top]."²⁷ Another enlisted man recalled, "The cockroaches were so thick on the ceiling that if you were drinking coffee you had to hold your hand over the top of it ... [and] the walls were covered with cockroaches ... [The Russian peasants] kept a couple chickens [in the house].... That was what the chickens fed on."²⁸

Captain Moore received word on January 8, 1919, that Lt. Donovan, along with the Second Platoon (Lt. Wieczorek) and the Third Platoon (Lt. Primm), had been pulled from their positions south of Obozerskaya and were heading for Archangel. Moore recorded, "We shall soon be more powerful."²⁹ But in the meantime, the temperature dropped to even crueler iciness. Lieutenant Stoner recorded the mercury on January 12, 1919, at -22° F and the next day -30° F.³⁰ The Americans were reluctant to spend much time outside; nevertheless, they manned their posts and ran patrols. One patrol returned thoroughly chilled but amused by what it had seen. A rifleman reported, "Two enemy patrols mistaken (*sic.*) [each other for Americans] and fired upon each other."³¹

Finally, on January 14, 1919, the balance of Cpt. Moore's company arrived. Walter Dundon wrote, "Today at 2:30 P.M., Lts. Donovan, Primm, and Wieczorek, 2nd and 3rd platoons, less 13 E.M. who were left [behind] ... reported for duty with Co. The detachment traveled 204 versts, marching most of the way, the men reported [it being a] very hard trip, the weather being 40 degrees below zero, Fahrenheit most of the journey."³² One participant in the march wrote, "No soldier who was in it will ever forget that mid-winter march from Archangel in gray days and cold, when the spruce trees cracked in the frost with the report of

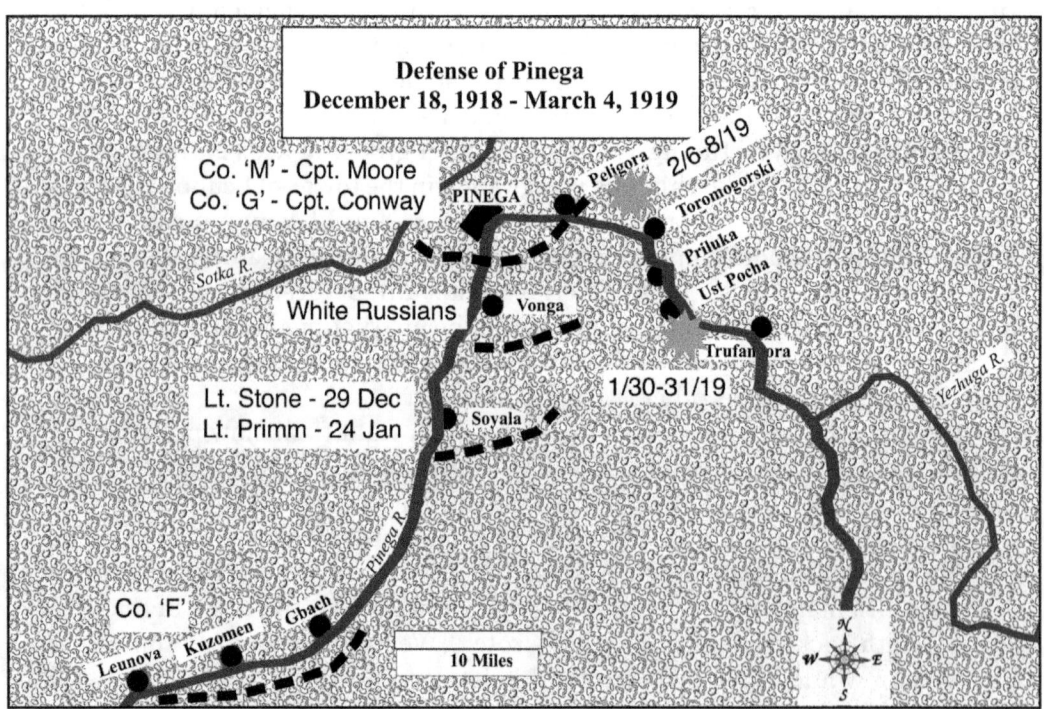

rifle shots."³³ Joel Moore now had his entire command, nearly 175 men, and his full complement of lieutenants. His men, along with Cpt. Conway's two platoons, made for a sizeable American presence in the Pinega River Valley.

The next morning, Cpt. Moore assigned the newly-arrived troops limited jobs of guard duty and defense construction. These doughboys, relieved not to be marching across Russia's frozen landscapes, settled into their new roles. They, along with the rest of the Yanks, were elated that afternoon when, as Lt. Stoner reported, "[the] YMCA man brought mail, cigarettes and tobacco."³⁴ That evening, Cpt. Moore, feeling better about their immediate situation, recorded, "One platoon 'F' Co. [Lt. Philip Sheridan] is at Leunova with detachments at.... Kuzomen and Gbach.... One platoon 'M' Co. with a strong detachment at Soyala.... Two platoons 'G' Co. and three platoons 'M' Co. are at Pinega.... One company [of] Akutin's volunteers is at Vonga." Moore wrote to Col. Stewart, "These Russian will someday be troops, but right now they are liabilities. They cannot be depended upon to hold the enemy back from Pinega. [The Bolsheviks] could make Pinega untenable for us if he got his artillery to Vonga."³⁵

The American riflemen continued with their responsibilities, and though the daylight hours were short and the temperatures brutally frigid, the Yanks manned outposts, ran patrols, built defenses around Pinega, and worked to train the White Russian volunteers. At night the Americans not on guard duty retreated to their assigned Russian homes. One wrote, "In the dismal huts of the village [we] are packed with the crowded *moujiks* like herd animals, where the atmosphere is dank and pestilent, with an odor like stale fish." He continued, "In January and February there are only a few hours of feeble shadowing light, then tragic blackness blots out the snows and mournful woods.... With night, the tiny windows are shrouded with board coverings, a candle flickers in the low-ceilinged room.... Through the long, dark unwholesome night ... black thoughts [about] ... the smug, pompous statesmen who with sonorous patriotic phrases sent [us] to [this] exile."³⁶

For the next week, the days went by, each like the one before. The weather remained frosty, curtailing everyone's outside activities, but it did not stop some routine activities. Lieutenant Clarence Primm wrote, "Washing of clothes is done in two processes, soaping and rubbing in hot water at home, and rinsing and rubbing in cold water at the riverbank ... through a hole cut in the ice. Although the result may please the eye, it ... frequently ... offend[ed] the nose because of the common use of fish-oil soap."³⁷

On January 23, 1918, Cpt. Moore received reports of Bolshevik advances near the town of Shenkursk, situated on a tributary of the Dvina River, some two hundred miles south of Archangel. Bolo forces attacked Company A, forcing the Americans to retreat, bringing with them nearly a hundred sick and wounded. This force also shepherded a throng of Russian civilians and, trudging through the deep snow, they retreated nearly eighty miles to the town of Shagovari. There, they reached the security provided by two more First Battalion companies. Joel Moore realized if the Bolsheviks continued to advance northward along the Dvina River, they could cut the line of communications between Pinega and Archangel. This would isolate Pinega. Moore also received word that Red sympathizers in Leunova and Kuzomen had heard about the Shenkursk retreat and were beginning to act aggressively. With this in mind, Moore dispatched Lt. Primm and the Third Platoon to Soyala to relieve Stoner and his boys.[38] Lieutenant George Stoner's troops were worn out by their constant duty, and many of the men were incapacitated by the pitiless cold.

Clarence Primm was aware of what had happened at Shenkursk, but he believed the establishment of First Battalion's new defense line would turn the situation around. Primm optimistically wrote, "Time passes by rapidly, with little flurries of excitement now and then. In all probability we shall 'hold the line.'" He added, "We are not here to sacrifice lives needlessly, we may have no more severe engagements unless attacked in force, because by the end of the frozen period the Bolshi regime is expected to be *hors-do-combat*."[39]

The British high command, wanting Cpt. Moore to do something to take the pressure off the embattled troops of First Battalion, ordered him to assemble a combat force and push southward along the Pinega River. The Brits chose Ust-Pocha as the town to capture. This village, about thirty-five miles upstream from Pinega and a few miles north of Trufangora, was now at the Bolsheviks' spear point. The British high command reasoned if Ust-Pocha could be taken, the Reds would have to retreat back to Trufangora, and this defeat might dampen the Bolshevik's ardor in their advance toward Archangel. Captain Moore and Maj. Akutin (who had been promoted) assembled an assault force composed of seven hundred White Russian infantrymen who would conduct the attack and two platoons (Stoner's and Wright's, 72 enlisted men) who would provide defensive support.[40] Moore remarked, "There is the very best of cooperation between American and ... Akutin's soldiers."[41]

Leaving Lt. Robert Wieczerok and his platoon, along with those of Cpt. Conway, to defend Pinega, the Moore-Akutin force left Pinega on January 28, 1919. They marched forward all day, and by darkness of the next day, they had reached a small village just north of Priluka, a settlement five miles from Ust-Pocha. Priluka was now occupied by Bolo outposts, who commenced skirmishing with Akutin's men. The following morning, January 30, 1919, the White Russians surged forward, drove the Reds out of Priluka and then advanced toward Ust-Pocha. Here, the Bolsheviks were protected by well-developed defensive positions, making it impossible for Maj. Akutin's troops to take the town that day. The White Russians tried again on January 31, 1919, but failed. Walter Dundon recorded, "The enemy was well fortified, and had us outnumbered two to one, so consequently the attack[s] proved unsuccessful."[42] Captain Moore noted, "We tried the enemy's works at Ust Pocha ... but were held with great losses."[43] A count of Akutin's casualties showed his men suffered severely—10 killed and over a hundred wounded.[44]

The Bolsheviks, emboldened by their successful defense of Ust-Pocha and buoyed by the realization they outnumbered the White Russians, advanced from their trenches and counterattacked. Major Akutin's volunteers became rattled and retreated, leaving the American riflemen in a forward position. The Yanks, well protected by trenches and machine-gun positions, opened fire upon the Reds, downing enough to break the assault. The Bolos fell back, out of range, while their war-experienced commanders sought ways to outflank the small platoon. The Americans, using this moment of quiet, slipped out of their defenses and fell back, but they had bought enough time for Akutin to rally his men. The White Russians had a new position, and resupplied with ample ammunition, they were once again ready to fight.[45]

Captain Joel Moore marched his two platoons past Akutin's line and established another defensive position, this one just outside Peligora, which he termed the "last stand" before Pinega. Here, Moore's men worked side by side with the town's citizens for the next couple days, hastily constructing a series of trenches, barbed wire entanglements, and blockhouses. The resilient officer brought in every piece of artillery and added a unit of White Russian machine gunners. Moore wrote to Lt. Stoner, "[The] enemy probably will attack our forces at Peligorskaya.... We want to inflict severe losses on the enemy and repulse him."[46] Meanwhile, Maj. Akutin's men slowly gave ground against the relentless Bolo attacks. Eventually, Akutin's soldiers fell back, seeking shelter among the newly created defenses. Joel Moore then wrote, "Our forces are rapidly strengthening [their] defense and gaining confidence.... I believe that [Maj.] Akutin and his officers are developing something of an *esprit de corps*." But he also observed, "[The] enemy [has] about 2000 strong [and] has [a] heavily fortified and equipped base."[47]

The Bolsheviks reached the Peligora defenses and, bolstered by their recent successes, immediately threw themselves against Moore's positions. The results were disastrous; Bolo corpses piled up on the frozen landscape. The Bolshevik commanders, following a series of bloody repulses, realized Peligora was not going to be taken. Knowing this, and with the frigid February weather murdering any wounded man not immediately removed to a warm location, the Bolos' leaders ordered their soldiers to retreat back to Trufangora. The unhappy soldiers destroyed Priluka as they passed through it, leaving the village nothing but a pile of embers.[48] Once it was obvious the Bolo army was gone, the Americans returned to Pinega. Walter Dundon, after assessing the men in his company, assigned duties and on February 10, 1919, wrote, "Three skeleton platoons (1st, 2nd, and 4th) in Pinega today doing street patrol, outpost duty and patrolling nearby villages."[49] Captain Joel Moore, his men at rest, remarked, "The withdrawal of the Reds to their stronghold at Trufangora in the second week of February disappointed their sympathizers in Pinega ... and from that time on the occupation of the Pinega Valley by the Americans was marked by cordial co-operation of the whole area."[50]

Captain Joel Moore ordered his Russian-speaking soldiers to resume the training of White Russian volunteers. Walter Dundon, on February 12, 1919, wrote, "The Russian White Guards are doing the Interior Guard in Pinega. This arrangement allows us to have a limited amount of close order drill, Lewis gun, machine gun and non-commissioned officers school, also Russian, English, and arithmetic classes in the evening."[51] The local White Russian government issued a decree ordering all men eighteen to forty-five to report for military duty, and when this new batch of recruits reported for duty, they were mixed among their experienced comrades. Akutin's force grew in size, reaching nearly two thousand. Joel Moore commented, "The White soldiers had gained their confidence back.... They wanted to be in the front and did not want the Americans to fight their battles for them."[52]

February's mid-month weather sank to brutally cold levels. Lieutenant George Stoner on February 15, 1919, recorded, "Thirty-five below [zero]." Three days later, on the 18th, he noted, "forty-two below zero," and the next day, "forty below zero, [and] snowing and blowing."[53] But this did not stop the Americans' activities. Regardless of how cold the temperature had become, the Yanks were mounting guard, conducting patrols, and drilling the Russian volunteers. First Sergeant Dundon wrote, "No changes. Usual day and night patrols sent to nearby villages. 40 to 50 degrees below zero."[54] The cold, though, had its effects on the doughboys. Private Alfred Lewis (Co. M) remarked, "It was cold ... you had a good hat on; you had a good coat on; you had heavy underwear. But your face—your nose—could freeze up and you wouldn't even know it. And your fingers—it's kind of hard to handle a gun ... if you've got big mittens on. So your hands and face freeze up." He added, "The Russian women, they were always glad to help you. Quite often they'd pour the oil from their lamp into a bowl and they'd bathe your hands or put some on your face and thaw you out ... [and] let you hang around the stove for a while."[55]

On February 20, 1919, Maj. Akutin and Cpt. Moore organized a parade through Pinega's main streets, showing off the Russian soldiers as well as a platoon of Americans. Moore, with all the soldiers standing in snappy formation, gave a speech. Afterward, the officer wrote, "[I made a speech] through my official interpreter to the men ... [I] impressed the men with [the] importance of their training ... and for their present enthusiasm and hard work ... [I] pointed out the fact that Pinega was now safe ... and that their big purpose is to ... help push [the] Bolsheviks out of this area.... [I] praised Akutin's force for its willingness to assume the responsibility for holding the front ... and that when the Russian mobilized army became trained fully, the Allied troops would not be necessary even in the reserve." Moore then noted, "I have two missions here. One is to make the defenses of Pinega so formidable as to discourage further advances of Reds in this area.... Second, I am to inspire and develop self-reliance among [the] Russian troops. I believe I am getting results."[56]

Another week went by with little difference from the previous day. Walter Dundon's notation in his log book from February 21 through February 27, 1919, read the same each day: "No changes. Usual day and night patrols sent to nearby villages. 40 to 50 degrees below zero."[57] The doughboys, their schedules routine and without much danger, looked forward to the end of winter and the dream of going home. A group of YMCA volunteers arrived on February 25, 1919, and entertained the troops with a dance. This activity buoyed the Yanks' spirits and, with the news that the entire company was going to be sent back to Archangel, the homesick boys began to think going home was a real possibility.[58] Company M's riflemen, as they returned to their bunks following the dance, also basked in the friendships they had made with the locals. Lieutenant Clarence Primm summed up this relationship, writing, "A single soldier or a very small patrol from such a unit could travel far, and spend each night in whatever village it found itself, without a thought of treachery, and being assisted at every turn by information and hospitality from the natives."[59] The American command believed it had accomplished its assignment; it was time to leave Pinega.

A few days later, on March 4, 1919, Lt. Stoner, with his platoon and part of the Second Platoon, left Pinega, their sleds and sleighs piled high with company equipment. They moved west, heading for the monastery at Kholmogory. Stoner's convoy arrived at Kholmogory on March 6, 1919.[60] The rest of Company M pulled out of Pinega on March 5, 1919, and marched into Kholmogory two days later. Captain Moore wrote, "When the Americans left the Pinega sector of defense in March they carried with them the good wishes of citizens and the Russian soldiers of that area."[61] Company M reached the Smolny barracks on March 9, 1919, their responsibilities in Pinega officially completed.

Once in the barracks, Moore's men were subject to the unwanted rules and restrictions of rear echelon life. First Sergeant Walter Dundon duly recorded, "March 10, 1919—3rd and 4th platoons had cootie and Venereal Inspection." This was followed by "instruction in morning, and usual drill schedule followed in afternoon."[62] Captain Joel Moore and his officers were called to meet with Col. George Stewart. Moore's lieutenants found their commanding officer frail looking, unsteady, and balding. He also appeared somewhat confused and bewildered. They came away from the 339th Regiment's headquarters baffled by the man who had absolute control over their lives. Lieutenant Harry Costello (MG Co.) was present when the officers from Pinega stood before Col. Stewart. Costello wrote, "I cite the famous 'hand-shaking episode.' Lieutenants George Stoner, Wesley Wright and Robert Wieczorek, of M Company ... were introduced three times in the same day to the colonel. On each occasion the colonel grasped the hand of the officer being introduced and said: 'How are you, lieutenant? When did you get in?' Even after three introductions."[63]

Chapter 14

Winter on the Railroad Front

February 1, 1919: Company I's First Lieutenant Gordon Reese slapped his hands together, trying to get some feeling back into them. He was cold, but he knew the men in his platoon were even colder; they had been on guard duty all night. Reese, on the other hand, had been in his heated blockhouse, catching up on paperwork while his men were outside in the frigid cold. Gordon Reese was no stranger to frosty temperatures; he was born in Minneapolis, Minnesota, on April 14, 1895, the last of five children of Charles and Annie Reese. His brothers and sisters did not spend much time with him, as he was eight years younger than his closest sibling, Annie, and fourteen years younger than the eldest, Daniel. In fact, with Gordon's mother in her mid-forties and away from the house much of the time, Gordon was raised by a Swedish servant, Anna Brinson.[1] The youngster's father was a Baptist minister and as such never stayed in one place very long. Once Charles Reese's ministry in Minneapolis was concluded, he shifted his family to Newton City, Massachusetts, where Gordon attended elementary school. A few years later, though, the Baptist minister moved again, this time to Milford, New Hampshire. Gordon grew up in this community, attending high school and graduating in 1913.[2]

The young man worked at odd jobs for the next few years, but when the United States declared war on Germany in 1916, he immediately applied for Officer Candidate School. He passed the examination and was sent to Fort Sheridan, Illinois, to begin the process of

Gordon Reese was enrolled at Fort Sheridan, Illinois, when he registered for the draft in 1917 (Library of Congress).

becoming an officer. Cadet Reese was still at Ft. Sheridan in June 1917 when he was required to register for the draft. Gordon Reese listed his occupation as "Candidate for Commission, R.O.T.C" and was identified as "of medium height, medium build, with blue eyes and dark brown hair."[3] Reese was commissioned second lieutenant in the summer of 1917 and sent to Camp Custer. His promotion to first lieutenant came a few months later, and by June 1918, he was assigned to Company I, 339th Infantry. The regiment was shipped to England, from there to Archangel, and in September 1918, Lt. Reese commanded Company I's Second Platoon near Obozerskaya.

Lieutenant Gordon Reese and his platoon were thrown into combat on September 16, 1918, not far from verst 464. He led his riflemen in a desperate bayonet charge that broke the Bolsheviks' attacking momentum, ultimately resulting in the Bolos being driven from the battlefield. For this action, Reese and several men under his command were awarded the British Military Cross. Later, the company would spend ten days in the Smolny barracks, the men resting and, when given a chance, taking liberty in Archangel. But now, once again back at the Railroad front's farthest point forward, Lt. Reese and his riflemen shivered in the bitter cold.

Northern Russia's Arctic weather had become more the enemy than the Bolsheviks. One rifleman remarked, "Snow! Good gracious there was no name for it! We was like wild Indians."[4] Corporal Clement Grobbel (Co. I), agreed, writing his family, "The weather is a snappy one, snow and more snow."[5] And another soldier commented, "This cold of Russia presses on the diaphragm like a ponderous weight and breathing becomes a gasping effort."[6] As Company I's riflemen struggled with winter's intensity, Cpt. Horatio Winslow cautioned his platoon commanders to make absolutely sure every one of their men was protected as best as could be. Private Russell Hershberger (MG Co.), who spent time on the Railroad front, summed up the efforts the officers and NCOs went through to safeguard their doughboys, commenting, "Everybody was supposed to keep watch ... if you seen anybody with frostbite, you're supposed to tell them about it." He added, "[I] wore the same pair of socks all that time ... [I] didn't dare take [my] shoes off and sleep without them, or they'd be frozen stiff in the morning."[7] And Pvt. Cleo Colburn (Co. I) also noted, "In February ... it was fifty-two below zero ... when on guard duty, we changed guards every fifteen minutes."[8]

Lieutenant Reese's platoon rotated away from its outpost duties at verst 445, replaced by another one of Company I's platoons. The Railway Force was headquartered at verst 455; however, the "rest" location was the train yard at Obozerskaya. Here, the Americans were housed in comfort, each squad bunking in a separate, well-heated boxcar, and once inside these vehicles the men of the Second Platoon crowded around their wood-burning stoves. They washed, changed clothes, and devoured a hot meal. Those who chose not to venture outside swarmed around the YMCA boxcars and buildings, because cigarettes and chocolate could be purchased there, and there was special entertainment. One Yank remarked, "[A] row of cars was maintained at Obozerskaya ... [by] the YMCA ... [plus] ... a canteen in Obozerskaya [where] movies became routine, and rum rations were issued."[9] The YMCA also had special cars for quieter activities, as recorded by Cpt. Moore, who wrote, "[There were] two cars equipped with tables for reading and writing and with a big cocoa urn."[10]

The men, though, were not allowed much free time; sergeants equipped with duty rosters would find them. The Yanks did guard mounts in Obozerskaya, weapons training, and platoon combat drills. Medical personnel inspected the soldiers for frostbite, lice, and any other condition capable of taking a rifleman away from his responsibilities. Nonetheless, for the men resting in Obozerskaya, they knew they were safe, for as one soldier recalled, "[When at the Front] there was a tautness, a certain hushed, dread expectancy in the air, and life [was] an uncertain thing [to be] lived ... for the day."[11]

Major J. Brooks Nichols, who split his time between his headquarters at verst 455 and at the forward positions, also wanted his riflemen to send a message to the locals. He accomplished this by having the men at "rest" spend time at the rifle range. Lieutenant Clarence Primm described the effectiveness of this activity in a letter to his parents: "We practice firing frequently, and are always glad when the Russians see us do well, because it has another salutary effect.... News spreads fast among the Russians, and spies hear things and carry them to Bolshevik headquarters. When the Bolos hear that there are Americans who are dead shots stationed in a village, they do not send raiding parties to that vicinity." Primm illustrated an example of this, writing, "An [American] soldier saw a crow from the jutting gable-end of a two-story house.... At the time, a middle-aged farmer stood nearby holding his horse. The soldier, fearing the horse might bolt, asked the old man's permission to fire. The farmer took a tight grip on his horse and said 'Korosho'—'O.K. by me,' and then looked upward.... One shot and the crow came down, kerplunk; the horse ran around the farmer twice, with the empty sled swinging wildly; but the old man stood there firmly anchored, not once taking his eyes off the crow nor shutting his mouth for a full minute.... [It] tickled him immensely." Lieutenant Primm added, "Whenever these people see our men shoot well it gives them great relief and confidence, because they feel that the Bolshevik chances in a raid are vanishing."[12]

The "resting" days of Lt. Reese's riflemen came to an end and they were ordered back to work. Reese's platoon headed west from Obozerskaya, following the snow-covered road to Bolshie Ozerki, a dozen miles away. This trail was the only physical link between Obozerskaya and Chekuevo, some forty miles to the west. There, at Chekuevo, Maj. Nichols had Company H stationed, that unit's four platoons tasked with protecting the Americans' right flank. In Bolshie Ozerki, Reese's men lived as guests of the locals. The village was small, with no more than a couple hundred inhabitants, so the Yanks were packed in with their hosts. This was accomplished when the platoon commander paid off the village leader. Joel Moore wrote, "The *starosta* ... was given several hearty draughts of rum to warm him up ... along with a small sack of sugar to appease his wife who, he said, always made things warmer for him when he returned home with the odor of rum about him."[13] The men crowded into the peasant homes, with "the cherished *samovar* [being] ... brought forth ... [to serve] the uninvited guest with steaming tea."[14]

Then, trading of foodstuffs occurred. One rifleman recalled, "If they ... wanted to make an exchange, many times I wouldn't even call [for] an interpreter, because I had seen their faces several times, and I knew that they had vegetables, potatoes, or carrots, or something ... [and] they were anxious to make an exchange." He added, "They wanted to get rid of [their excess] and we needed it.... [Our] split peas would dry and [they] could keep under their house."[15] Following this, the bedding came out and everyone staked out places near the great stove in the house's main room. One doughboy wrote, "Each member of the family has a pallet of coarse cloth stuffed with fluffy flax, which is placed at night on the floor, on benches, or on part of the top of the huge stove.... The place on the stove is reserved for the aged and babies. It is the best bed in the house."[16] Another Yank bragged, "If you got good and friendly with the madam of the house ... you [might] have a private place to sleep on the top of the stove."[17] The doughboys appreciated being able to sleep in these warm and protected abodes, however; most were dismayed by the housing conditions. Private Sam Safer (Co. E) remarked, "The houses were not the cleanest places on earth.... They were infested with cockroaches."[18]

Bolshie Ozerki was manned by a permanent contingent of French soldiers. These fellows were all old-timers from the Western Front, sent to northern Russia before the Great War ended. But now, with the war over, these veterans detested being trapped in this frozen wasteland and their attitudes bordered on insolent. A doughboy, shocked by the French soldiers' lack of purpose, wrote, "One night ... a Bolshevik got tangled up in the barbed wire outside a French blockhouse, and he was a-moaning and a-hollering ... out there till the Frenchmen couldn't sleep. One of the Frenchmen got mad and he got up and took an axe right out and knocked the Bolshevik's brains out, and went back in and went to sleep."[19]

This action did not impress the Bolsheviks, nor did it set well with the local citizens. However, the Bolos had discovered the Americans were of a different mindset. The Reds had learned the hard way; to attack a Yank-held position only meant one thing—horrendous casualties. But the Bolos had also noticed, once the fight ended, the Americans would gently tend to wounded Reds. Thus, the relationship between the Bolshevik riflemen and the Yanks seemed almost cordial. A doughboy remarked, "We'd go out on patrol and meet them on the road and holler at them, and we'd wave."[20] Other Yanks joined in. "One night ... an orator came out ... and boy, did he talk. He'd holler, 'Americans! Americans!' and finally one of the Americans hollered [back].... The Red ... seized the opportunity to tell [us] ... that the war was over and asked us what we were fighting for.... [Our] best answer [was] ... 'We're here because we're here.'"[21] The Bolsheviks, who usually knew where the American patrols were going, left behind leaflets for the Yanks to find. One read, "You soldiers are fighting on the side of the employers against us, the working people of Russia.... You are kidding yourself that you are fighting for your country." The Americans used the leaflets as fodder for fires and as toilet paper, because, as one rifleman opined, "needless to say this was not taken seriously."[22]

After a week at Bolshie Ozerki, Reese's platoon was replaced and the unit returned to Obozerskaya, where it boarded a train and traveled to verst 455. Here, the platoon would act as a backup to the force manning the front line at verst 445. Verst 455 was no longer the lonely railroad siding it had been when the Allies secured it back in October 1918. Now, in February 1919, it was the vital military center of the Railroad front, commanded by a British senior officer and his staff. A Yank described the base, writing, "The headquarters of the Railway Force was at Verst 455, where the armored train was kept most of the time." He continued, "The camp was well fortified with barbed wire, blockhouses, and outposts manned by infantry units." By February, there was an observation tower that could be used to keep a watchful eye out for Bolshevik movements.

Major J. Brooks Nichols ignored much of what the Brits demanded and ran operations for the 339th's Second Battalion. Nichols, though, was in a tough situation; the British were still in charge of the Americans and continued to tell the Yanks what to do, and Col. Stewart from his warm office in Archangel often sent messages, recommending Nichols conform to what the British wanted. But Nichols, as long as rations and supplies were assured, only did what he felt best to protect and maintain his troops. The American major struggled, knowing at any time the British might demand his replacement, while at the same time, he also felt as one rifleman, who spoke for his comrades, grumbled, "he was abandoned by his country, [and] that he was forgotten and left to his fate."[23]

Major Nichols was also dealing with a problem that had arisen because his young American riflemen detested being under British rule. Company I's First Lieutenant Albert May reported, "An American soldier ... killed a British officer at Verst 445." An inquiry was opened to determine what had happened. Lieutenant May, who was part of the investigation, concluded, "The American either just went nuts, or mistook the officer for the enemy. When the Britisher stuck his head out of his dugout he was shot and killed."[24] This inquest eventually was "swept under the rug." Nichols knew, though, what had happened was but a reflection of the feelings between the Americans and the British.

The American soldiers were also aware that, back home in the United States, a flood of anger was growing—people were coming out against their young men's involvement in Russia's civil war. Hundreds of relatives of men in the 339th Infantry had become forcefully vocal in their opposition of this war, and their entreaties had reached the hearts of thousands more. A *Chicago Tribune* article reflected this growing development: "Our men are dying for a cause, the purpose of which they are no more certain than we in America. America has not declared war on Russia, but Americans are killing Russians and are being killed by them."[25] William C. Bullitt, of the American State Department, added his distaste for the involvement, declaring on January 30, 1919, "The 12,000 American, British and French troops at Archangel are no longer serving any useful purpose.... They are in considerable danger of destruction by the Bolsheviki.... Unless they are saved by prompt action, we shall have another Gallipoli."[26]

The United States Congress heard the uproar, and debates commenced on the Senate floor, with Senator Robert La Follette (R-WI) shouting, "No government ought to intrude itself into [other governments'] affairs. Under what rule of international law can you justify our action?" He then added, "Total deaths among the American Expeditionary Forces in Northern Russia to Jan. 4 ... [are] 6 officers and 126 men."[27] President Woodrow Wilson heard the ruckus coming from the Senate building and, feeling the heat from voters in Michigan and Wisconsin, announced on February 16, 1919, that he had "decided to call off the North Russian campaign and ... cabled that information to Secretary of War, Newton Baker, who began preparations for withdrawal."[28]

President Wilson's announcement to pull American troops out of Russia eventually reached the doughboys at verst 455, but it did not change their situation. The riflemen knew they were stuck in this frozen world, but they also understood their enemy. The Americans did not believe the Bolos had the means or the will to force them to leave, because, as many Bolshevik prisoners had stated, "our losses are terrible. The commissars cannot understand [American] resistance. We [the Bolsheviks] are 20 to 1 and have more guns ... but the soldiers will not attack any more over the snow against your awful machine guns."[29] The Yanks knew their most pressing enemy was the northern Russian winter; it was the frozen wasteland that controlled when they could leave. Then, in an announcement the riflemen found ironic, they were notified they could wear a new service stripe. Clarence Primm wrote, "We are now permitted to wear a gold chevron on the lower part of the sleeve, to indicate six months' service abroad ... but there are no gold chevrons in our supply list, so we are as bare as before."[30]

Regardless of whether they had the service chevron sewn to their sleeves, Lt. Reese's men were shifted from the "palace guard" slot at verst 455 to the front, ten versts farther south. They traveled by rail, passing through verst 448, which had its own assortment of defensive constructions—barbed wire, blockhouses, trenches, and dugouts. The Canadians had their artillery pieces dug in here, and their guns could support just about any need arising at the forward outposts. And if more artillery was needed than what the Canadians had to give, the armored train could run up to this position and add its heavier shells to the fray. The riflemen climbed down from their transport and hiked the last three versts. There, at verst 445, they slid into, as one soldier described, "a series of interconnecting trenches with communications linked to all outposts and dugouts." He did add, "All the works were well-heated."[31]

Lieutenant Reese, once he was certain his men were where they were supposed to be, and after acknowledging the departure of his fellow lieutenant's platoon, made sure communications with the Canadian gunners were working and checked the phone lines connecting him with the supporting machine-gun posts. The officer sent out patrols to monitor the snow-covered terrain between verst 445 and the village of Emtsa, several versts farther south. This land between the Americans' positions and the Bolsheviks' positions at Emtsa was where the action might take place; the homesick doughboys called this area "No Woman's Land."[32] There was a creek in this wild space and its frozen surface often became the demarcation between the two forces' patrols. One Yank wrote, "We [would] stay on one side of the river and the Bolsheviks stay on the other side.... Some of

The blockhouses were solidly built, both for protection and for warmth (U.S. Army Signal Corps).

them Bolsheviks, they used to come to the river in the morning to get water. They [would] say, 'Hello! Good morning, Americans!'"[33]

Though there was always the danger of being shelled by artillery, the American riflemen knew their worst enemy was the cold. Everyone was safely warm in their blockhouses; the peril came when the soldiers had to remain outside. One rifleman remarked, "Some of the boys were hiking in their sock feet, their shoes over their shoulders. I've done it for a while myself. Of course, you had three or four pair of heavy socks on. Walking in your stocking feet, you didn't slip."[34] Another, though, looked at the footwear problem differently. He wrote, "Let it be said that many a footsore doughboy helped himself to a dry pair of boots from a dead Red Guard ... or a pair of *valenkas*, or warm felt boots.... [They] hated the ill-fitting British army shoe [Shackleton boot]." The soldier added, probably with a grin, "One thing the Americans never did take from the dead Bolo was his Russian tobacco, for it was worse than the British issue tobacco."[35] The Americans, though, as the winter ground on, grew to look more like their foes than their comrades back in Archangel. One soldier stated, "Our clothes ... they looked like rags.... Some of our boys, like the Russians, wore sheepskin coats.... We had nothing. Dirty clothes, filthy! For weeks we didn't shave."[36]

Not only did the Americans often appear like their enemy, their feelings about who they faced off against were also frequently similar—both sides just wanted to be left alone to deal with surviving the miserable cold. This unofficial truce between the Reds and Yanks proved to have another benefit. A rifleman wrote, "One time they [Bolos] came over and asked if anyone knew a prisoner by the name of George Albers [Co. I] ... I got to talk with him alone. He told me that he was treated very well—that he was allowed to walk around Moscow, and all he had to do was report in at dark. Otherwise he could do as he pleased."[37] Albers explained more about his experiences, saying, "I was a sentry ... [when] a guy wearing a white night coat crawled through the snow on a moonlit night.... [He] gun-butted me ... when I came to I was being carried on a stretcher.... The first thing they did to me when I came in the Bolshevik camp was to swipe my fur coat, smock, and uniform. The gave me a Bolshevik uniform." Albers continued, "I started on a terrible hike ... more than 150 miles to Vologda.... We were fed irregularly with black bread and fish soup.... From Vologda I was taken to Moscow.... I was the first American to get to Moscow." The prisoner added, "We had as much as anybody to eat, and they paid us when we worked.... We dug graves for people who had starved to death." George Albers then shared, "Sunday [was] a scream in Bolsheviki-land. Every Sunday all the prisoners would be taken to an official's house, where we were lectured on Bolshevikism."[38]

This sighting of Company I's captured comrade filled Cpt. Winslow's men with some comfort, and Lt. Gordon Reese immediately wrote Albers' family. His message soon appeared in a local Michigan newspaper: "George Albers, captured by the Bolsheviki, Nov. 7, is alive and being well treated.... Gordon Reese, lieutenant of the 339th infantry ... says [in a letter to Albers' wife] that the enemy ... brought Albers to an American front to prove that they were giving prisoners excellent [care]."[39]

Once the positions at verst 445 were deemed safe enough for representatives from the YMCA to visit. These occasions brought brief interruptions to the boredom and stress accompanying life in close quarters with the enemy. Russell Hershberger remarked, "They had their Victrola and records, and they'd come out and play that for us and give us a little entertainment."[40] Joel Moore added, "One YMCA secretary made the trip around the blockhouses and outposts daily with a couple of packsacks filled with gum, candy and cigarettes, which were distributed as generously as the small capacity of the sacks permitted."[41] These little nuggets from home helped the homesick boys get through this period of time.

Captain Horatio Winslow was ordered to pull his four platoons back to Obozerskaya at the end of February 1919, as French troops were to take over Company I's responsibilities. Lieutenant Reese's platoon hiked away from verst 445, the riflemen glad to be free from that frozen front line. Private William Robbins (Co. I), reminiscing about that station's incredible cold, wrote, "It was so cold that the soldiers had to light small bonfires to keep warm. They would drag snow-covered logs over near the fire on which to sit while they warmed themselves. When spring came, at least one 'log' turned out to be a frozen corpse."[42] But this did not bother Winslow's riflemen as they boarded a troop train, heading for Archangel and the Smolny barracks. They were going to be away from the war and provided with the opportunity to clean up, relax, and get into the city with all its delights!

Chapter 15

A Mutiny in Name Only

March 30, 1919: First Sergeant Whitney S. McGuire glanced at his company commander, Cpt. Horatio Winslow, and frowned, saying, "The boys did not like the order, because to them, '[the army is] reneging on their vacation.'"[1] Captain Winslow thought for a moment, then turned away from his first sergeant and snatched up the telephone. Winslow knew his first sergeant was right; after all, the young NCO had been raised from an early age to meet leadership's demands. Whitney McGuire was born September 6, 1898, in New Paris, Ohio. The youth's parents, Charles and Blanche, were no strangers to being in charge, as Charles was the vice president for Dille & McGuire Manufacturing, a company that had put Richmond, Indiana, on the map as the "the lawn mower capital of the world" by producing almost twenty-five million mowers.[2]

Young Whitney grew up in Richmond, along with a younger brother and sister. The three attended local schools, with Whitney graduating from Richmond High School in 1916. He went to Cornell University, where he studied mechanical engineering; by the time he registered for the draft in September 1917, he identified himself as a mechanical engineer in the family-owned lawn mower company. The draft officer described McGuire as tall, with blue eyes and dark brown hair.[3]

McGuire reported to Camp Custer and was assigned to Company I. He did well in those hectic weeks before the 339th regiment was shipped to England, and by the time the Yanks boarded transportation to cross the Atlantic, McGuire had been promoted to corporal. His promotion to sergeant came in the fall of 1918, which was soon followed by being elevated to the company's top sergeant position, and from that point on he worked closely with Cpt. Horatio Winslow.

Company I, by early March 1919, was due its turn for an extended period of rest at Camp Smolny, with the men moving into the barracks on the evening of March 12, 1919. The doughboys cleaned up, rested, endured medical check-ups, close order drill, and fatigue duties, happy to be away from the rigors of life at the front. The weather improved, with the temperature creeping above zero, the mercury reaching as high as 25°F.[4] Lieutenant Clarence Primm, his company also relaxing at the Smolny barracks, wrote, "[It] seems quite warm; snowing too. Pretty soon, perhaps in a month or so, sleighing will be over."[5]

As always, the American soldiers set about having a good time, and in this, the Red Cross and the YMCA were well prepared to help take care of the men. Joel Moore recorded, "The Central YMCA hut at Archangel had been remodeled and fully equipped for handling large crowds, and it served several hundred allied soldiers daily." He also added, "Whenever a company of Americans came in from the front, a special night was arranged for them to have a program in the theater hall, with movies, songs, stunts, and eats."[6] And of course, the engineer-built toboggan run continued to create excitement. Lieutenant Clarence Primm exclaimed, "The after hours have been spent in hilarious frivolity ... mostly sliding down a steep toboggan on pieces of very thin veneer wallboard for sleds ... we go fast and far, and the effect is usually surprising."[7] Elsewhere, Cpl. Clement Grobbel described his activities, writing his parents, "We are playing basketball, skiing, and snowshoeing.... Basketball is some game, each platoon of the Company has a team. One platoon plays against the other. I am in the team of the second platoon. Played a couple games but lost."[8] Another remarked, "While I am writing, Lt. Wright is showing my collection of American picture postcards to a Russian Red Cross nurse. He can't talk enough Russian to explain them, and she can't understand a word of American. It is a scream."[9] And a third, Pvt. Henry Abel (Co. I), noted, "I go down to the YMCA quite often. It is about three miles from our barracks. I take the street car for the simple reason they have some good looking girls for conductors."[10]

However, as the young soldiers in Company I explored Archangel's amusements, they noticed an undercurrent of discord that had not been present before. Certainly, the tension between the Yanks and the Brits had not eased, but now it seemed that the Russian businessmen were beginning to look upon the American soldiers as nothing but wallets to be emptied. Captain Moore saw this and wrote, "When a soldier in search of a meal ... is lucky enough ... to stumble across a place where he can get something to eat, but when he looks at the bill of fare and learns that it cost him about $7.50 for a sandwich and a cup of coffee, he beats it back to the barracks."[11] This state of affairs did not set well with the underpaid riflemen, and when this inequality was emphasized by the fact that some of the 339th's companies had never left Archangel, one combat-experienced veteran grumbled, "Across the harbor at Bakharitza, a well-fed Supply Company watched over mountains of rations and supplies that had been brought all the way from far off America.... These supplies never reached the front, but the [men in] Supply Company, with American business shrewdness and American aptitude for trading, acquired great bundles of rubles, and ... converted these into stable sterling."[12] Sergeant Matthew Grahek (Co. M) added his criticisms, writing, "Headquarters Company, they were stationed where they would load the supplies onto the train to take it to the front. They had a chance to steal and peddle the stuff."[13]

Company I's riflemen also looked upon the nicely dressed White Russian soldiers strutting around Archangel, their uniforms clean and unweathered, and wondered why these local soldiers had never spent any time at the front. Captain Moore noted, "The Russian Army of the North ... the Slavo-British Allied League [SBAL] ... never distinguished themselves except in the slow goose step— much admired by Col. Stewart, who pointed them out ... to his officers as wonders of precision." Moore growled, "They were trained under British officers.... They failed several times under fire ... [but] distinguished themselves in eating"[14]

The fact that Archangel's Russian soldiers were only good for parades and nothing else was brought home to Cpt. Horatio Winslow's riflemen when the Russians threatened to riot. Private Cleo Colburn (Co. I) objected, writing, "[Our] Company [was] ordered to stay in to be ready at minutes' notice. Riot expected uptown."[15] However, though nothing happened, except Company I's men were confined to quarters, it did not lessen the fact something had soured for the Allies during the past couple of months. Joel Moore recorded, "Rumors were rife at Archangel and Smolny and the gloom was thick enough to cut.... A great Bolo sympathetic strike and riot was imminent."[16] Lieutenant Primm also felt this unrest and wrote, "Our work in Russia is not over, in spite of the agitation at home. In many ways I ... regret that agitation ... there will always be a feeling ... that we were pulled out by politics before our work was done."

The local Russian battalion in Archangel had demonstrated that it was not dependable when two companies from that force refused to form up and go to the front. Captain Joseph Taylor (HQ Co.) recorded what happened next: "Col. Sutherland came to Olga Barracks and asked that [HQ] Company move out at once and take up a position to attack the west end of Alexandra Nevsky Barrack.... At 1:53 P.M. a message was received from Col. Sutherland to open fire at exactly 2:00 P.M. At 2:00 P.M. the order was given to commence fire."[17] The shooting lasted for about twenty minutes. Captain Taylor recorded, "[The Russians] returned fire from the windows of the barracks at the opening of the engagement but this was ineffective and soon ceased." Taylor added, "At the end of which time the mutineers, bearing a white flag and with their hands in the air, came out ... and surrendered." He also noted, "13 of the ringleaders suffered the death penalty."[18]

The Russians mutinied again, this time on March 1, 1919. Captain Hugh Martin, a staff officer for the Allies, recorded, "The Second Russian mutiny occurred in the Pechora district.... One company refused to go into the front lines.... There were a number of Bolshevik agitators among them and they took advantage of the situation to stir up mutiny." He continued, "The company ... when ordered to the front refused to move, the men stating that they would do no further fighting until they were better provided for ... [were brought in and] the leaders of the mutiny were shot."[19]

Unfortunately, the Archangel Russian soldiers were not the only ones balking at taking the Americans' places at the front, the French also were proving to be reluctant. Captain Hugh Martin recorded, "[A company of Frenchmen] absolutely refused to go to the front when the time came for the French Battalion to relieve the American Battalion on the Railway Front. Another company was sent to replace them and the men of that company likewise showed a mutinous spirit.... They constantly protested that they should not be kept on active military duty here while men of the same class were being demobilized in France.... They stated ... that they would go to verst post 455 but would go no further." Martin added, "It was currently stated that the French officers were in great danger of being killed by their men. The men of the mutinous companies began drinking very heavily and creating [a] great disturbance. The officers made no attempt to discipline them ... [and] during this time the men broke into the Y.M.C.A. building, stole a large quantity of goods, broke the piano and messed things up."[20] Ultimately, 113 mutineers were arrested, sent to Archangel, and placed under guard.

And for the Americans, the endless winter's brutality, the lethal Bolshevik pressures, and the growing belief that their allies were not doing their share battered at their morale. By March 1919, some of the Yanks were beginning to outwardly express their distrust in their leadership. On March 4, 1919, four riflemen in Company B put together a list of complaints in a petition that ultimately threatened mutiny. One of these four, Pvt. William Henkleman (Co. B), stated, "He would cross enemy lines alone, carrying a white flag. He would invite the Bolsheviks to a goodbye party. Then he and his co-conspirators would walk away from the war."[21] Four days later, Henkleman, along with Sgt. Silver Parris (Co. B) and two other conspirators, were arrested.

The four were placed before a court martial trial, charged with "treason, desertion and mutiny—crimes punishable by death."[22] Major Charles Young, the Third Battalion's ex-commander who now led the companies stationed in Archangel, had also been given the regimental responsibilities of chairing all court martials. He was in no mood for leniency, and the 339th's men knew that of him, for as one rifleman noted, "this ... responsibility he relished."[23] Colonel Stewart, aware of Maj. Young's inclinations, came to the trial and took over the hearings, as he outranked the major. Private Henkleman was called to the witness stand, and he "tore open his uniform blouse and exposed his chest to the judges: 'Look at the lice, the dirt, the filth. We are half-starved,' he said in his defense. 'But none of you have lice or go hungry.'"[24] An observer recorded, "Upon witnessing such a powerful argument, the courtroom went dead quiet. The head officer of the court asked the private if he were to promise to use his influence to keep the mutinous animosity down, they would leave Toulgas in less than ten days. The private agreed to their conditions and was excused."[25] Colonel Stewart then sent for Sgt. Parris, who just four days earlier had been decorated by the British with a medal for bravery, read the punishment for inciting mutiny—death—and gave him the same offer that Henkleman had received. Parrish also agreed, as did the other two conspirators. A mutiny had been shunted onto a side track, but the tension remained.

Company I's riflemen enjoyed another week, carrying out work details, drilling, and escaping the Smolny barracks by slipping into Archangel. During these days, only one thing of note happened: the men received a mail shipment from home. Mail was still arriving, though coming by way of a slow and convoluted passage. The White Sea and Dvina Bay were frozen over; thus no ships were moving in or out of Archangel. However, the port at Murmansk remained open. Small numbers of men, mail, and supplies were loaded onto the rickety train line that ran south from Murmansk and transported about 150 miles before being unloaded onto sleighs and hauled east to Onega and from there farther east to the Archangel-Vologda Railroad. Though the mail was slow in coming, the homesick Americans treasured each letter. Lieutenant Clarence Primm began one of his return letters on March 15, 1919, with "More mail today! Yours of Oct. 12 arrived."[26]

This latest batch of correspondence, though lovingly received, also contained a number of unsettling newspaper articles, all pertaining to the 339th Infantry's presence in Russia. The soldiers were aware that President Wilson had issued an order to get them home, and they had heard stories of the drama playing out in Congress, and yet, here they were, stuck in northern Russia. Many agreed with Senator Hiram Johnson (R-CA) who proclaimed, "We have sacrificed our own blood to no purpose, and into American homes have brought sorrow, anguish, and suffering."[27] The men's grousing increased as sickness and weather-related infirmities stripped more comrades from the ranks, for as one soldier, speaking for many, growled, "The men ... didn't understand why they were fighting in Russia when the war was over."[28]

The riflemen in Company I were entertained by the YMCA with an amusing minstrel show on the evening of March 27, 1919, but then a few hours later, they were forced from their sleeping quarters by a fire that destroyed their barracks. Captain Joel Moore, his company's lodgings not far from the destroyed buildings, wrote of the incident: "Fire broke out in the guard house at 2:00 A.M. [It] burned [the] Guard House and the barracks of 'I' Co." He added, "Vigorous work by American soldiers saved the adjacent buildings ... [they used] buckets and snow."[29] Captain Winslow's officers scrambled, searching for places to house their platoons, and by sunrise they accomplished the task, though now two platoons (the first and fourth) were bunked in one building while the other two platoons (the second and third) were housed in another that was some distance away. Joel Moore summed up this command difficulty, writing, "[The fire] result[ed] in the splitting of the company into two separated parts."[30] This would severely affect the events to come.

Colonel George Stewart, on March 16, 1919, received word from Gen. Ironside that the situation on the Railroad front had deteriorated. The British general rushed to Obozerskaya after learning that the Bolsheviks were intent upon severing the supply line between Obozerskaya and Chekuevo. The Bolos overwhelmed the French force holding the town of Bolshie Ozerki and drove off Company H's attempts to recover that position. Company E had been dispatched from the Smolny barracks to strike the Bolos, but this unit crumbled under fire. General Ironside ordered Col. Stewart to send another company; Stewart contacted Cpt. Joel Moore, telling him to get his men ready to move. Captain Joel Moore wrote, "'E' Company of Americans resolutely floundered.... [Then] the order came to move [Company M] ... to Archangel ... [and] thence to Obozerskaya as quickly as possible."[31]

As soon as Company M's riflemen became engaged on the Obozerskaya-Chekuevo road another force of Bolsheviks was located, this one moving northward along the Archangel-Vologda Railway, its goal Obozerskaya. General Ironside wanted more men, and he wanted combat veterans, not other rear echelon troops similar to Company E or Archangel's Russian troops. Captain Horatio Winslow's riflemen were the only troops remaining in Archangel that qualified.

Ironside notified Col. Stewart, who gave Winslow the command to send his boys back to the front at 9:30 a.m. on March 30, 1919.[32]

Company I's riflemen were edgy that morning; they had seen Company E leave and had watched as their Third Battalion brothers in Company M had been snatched away. Captain Winslow's doughboys, now pummeled by dozens of rumors, loathed the thought of having their R and R interrupted, especially when they knew countless numbers of White Russian soldiers strolled Archangel's streets, having never heard a shot fired in anger. They also knew there were several American companies whose men had done nothing but guard Archangel's buildings. Private James Siplon (Co. I), his sentiments echoed by many of his fellow comrades, recalled, "We felt imposed upon, and felt that some of those other companies that had just been on guard duty around Archangel and Bakharitza could replace them."[33] But orders were orders, and Cpt. Winslow gave the command for his men to load their gear onto sleds in preparation to cross the ice to the train station and from there south to Obozerskaya.

Rumors exploded upon this directive; the men in each location soon believed their comrades in the other barracks were not doing what they had been ordered. Thus both groups were reluctant to respond. One sergeant "described that morning's atmosphere [as] filled with half-truths and rumors."[34] Eventually even those fellows who had packed their gear onto the sleds stopped their work. Captain Winslow, when he realized his command was not being carried out, sent 1st Sgt. McGuire to take care of the problem. The young first sergeant went into the barracks and ordered the men to immediately load their gear onto the sleds. Private Henry Abel (Co. I) recalled, "When the top sergeant transmitted these instructions to the men in the barracks they refused to put on their packs, asking, 'why in the hell are we here?'"[35] Whitney McGuire returned to his captain, informing him that the men did not see why they should be the ones sent back to fight, adding, "The boys [don't] understand why they are not reinforced with an army sufficiently large enough to assure the defeat of the bolsheviki."[36]

Captain Horatio Winslow, struggling with the fear of a possible mutiny, marched into one of the barracks and faced the men of those two platoons. He asked his riflemen what the trouble was; his veterans immediately replied that "they did not see why they should [be] ... fighting on the front lines while the Russians remained in Archangel."[37] Winslow returned to his office, and along with 1st Sgt. McGuire and Lt. Albert May, sought a solution to what could become a serious problem. The men had refused an order; Winslow knew "if a mutiny were to happen, or even the conspiracy to prompt mutiny were to occur, the captain would have to report it as mutiny.... If the captain did not report the possibility of a mutiny, he would be guilty of mutiny."[38]

Winslow was faced with a terrible choice; he knew this situation must be reported to the battalion commander in charge of the American troops in Archangel, Maj. Charles Young. But Winslow knew Maj. Young did not like the boys in Company I, and this animosity ran deep. Major Young's negative sentiment toward Company I, along with the intolerant attitude he had shown in court martial hearings, contributed to the possibility of a vindictive outcome against the company's men. Therefore, Horatio Winslow chose to go over Charles Young's head; Wilson picked up the phone and called Col. George Stewart, who immediately replied he would come to the Smolny barracks.[39]

First Lieutenant Albert May, privy to what had just taken place and hoping to ease the situation before Col. Stewart arrived, went to the barracks where his men (First Platoon) and the Fourth Platoon lurked about, uneasy and angry. Private James Siplon of the Fourth Platoon grumbled, "We felt it wasn't right ... they should send one of the other companies out." He continued, "[When] the Bolos made several small attacks up there, and the White Russians began to run.... The first thing that the commander in Archangel thought was to send [us] back ... to [bail out] these fellows."[40] Lieutenant May listened to his men's objections, and after talking with them for some time and using his skills as a lawyer, decided to split hairs. He recalled, "[I] ordered the men to load the *droskys* [sleds], stating that loading *droskys* was not going to the front."[41] His men were puzzled at first, but reluctantly complied, knowing they had been given a simple order they needed to obey. One soldier, though, 27-year-old Pvt. John Petrowskas, did not begin loading his gear. Albert May faced off against the solitary soldier, addressing him personally, but the man did not budge. Lieutenant May immediately placed Petrowskas under arrest.[42]

Colonel George Stewart arrived a few minutes later and had Cpt. Winslow's sergeants round up all the men and set them down on chairs in the YMCA building; Stewart wanted all the men to hear exactly the same thing at the same time. Colonel Stewart addressed the entire company, letting them know what mutiny would mean. Private James Siplon was impressed by this discourse, recalling, "Col. Stewart came down [to us] to read the Articles of War."[43] Stewart talked for some time, instructing the soldiers on the importance of following orders without question, but at the end of his speech, he encouraged his troops to explain why this morning's actions had occurred. Winslow's men, surprised at first that their regimental colonel was willing to listen to their complaints, repeated what they had told 1st Sgt. McGuire and Lt. May, concluding with, as one soldier summed it up, "Why do we have to go to the front and fight for the Russians when they won't fight for themselves? We are willing to risk our lives for Americans, but why should we fight for Russians?"[44] Lieutenant Albert May noted Stewart's reply, an answer that calmed the storm with its openness and vulnerability: "The colonel answered that he had never been supplied with an answer as to why they were there." He added, "[Regardless of] whatever reasons there may be [for being in Russia] there is one good reason why we must fight now. We must fight now for our lives. If we don't fight we will all be wiped out."[45] Then 1st Sgt. Whitney McGuire stood up and spoke, presenting Col. Stewart with a way to ease the men back to Obozerskaya. James Siplon recorded McGuire's words, writing, "He talked for the men and made the men's condition on the proposition that the men were perfectly willing to go back to be in reserve ... and they weren't refusing to fight if they had to. They were just simply disappointed because [the army] was reneging on their vacation."[46] Sensing the change in atmosphere, Col. Stewart then asked the men if there was anyone among them who refused to go to

Obozerskaya. No one stepped forward. Corporal Cleo Colburn wrote in his journal, "all decided to make another trip to [the] front."[47] Stewart then praised the company for its accomplishments and attitude. He added, "if [the men] were just willing to go back to ... [Obozerskaya] and be in reserve, [the army] would just simply forget about [what had just happened]."[48] With that, Col. George Stewart left and the men loaded their sleds.[49]

As the men of Company I were packing their sleds, 1st Sgt. McGuire approached Lt. May. He pleaded for Pvt. Petrowskas, stating, "Private Petrowskas (of Polish decent, speaking English imperfectly), had not understood the order given by Lieut. May and asked that, if in view of this fact, the arrest might not be reconsidered. The two other Platoon Sergeants, being questioned, agreed that Private Petrowskas, who had just come into the room when the order was given, had not understood it."[50] Lieutenant May stated, "such a misunderstanding was possible, as the man had been arrested upon the slightest hesitancy, and no opportunity had been given to him at that time to make an explanation."[51] Private Petrowskas was released and allowed to join his platoon, and he went with them when the company traveled across the ice to the train station. Joel Moore finished the episode, writing, "Cpt. Winslow moved his men off across the frozen Dvina, proceeded as per schedule to Obozerskaya ... and took over the front line at a critical time."[52]

Later, when members of the press became aware of the event, they attempted to brand Company I as the unit that had mutinied. Colonel Stewart fought back, reporting, "I did not have to take any disciplinary action against either an officer or soldier of the regiment in connection with the matter, so you may judge that the reports that have appeared [in the press] have been very, very greatly exaggerated. Every soldier connected with the incident performed his duty as a soldier. And as far as I am concerned, I think the matter should be closed."[53] The army conducted an investigation and, when it concluded, determined "the alleged mutiny was nothing as serious as had been reported ... [and the] recommendation to the Commanding General of American Forces in North Russia [is] that this matter be dropped."[54] First Sergeant Whitney McGuire remarked, "They kicked like hell, but they went and never did a better job than they did that same day. Never was a more unjust charge laid against brave men."[55]

Chapter 16

The Fight for Bolshie Ozerki

March 17, 1919: Corporal Earl W. Collins was in charge of a five-man patrol, their job making sure the route between the little town of Bolshie Ozerki and Chekuevo was open. The day had been quiet, but then they heard the chatter of a machine gun shatter the early afternoon. Collins looked at Pvt. Earl Fulcher, whose eyes were wide with surprise. "I'm going to headquarters," Cpl. Collins said. He bundled up and went outside.[1] Earl Collins was born July 20, 1890, in Detroit, Michigan, to Samuel and Clara Bell Collins. Earl's father was an English immigrant, coming in 1885 to Detroit, where he secured a job as a hardware store clerk. Collins married Clara Bell, and the couple would have three boys. Earl attended schools in Detroit, and he demonstrated a good grasp for numbers and financial columns before graduating from high school in 1907. He joined the Michigan Naval Reserve and served as a seaman for three years. Once his enlistment with the Michigan Naval Reserve ended, the young man found a job as a clerk, and by 1917 he was at the Detroit Savings Bank, located in the Penobscot Building on West Fort Street.[2]

Earl, like thousands of young men living in Detroit, registered for the draft on June 5, 1917. The registrar described Earl as short in height, of slender build, and with blue eyes and light brown hair.[3] His orders to report to Camp Custer arrived in late May 1918; he was assigned to Cpt. Carl Gevers' Company H, 339th Infantry. Then, because of his past military experience, he was promoted to private first class. Company H shipped out of the United States on July 22, 1918, aboard the *Northumberland*, heading for Great Britain and from there to Archangel.

Company H, in mid–September 1918, was sent to Onega to support a small force of British troops protecting this port town. Onega was also important as a railroad station on the Murmansk to Archangel Railway. Thus, keeping this town out of the Bolsheviks' hands became important. The Reds understood Onega's value and began a push toward it. The British commander in Onega responded, ordering Captain Gevers to advance two platoons (about 140 men) up the Onega River to Chekuevo, and there, on September 24, 1918, the Americans ran into a Bolshevik force and, in a sharp fight, routed them. The Yanks chased the Bolos for nearly five miles eastward along the Chekuevo-Bolshie Ozerki Road before turning back. Company H then spent the next seven months rotating between Onega and Chekuevo, working to keep the western half of the line of communications between Onega and Obozerskaya open. During this time, the company's riflemen patrolled the line and battled the frigid cold.

On March 16, 1919, Cpl. Earl Collins (he had been promoted) led a squad of five men out of Chekuevo, their assignment to patrol the road between Chekuevo and Bolshie Ozerki. Private Earl Fulcher (Co. H), a member of this patrol, noted, "I left Chekuevo with a patrol consisting of myself and the following men; Corporal Earl W. Collins ... Pfc. Joseph Ramotowske ... Pvt. William Scheulke ... [and] Pvt. John Fruse." He continued, "At this time patrols left Chekuevo daily and proceeded along the Chekuevo-Bolshie Ozerki road to Bolshie Ozerki. The time required to go and return was about three days."[4] Collins' patrol was in Bolshie Ozerki the next day, resting, when the Reds attacked. This is when Cpl. Collins left his squad to find out what was happening. Private Fulcher stated, "This is the last I saw [him]."[5]

A sizeable force of Bolos advanced upon Bolshie Ozerki, overwhelming the French and White Russian outpost positions. As the Reds closed in on the position where the Americans were sheltered, Pfc. Josef Ramostowske (Co. H), now the squad's senior rifleman, led the four out of the house and to a nearby trench. Earl Fulcher wrote, "we were attached to the French detachment by a French officer and held an entrenched position until sunset ... at which time the enemy began shelling [us] and we withdrew to a position across the river."[6] Darkness cooled the shooting but resumed the next morning. Private Fulcher was shot through both thighs around noon, and not long after this the Bolsheviks zeroed in on the Allies' position with artillery. The wounded Fulcher recorded, "The enemy artillery reached our position and the French officer in command went out with a white flag and surrendered the entire detachment, consisting of about 50 French, Americans, and Russian troops."[7]

Captain Ballensinger, now the commander of Company H, along with the senior British commander in Chekuevo, received word that this Allied force in Bolshie Ozerki had been captured. The British leadership, though, did not express great concern, for, as one American officer noted, "it was thought [Bolshie Ozerki had been struck] ... by a strong raiding party, bent upon capture of the ration and ammunition convoys."[8] But the Bolsheviks were in Bolshie Ozerki to stay. They severed the telephone line between Obozerskaya and Chekuevo, immediately worsening the situation. Matters grew worse for the Allies when they discovered the French commander at Obozerskaya, Col. Lucas, who had traveled to Bolshie Ozerki to inspect the French positions there, was discovered to be missing.

Colonel Lucas, though, was alive and well. One writer noted later, "By a stroke of luck, Col. Lucas ... just missed being taken with the French defenders, having passed through the area a few hours before the Red attack. He was ... several miles west of Bolshie-Ozerki, still unaware that a large Soviet force was between him and his Railroad Force command."[9] Lucas and his small force approached Bolshie Ozerki from the west, only to be ambushed. Joel Moore wrote, "They were met by a sudden burst ... of machine gun [fire]. Luckily the range was wrong. The horses bolted, upsetting the sleighs and throwing Col. Lucas into the neck-deep snow."[10] An American rifleman beside him was not as fortunate; Cpl. Nathan Redmond

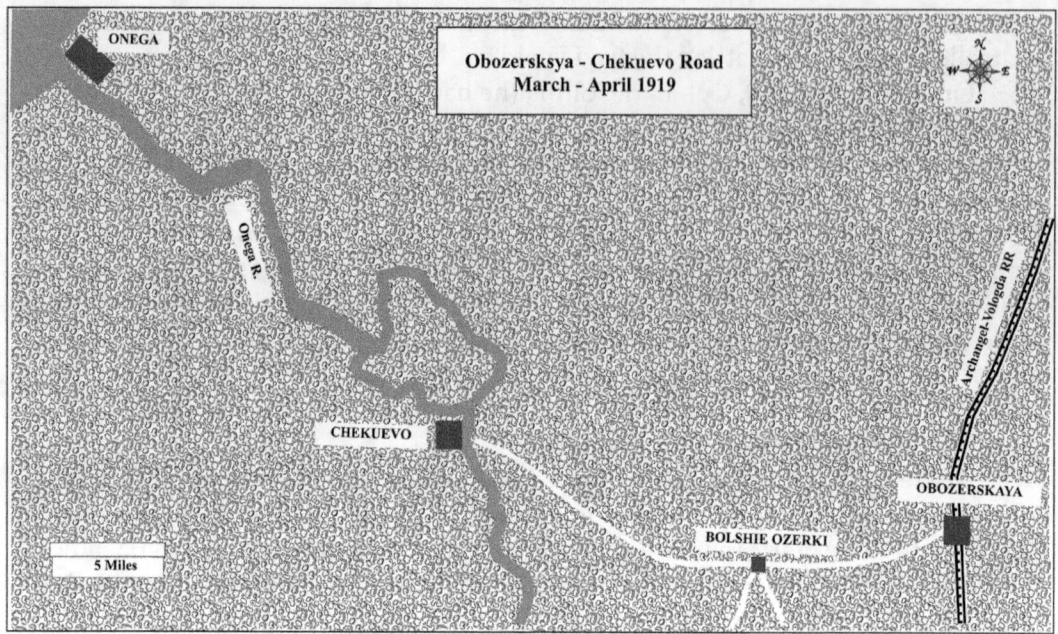

(Co. H) was killed. The Americans retreated west to Chekuevo while Lucas, who had become separated from his escort, stumbled around in the forest, bewildered. A British staff officer noted, "He wandered about for twenty-four hours in the forest, until he was happily picked up by a patrol and brought into the railway. Both his hands were badly frost-bitten and he had to report sick."[11] General William Ironside, aware the line between Obozerskaya and Onega had been cut and displeased with Lucas' performance, immediately relieved the French colonel, and, as Ironside remarked, "I then decided to take over the command myself."[12]

General Ironside ordered an all-out assault to retake Bolshie Ozerki, directing the force at Chekuevo to march east with a combat group, while another would leave Obozerskaya and march west. At Chekuevo, Company H's two platoons, led by lieutenants Edmund Collins and Clifford Phillips, along with a force of British troops, readied to attack. Meanwhile, Company E was "rousted from Smolny barracks and sent down the railway with a force of Whites and a half-company of Yorks."[13] Both forces, 70 Americans and 300 Brits and Russians, were to strike the Bolsheviks (nearly 1,200 men) at Bolshie Ozerki on March 23, 1919. Company H's platoons approached Bolshie Ozerki at 9:00 a.m., only to be fired upon when they were about 1,000 yards west of the town. Lieutenant Collins sent one Brit company to the left and the other to the right, with the Yanks to go straight up the middle. The Bolo machine guns stitched the Allied line with lethal steel, causing one American to write, "[We] were easy to shoot at as [we] floundered in the waist-deep snow. [We] crossed 500 yards before getting no farther."[14]

Lieutenant Edmund Collins was mortally wounded by a sniper, and two British line officers were also felled. A doughboy recorded, "the men made 400 yards; here the American officer was [wounded], two British officers were hit ... [and] the little company, facing utter massacre, burrowed in the deep snow, and in the stifling cold, hung on to the last round, till the retirement order came at dusk."[15] Private Edward McConvill (Co. H) was killed, dying from wounds to his shoulder and arms, and a handful of other Yanks suffered wounds. The battered Allies drifted westward, stung by their losses, and, as Lt. Harry Ketcham (Co. H) remarked, "many American and British soldiers were frostbitten."[16] Regrettably, Lt. Collins died from his wounds before reaching Chekuevo.

Meanwhile, Company E, along with a force of White Russian soldiers, marched from Obozerskaya. Private Donald Carey (Co. E) noted they were "in their dreaded Shackleton boots with depressed spirits and with ... morale at an exceedingly low point."[17] The riflemen's resolve was low; the men did not want to be away from Archangel, and they were poorly led by Cpt. Bernard Heil, who was "already a pariah among his troops for leading from behind."[18] The formation did not reach Bolshie Ozerki that day; instead, it bivouacked several miles east of the Bolshevik position. Private Carey recorded, "[The] company stopped [for the night] ... they built fires and warmed themselves while a number of White Russians [headed] west for Bolshie Ozerki, each man dressed in a white sheet-like hood and cape which at once recalled to my mind accounts of the Ku Klux Klan."[19]

The men were awakened early on March 24, 1919, and pushed westward, led by, as Pvt. Carey growled, "a couple of noble lieutenants stupefied with liquor."[20] The men struggled in the darkness and heavy snow, following a force of White Russians. Donald Carey wrote, "at a turn in the road [I] noticed dark forms ahead in the early morning gloom, and the red glow of cigarettes—White [Russian] soldiers." He continued, "Word was passed back to Company E that the Russians would attack and the Yanks would be in support.... The Whites advanced, and the air filled with bullets and artillery shells ... [Carey at a high point on the road] hugged the ground as shells burst about the company."[21] Company E's riflemen looked around for their commander, but Cpt. Heil, as Cpl. Fred Kooyers (Co. E) complained, "had stayed about two miles back of the men, trying to dodge the battle."[22]

The White Russians' assault floundered as the men sank into the deep snow, many as casualties. Plus, the leaderless riflemen of Company E became grounded by the Bolsheviks' heavy fire. Major J. Brooks Nichols arrived and moved through the stalled formation. He concluded the attack was futile, as the Bolos' position was well fortified, and the Reds far outnumbered the Allies. Nichols ordered Company E to withdraw. The Yanks crept away from their dangerous location, expecting to return to Obozerskaya. Major Nichols, though, directed the doughboys to swing to the right and attempt to get around the Bolo left flank. The dispirited riflemen floundered in the deep snow for an hour before Nichols realized this group of Americans was not going to get the job done. Nichols called off the attack and led the men back to the Allied artillery emplacements near verst 18. Major Nichols conferred with Gen. Ironside and the two agreed; this position would be held until reinforcements could be brought in. But the day's fight was over; the White Russians had suffered a number of killed and wounded, though Company E had lost none. That evening, American combat engineers arrived,

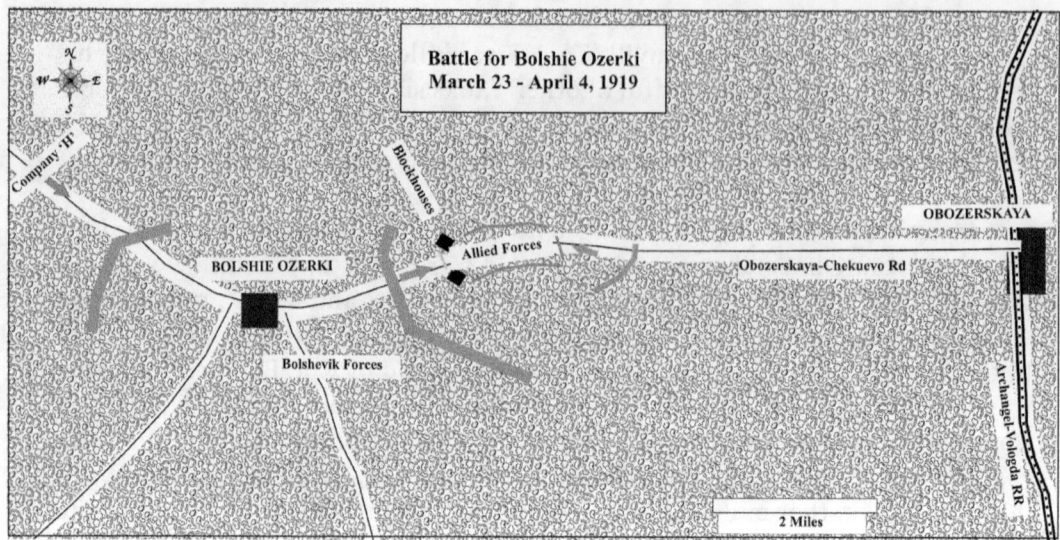

armed with axes, saws, and barbed wire, plus the energy and knowhow to rapidly construct defenses.

The men in Company E griped about their misfortunes, with one American writing, "after our unsuccessful attempt to take Bolshie Ozerki, the British and American sergeants got together and agreed that, if they were ordered to make a further attack, they would refuse to go into action."[23] Major Nichols, accurately assessing this rifle company's intentions, realized nothing good would come out of trying to push it forward against the Bolos. He informed the men of Company E that they were to hold until reinforcements arrived; then they would be sent away. A member of Company E recorded, "The attack at that time was called off, so that they did not have an opportunity to put their threat into force."[24] The next morning, March 26, 1919, Company E's disharmony roared loudly, Pvt. Donald Carey (Co. E) noting, "The men had had enough.... When Lt. Edwin Broer ordered [Cpl. James W.] Sanders to lead a relief platoon toward the front line, he balked and said he and his men would not go unless a commissioned officer accompanied them.... A heated argument ensued ... but Broer finally agreed to lead the patrol." Carey continued, "Broer began leading the 80-man detail, but turned back because he had forgotten to bring his overcoat. When the men began to turn back with him, Broer ordered them to continue on ... the men refused, complaining they were being mistreated. Once more Broer backed down. He would spend his night coatless."[25]

Captain Joel Moore's Company M arrived in Obozerskaya at 2:00 a.m., March 28, 1919, and after a short rest, marched the twelve miles to verst 18.[26] Lieutenant George Stoner's platoon went forward and took over the responsibility of guarding the front line. Meanwhile, the dispirited men of Company E abandoned their positions and hiked toward Obozerskaya, with Donald Carey remarking, "no time was wasted in bidding the much cursed place a ceremonious farewell."[27] Captain Moore, knowing his front was protected by George Stoner's riflemen, recorded,

"[My] men began building shell splinter proofs and shelters to rest in at the various posts."[28] Moore's riflemen pitched tents amid the tall trees and prepared to endure the deep snow and miserable cold. Joel Moore reminisced, "Who will ever forget that tented camp we went into that day?" He continued, "[We] were a resourceful outfit which soon improved its barricades and built brush shelters within which they could conceal their warm fires."[29]

Company M was up early the next morning, with 1st Sgt. Walter Dundon recording, "Stood to at 4:00 A.M. Outpost duty and patrols."[30] Major Nichols and Cpt. Moore, along with the combat engineers, developed an extensive series of defensive layers, each one supporting the next. Moore sent Supply Sgt. Glenn Leitzell back to Obozerskaya to get extra saws and axes. Lieutenant Clarence Primm described their construction, writing, "[We built] the usual type of blockhouse ... trees on the site furnished all the material except barbed wire, which was used both to bind the longs together and to erect entanglements at a little distance from the blockhouse.... The walls are nearly four feet thick. A good double roof, slanting and well covered with ... many layers of logs to resist shrapnel and light artillery shells." He added, "Long straight lanes would be opened in the forest leading in different directions from the blockhouse, so the enemy could not approach without crossing one or more of these lanes, when machine gun fire would be opened on them. If the enemy came very close, so as to be visible among the trees near the blockhouse, the riflemen got busy acting as sharpshooters."[31]

The Bolsheviks made no movements against the American positions; they too were fortifying their position as well as bringing in reinforcements. The Reds

Americans camped out in tents near Bolshie Ozerki (U.S. Army Signal Corps).

now had brought in three full-strength formations: the 9th Saratov Regiment, the 2nd Moscow Regiment, and the Kamyshin Brigade, over 7,000 men, led by the 50-year-old Maj. Gen. Aleksanr Samoylo, a veteran of the czar's Imperial Army.

Though the infantries of both sides wielded only axes and saws, their artillerymen were busy. Lieutenant Primm noted, "[The] big guns [blasted] away from behind us at an enemy somewhere ahead of us." The young officer, in a moment of reflection, continued, "[It was] the most beautiful winter day, just below freezing, but bright. For the first time in Russia our company is living as many folks at home might imagine soldiers in the snowy forests would be apt to live—in tents and bough shelters banked with snow."[32] A rifleman added, "That's the only time that I was in the army up there that was real snow and cold, and we were in our pup-tents out there in the woods."[33]

The Allies' defenses straddled the Obozerskaya-Chekuevo road several hundred yards west of the verst 18 road sign, with its westward-most point being two sturdy blockhouses. A well-built log barricade protected a deep trench that connected the two blockhouses as well as log-built entrenchments protecting the blockhouses' flanks, these positions bolstered by Lewis gun positions. Captain Joel Moore's riflemen held these critical posts, as both Maj. Nichols and Gen. Ironside knew these experienced veterans were the best they had. From the point of the defensive spear, the entrenchments curved eastward from each blockhouse and zigzagged their way for almost a mile, these rifle pits to be held by the White Russians and a scattering of British troops, their main job to protect the Allies' center—the location where the tented bivouac was located. From there, farther east, the Allies' defenses consisted of an artillery emplacement and another line of barricades. The White Russians worked the 75mm guns while Cpt. Moore's riflemen manned the barricade. Lieutenant John Cudahy explained the logic for this defensive setup, writing, "It was a tactical custom of the enemy to attack the front and rear positions, sometimes he struck both simultaneously, but seldom the flanks.... Therefore Gen. Ironside placed his Americans forward and back." He continued, "On the flanks ... the Yorkmen were scattered among [the White Russian soldiers] as bolsters [because] the Russians were green ... [and] as yet untried."[34] Lieutenant Clarence Primm surveyed their defenses and noted, "Our position was over a mile long, but only 200 yards wide, [and] stretched along the country road."[35]

March 30, 1919, dawned quiet—"too quiet," Cpt. Moore cautioned. The White Russian artillery soon began shelling the Bolshevik positions near Bolshie Ozerki, causing Moore to state, "We shelled him vigorously."[36] More supplies were hauled into the Allied position, enabling the artillery to expend ammunition without fear of running low. A mission of YMCA members arrived, led by Bryant Ryall and Frank Olmstead. They assembled a canteen to serve the soldiers. Clarence Primm, appreciating their efforts, wrote, "It is good to find a Y outfit on the job here. They serve us hot cocoa and crackers, and hand out chocolate and cigarettes when we run short."[37]

The situation changed early the next morning, March 31, 1919. Bolshevik movement noises woke the Allies, causing 1st Sgt. Walter Dundon to record,

"Stood to at 4:00 A.M."[38] It was obvious the Bolos were moving about, out beyond the Allies' perimeter, but there was no way to know where they would strike. Captain Moore sent Lt. Wright's Fourth Platoon to relieve Lt. Stoner's riflemen who had been manning the blockhouses and western-most posts. But then the forests grew quiet again, leaving the Americans, Brits, and White Russians wondering what would happen next.

The Bolsheviks cut the telephone line connecting the Allies with headquarters at Obozerskaya at 8:30 a.m., and not long after this a quick flurry of rifle and machine gun fire erupted five hundred yards east of the Allied perimeter. Supply Sgt. Glenn Leitzell (Co. M) explained what happened: "I left the front lines with a comrade, Freeman Hogan, and a Russian driver, on my way back to Obozerskaya for supplies. About a quarter of a verst, 500 yards, from our rear artillery, we were surprised by a patrol of Bolos." He continued, "[They] leaped out of the snow banks and held us up at the point of pistols, grenades, and rifles. Then they stripped us of our arms and hurried us off the road and into the woods." Sergeant Leitzell, along with Pvt. Freeman Hogan, was marched away, a prisoner, and as Leitzell then exclaimed, "to our great surprise we were joined by Mr. Ryall, the Y.M.C.A. Secretary who had been [captured] just [moments] ahead of us."[39]

This ambush tipped the Allied commanders that their entire position was surrounded. Captain Moore shifted Lt. Clarence Primm's Third Platoon to bolster the defenders at the perimeter's eastern end. They arrived just as a mob of Bolshevik riflemen emerged from the southeast, rushing toward the artillery pieces. Joel Moore reported, "At about 9:00 A.M. Three [companies] of the 2nd Moscow Regiment came around by our right flank and made a push for our two 3-inch pieces at the rear." Moore continued, "Corporal [Robert] Pratt took his Lewis Gun team to a vantage point 200 yards in front of the guns to engage the enemy's two machine guns. [The] officer in command of the [artillery] pieces, Lt. Lukovski, turned them [around] and gave the enemy muzzle burst, direct fire."[40] The blank-point artillery, along with Pratt's accurate machine gun fire, stunned the attackers. They pressed forward for a few more minutes, severely wounding Cpl. Pratt, but then fell back, demoralized, leaving the snow covered with dead and wounded. Once this battle site quieted, the Americans slipped out of the positions and went about the Bolo casualties, retrieving any wounded man with a chance of living. One of these casualties turned out to be the 2nd Moscow's commissar.

Meanwhile, Bolshevik artillery began pounding the entire Allied perimeter. Walter Dundon noted, "[The] enemy opened up at 9:00 A.M. with ... a heavy barrage." Then, a skirmish line moved forward, but it was quickly repulsed. More Bolsheviks emerged from the woods, mainly west of the blockhouses, moving straight east on the Obozerskaya-Chekuevo road. Howling and shooting, an entire battalion of Bolsheviks pushed forward slowly, the Reds struggling in the deep snow as they scurried from cover to cover. They inched forward, taking casualties from the accurate fire put down by the well-protected riflemen of Lt. Wright's platoon. Joel Moore remarked, "About 10:00 A.M. an enemy attack developed [against the] front line and lasted intermittently all day. [The] enemy centered [their] attack on the forward blockhouse and the barricade in the road."

He added, "Fortunately the Reds directed their attack at the points held by the Americans rather than at the four flank positions held by the green Archangel troops."[41] The assault lasted for hours, but as the sun began to set, the battered Bolsheviks retreated. Captain Moore noted, "All attacks repelled with severe losses to [the] enemy."[42] The doughboys of the Fourth Platoon relaxed, standing amid piles of spent brass. They had fired thousands of rounds and shot down countless attackers and had done so without a single casualty! An American rifleman summed it up, writing, "The shooting was good that day."[43]

That afternoon, though, beyond the eastern perimeter, disaster struck again. Company M's Jens Laursen, along with Pvt. Charles Dial and a small complement of Russian sleigh drivers, had left Obozerskaya with a load of supplies, bound for the Allied position at verst 18. Lens Laursen stated, "[We] were ambushed ... two miles from supporting lines ... [and] brave, courteous Dial was shot through the head." He continued, "[I] sought safety by rolling into the deep snow by the side of the road, and when the chase got too hot, [I] held up [my] rifle and belt as a token of surrender."[44]

Darkness silenced the sounds of war, leaving only the cries from the wounded. These pitiful noises decreased as the night's plunging temperatures took effect. Lieutenant John Cudahy reported, "The sun went down upon the tumult of a bloody, gruesome day; it became cold again ... the unfortunate Bolsheviks passed the acme of mortal misery ... they lay out through the endless, black hours of terrible cold and frost ... [which] took a greater toll than all the gunshot wounds."[45]

The fighting on April 1, 1919, started early when Bolo machine guns and mortars opened up at 3:30 a.m. The Yanks manned their shooting positions, ready to repel more attacks. This morning, it would be the men of the 9th Saratov Regiment who attempted to break through the Yank positions. They pushed forward, passing the frozen bodies of the victims of the previous day's attacks and using the early morning's darkness as cover, and crept to within two hundred yards of the blockhouses. Then, the Americans opened up, ripping lethal steel into the Bolo ranks. The Bolsheviks inched forward, firing as they slowly advanced. Sadly, some of the Reds' bullets found American flesh; Pvt. Alva Crook (Co. M) fell, mortally wounded. The 26-year-old from Lakeview, Michigan, died within minutes. Then, the attack collapsed, the Russian infantrymen not wanting to be slaughtered like their brothers had the day before.

A few minutes later another battalion from the 9th Saratov Regiment passed through the broken remnants of the first wave and pushed closer to the American positions. One company got within seventy yards of the barricade, with a dangerous group slipping around to its rear. Corporal Frank Sapp (Co. M), manning a Lewis gun, held to his position as the Reds neared his location. He killed a number before Bolo bullets ripped through his body, killing him.[46] Not far from Cpl. Sapp, Cpl. William Russell (Co. M) watched in alarm as the approaching Reds frightened a White Russian machine-gun crew. Russell took command of the team and steadied them, enabling them to hold off the attackers. The Bolsheviks pushed closer, firing rifle grenades and relying on the sheer weight of their numbers. They forced the White Russians to flee from their machine guns, but Cpl. Russell took charge of the weapon and continued to fire. He held the position by himself. Moore wrote, "The stoutly fortified [Americans] did not bulge but worked every death-dealing weapon with great severity."[47] The assault fell apart, only to be followed by a third, but again, Bolshevik fervor was not able to overcome American steel. The fighting was over by 8:00 a.m. Later, Cpl. William Russell would be awarded the Distinguished Service Cross for his actions.[48]

The battlefield grew quiet, so much so that many thought the fight might be over. Company M's Sgt. Matthew Grahek recorded what happened next: "Evidently their commanding officer thought that [his] men had gained their objectives.... I saw [him] coming on horseback ... [my] men wanted to start taking potshots at him. I says, 'Heck no, let him keep coming closer. The closer he comes the better shot he'll be.'" Sergeant Grahek continued, "I sent a runner over to [the] headquarters tent. Lieutenant Wright, another sergeant, and a translator come over and we lay down out of sight. He kept coming. We thought he was going to give himself up. The lieutenant gave the translator the order to ... motion him in.... As soon as the guy seen the spot he was in, he ... took off with the horse. What chance did he have?—Two Lewis guns and a platoon of rifles trained on him." Grahek added, "He was holding a lot of valuable papers."[49] The Yanks also took the Bolshevik officer's sword, which they presented to Cpt. Moore. That night Company M's commander wrote, "The [Bolo] commanding officer [came] riding up on his white horse ... to his death." Moore added, "Every attacking line of the enemy was repulsed. Darkness closed the scene at 9:00 PM with the little force still intact."[50] Lieutenant John Cudahy admitted, "It was a glorious thing to be in the blockhouses and the log barriers and to witness those human multitudes surge on, then slacken, and falter and fail and shrivel as they came."[51] That night scores of wounded Bolsheviks, as well as Reds who no longer wanted any part of this battle, crawled into the American lines and surrendered. They reported that the entire Bolo army was going to attack "on the front and the two flanks." The Allied officers, hearing this, had every man who could handle a weapon manning a position all along the perimeter.[52]

Even though the Allies were prepared for a pre-dawn assault on April 2, 1919, the Reds did nothing until 6 o'clock when their artillery began pounding the defenses. Captain Moore shifted Lt. Robert Wieczorek's Second Platoon to relieve the western positions, enabling Lt. Wright's men to stand down.[53] The Bolo artillery continued to pulverize the Allied lines, but once the morning's light strengthened, their shelling changed from random firing to highly directed fire aimed at the blockhouses. The Bolshevik guns began to score direct hits; one at a location along the front barricade shattered the defenses, with the blast's concussion seriously injuring Cpl. Joseph Ryduchowski's head. He was carried to the aid station suffering from shell shock. Another shell destroyed the wooden barrier at Post No. 1. Here, Pvt. George Manders was severely hurt. He too was carted away, requiring medical help for shell shock. The pounding continued; Pvt. Martin Nichols at Post No. 9 was also wounded, suffering from head wounds.[54]

The Allies' two 75mm guns returned fire against the Reds' guns, forcing the

Captain Joel Moore celebrates with a Bolshevik officer's sword that his men captured on April 1, 1919 (U.S. Army Signal Corps).

Bolsheviks to concentrate their fire on the White Russian gunners. This duel continued for some time, enabling the Americans to recover from the pounding they had received. Lieutenant John Cudahy wrote, "The Bolsheviks ... now commenced a blasting duel between the opposing batteries that tossed skyward mountainous geysers of snow, made fragments of the trees, and ... shook the forest end to end with a ceaseless, reverberating roar."[55]

The Bolo infantry west of the blockhouses crept out of their positions and moved forward, the Bolshevik officers wanting one more massive assault to overwhelm the Yanks. Lieutenant Wieczorek's riflemen and Lewis gun teams opened fire. The Reds quickly sought shelter and the attack melted away. Joel Moore recalled, "The attack which followed was weak ... 2nd platoon with Lewis Gun and V.B.'s easily handled the attack of the enemy.... [The] enemy evidently could not get his men to do the attack and only slow intermittent fire continued during the day."[56]

General William Ironside, fully aware of the Bolsheviks' focus on battering through the Allies' position, believed it might be possible to strike the enemy at its rear and retake Bolshie Ozerki. He ordered the Americans and Brits at Chekuevo to resume their attack. The assault was to be made in three prongs. A company from the 6th Yorkshire Regiment was to advance along a trail through the woods to flank Bolshie Ozerki from the north. A second company of Yorkshires, along with American mortars and a machine gun team, would move to strike the Reds from the south. And finally, a third force, this one composed of Polish troops, was to advance east on the road and hit the Bolos head on. Captain Richard Ballensinger's two Company H platoons would follow behind and act as a reserve.[57]

The three battle groups advanced during the pre-dawn darkness on April 2, 1919, but things quickly fell apart. The British company, slated to strike from the north, reported at 2:00 a.m. it "was lost in the woods ... belly-deep in snow ... [and] could not proceed."[58] The Poles marched forward, unaware their left flank force was not where it was supposed to be, and ran into trouble. Their surprise attack was thwarted because, as Lt. Cudahy reported, "dogs, tied to trees by the Bolsheviks, [hearing] the approaching ... attack, gave boisterous, barking alarm ... [and] the woods were made hideous with the rasping rattle of many machine guns."[59] The Poles were caught out in the open and, as one officer reported, "suffered heavily and had to retire from the battle."[60]

With both the left flank and center crushed and in disarray, the right-flank group, the Yorkshire company, commanded by Cpt. Thomas Bailey, moved forward, only to find Bolos coming from their front, left, and right. By 6:00 a.m. Bailey's men were nearly surrounded, two soldiers had been killed, and a number wounded. Captain Thomas Bailey, as Lt. Cudahy recorded, "rose to lead a rush at the machine gun positions and was killed in his tracks."[61] Then, as more men fell, the surviving British officer ordered the Yorkshire men to pull back. They passed through Company H's platoon, commanded by Lt. Clifford Phillips. The young officer from Falls Creek, Nebraska, led his men forward, established a battle line and faced the Bolsheviks, who swarmed forward like a horde of angry hornets. The American platoon was greatly outnumbered and in immediate danger of being flanked. Captain Richard Ballensinger recorded, "the enemy's counter attack was extremely heavy, and all of his fire swept the road continuously."[62] Lieutenant Phillips kept his men under control and, by directing their Lewis guns effectively to hinder the Bolo attackers, led the platoon as it slowly retreated. Unfortunately, "during the fighting Lt. Phillips received a chest wound, which nicked an artery of his lung ... it knocked him down as if a ton of bricks had fallen on him."[63] The Americans' action enabled the Yorkshire riflemen and Polish troops to pull back, and eventually the entire force retreated back to Chekuevo. Lieutenant Phillips' men loaded their wounded officer onto a sled and pulled him to safety. He would die a month later in a field hospital in Onega.[64]

April 3, 1919, opened at 2:00 a.m. with machine-gun fire, but once the Allies had rushed to their posts, there was nothing to see. Joel Moore noted, "The [White Russians] opened on the shadows with automatics. False alarm."[65] The men stood down for another two hours before returning to their defenses at 4:00 a.m. Captain Moore rotated Lt. Clarence Primm's Third Platoon to the blockhouses and western barricades, and then the Allies waited. Once the sun rose, Cpt. Moore recorded, "[The] enemy during the night [had] carried off his dead and wounded from the woods, leaving only 28 dead in the road."[66] The morning remained quiet, and as the hours slowly passed, the Allies grew confident that the Bolsheviks were pulling back. Later that afternoon, a small force of Americans marched into the perimeter, having come from Obozerskaya, proof that the Reds were retreating.

Nothing happened on April 4, 1919, as the Bolos were content to lick their wounds. General Ironside sent a contingent of Yorkshire troops and White Russians to reinforce the verst 18 position. Lieutenant Stoner's platoon rotated into the blockhouses and forward posts; meanwhile, the rest of the company was employed doing defense maintenance. George Stoner wrote, "1st platoon on front—wire laying party."[67] Captain Moore received word to let the newly-arrived British riflemen assume the defenses; Company M was to pull out and return to Obozerskaya. Captain Moore noted, "Relief came out from the base in the afternoon, arriving about 3:30 P.M., and completing relief at 8:45 P.M. [It was a] mixed force of Russians and British."[68] Moore and his men made the hike back to Obozerskaya.

That evening, a number of Bolsheviks slipped into the Allies' perimeter and surrendered. An Allied officer wrote, "Bolshevik deserters came across to the Allied lines in large numbers with reports of heavy casualties, mutiny and intense suffering from the cold."[69] These men told stories of horrendous casualties; Joel Moore recorded, "The old Russian general [Aleksandr Samoylo] massed up in all over 7,000 men … and his losses … were admitted by the Bolshevik reports to be over 2,000."[70] Later, a Soviet source acknowledged that more than five hundred Bolo soldiers were also disabled by frostbite, meaning the Reds' campaign to break the Obozerskaya-Chekuevo road cost them over a third of that army.[71] The battered and demoralized Bolsheviks withdrew from Bolshie Ozerki during the night of April 4 and 5, leaving the field to the Allies. Company M's riflemen rested on April 5, 1919, in Obozerskaya, spending time cleaning their weapons and relishing the clean, hot waters of the Russian *bahnia*. Lieutenant Clarence Primm, once he finished overseeing his platoon, returned to his train car billet and remarked, "The Americans had never seen such shooting."[72]

CHAPTER 17

Prisoners

March 31, 1919: Jens C. Laursen, a mechanic in Company M, 339th Infantry, stared at the body of a British officer. The 23-year-old American soldier figured he would be next. Laursen, in desperation, "took from his pockets his entire supply of tobacco, cigarettes, and gum [and] with a nonchalant air proceeded to treat the Bolos."[1] The Bolshevik soldiers took Laursen's offerings, their faces expressionless, but most importantly, they did not shoot him; instead, they threw him into a dugout. He took refuge near the shelter's rear, relieved to still be alive. However, Laursen figured the Bolos would come for him eventually, and when they did, that would be the end.

Jens Laursen was born November 11, 1894. His parents, Christian and Annie, were Danish immigrants who had settled in a rural area just outside Detroit. Jens was their second child—there were seven kids all together, all raised on the Laursen farm. The children attended a local school, with Jens graduating from high school in 1913.[2] He went to work for a neighbor as a carpenter's assistant, and in 1917, when he registered for the draft, the registrar recorded that he worked as a carpenter for James Temperly of Detroit. The draftee was described as of medium height and slender build and with dark blue eyes and light hair.[3] Jens reported to Camp Custer in May 1918. He was assigned to Company M, 339th Infantry, and because of his skills as a carpenter, he became one of five soldiers designated as the company's mechanics.

Mechanic Laursen, along with the rest of the Americans in the 339th Infantry, shipped out to England and from there to Russia. Laursen, because of his position, often found himself and a small team separated from the company,

Jens Laursen (Co. M) was captured while bringing a load of supplies to the front (Passport Application, 1919; National Archives).

responsible for transporting supplies and building materials to whatever location Company M was defending. And this is what he and Mech. Charles Dial were doing on March 31, 1919, when they ran into Bolshevik soldiers. Dial was shot and killed, but in the confusion, Laursen had been able to dive into the deep snow and crawl away. The Bolos pursued Laursen, as he left an easy-to-follow trail in the snow, and it did not take long before they surrounded him, forcing him to surrender. Laursen recalled, "After being searched they took me into the woods ... where there were about 100 Bolos, and there I treated some of the officers, who were on horseback, with what cigarettes I had."[4] He eventually found himself imprisoned inside a dugout, worried about his future.

Jens Laursen noticed he was not alone. There, just a few feet away, sat another prisoner, the 35-year-old Bryant Ryall, a senior official for the American YMCA. Ryall, who had been captured less than an hour before Laursen, was from Wisconsin, the son of Esau and Susanna Ryall, both English immigrants. Ryall was a graduate of the University of Wisconsin and had just recently married the adventurous 36-year-old Catherine Childs. Catherine, a former director of the cafeteria of the Cleveland YWCA, had come to Archangel with the YWCA in the fall of 1918. She recalled, "[We] married in December [1918] in Archangel and a few days later [I] started housekeeping in ... Obozerskaya ... in a box car." She added, "It's a world of fun—living in a freight car.... I would not exchange with any bride in all America my cozy little box car."[5]

Jens Laursen and Bryant Ryall were given a frozen fish and a frozen loaf of black bread that evening. The next morning, the two were rousted out of the dugout and taken to a building where, as Laursen remembered, "their clothes were taken from them and dirty, 'cootie'-infested clothes substituted."[6] Laursen and Ryall were marched to another building, and once inside they were added to a small group of Allied prisoners, including Sgt. Glenn Leitzell (Co. M) and Pvt. Freeman Hogan (Co. M). Leitzell and Hogan's first experiences with their Bolo captors had been just as unsettling as Laursen and Ryall's. Glenn Leitzell noted, "I was surprised by a patrol of Bolos, ten or twelve in number, who leaped out of the snow banks and held us up at the point of pistols, hand grenades and rifles. They then stripped us of our arms and hurried us off the road and into the woods." He continued, "On our arrival there we were met by a great many Bolshevists who occupied [Bolshie Ozerki] and who tried to beat us with sticks, and cursed and spat on us as we were shoved along to the Commandant." Leitzell added, "One of the camp loiterer's scowling eyes caught sight of [my] ... gold teeth.... Raising a brass-bound whipstock he struck at [my] ... mouth.... But the prisoner guard saved [me] ... from the blow by shoving him so vigorously that he sprawled in the snow."[7] Following this, Leitzell and Hogan had their coats, fur hats, rings, and watches taken from them. The two were thrown into a "shack where [they] were billeted ... with a lot of Russian prisoners." Leitzell continued, "We were given half a salt fish, sour black bread and water for our meal. The bread was so hard and frozen we had to break it apart and cut it up with an axe. We managed to eat some of this by washing it down with water."[8]

On April 1, 1919, the three soldiers, Laursen, Leitzell, and Hogan, plus Bryant

Ryall, were marched to a building guarded by, as Hogan noticed, "a former loyal Russian they knew who had gone over to the Reds."[9] This guard, along with several others, "relieved [the prisoners] of [their] small pocket change and trinkets," convincing Laursen that the Bolsheviks were "a bunch of thieves and robbers."[10] Then they "received rations for the day, consisting of half a can of horse meat, salt fish, and 12 ounces of black bread."[11] The Americans were herded into another building where they met a senior Bolshevik officer, Aleksi Kuropatkin. He gave the prisoners cigarettes. Glenn Leitzell remarked, "This was very acceptable as we were quite unnerved, not knowing what would happen to us and fearing we would be shot."[12] The Russian officer questioned the Yanks about the Allies' defensive positions at verst 18, but they refused to divulge anything. Leitzell noted, "he got no information from us as we pleaded that we were soldiers of supply and were not familiar with the details of the scheme of defense."[13]

The prisoners were informed that they were going to be sent to Moscow, and soon after learning this, they were pushed out of the building and driven southward, heading for Emtsa. Leitzell recorded, "That day we walked 35 versts." He added, "We could hear the distant cannonading on the 445 front as we marched along during the day." Leitzell continued, "When we reached a log hut along the road at 10 P.M. we built a fire on the outside. We would sleep a half hour in the hut and then go out and warm ourselves, and so on through the night."[14] The doughboys were awakened and back on the road at 4:00 a.m. after being given a ration of bread and water. They hiked 27 versts to a village called Sheleska. They noted, "We were searched ... and all papers thought to be valuable taken." Leitzell added, "After a meal of salt fish, black bread and fish oil (for grease) and hot water, we were given a rest of one hour and then started on the road for Emtsa, 24 versts away."[15]

Once in Emtsa, the Americans were locked inside a boxcar. Later, the car's doors were opened, revealing a crowd of angry Bolos who attempted to get at the prisoners. The Reds guarding the Americans were forced to use the butts of their rifles to push the mob away. That afternoon, the train left Emsta, heading south,

  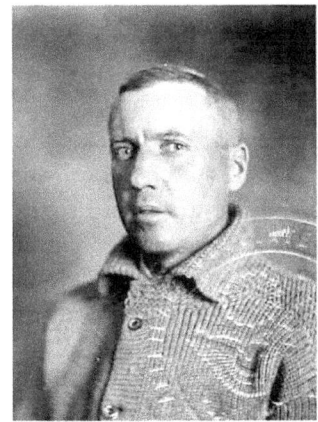

(From left) Bryant R. Ryall (YMCA), Glenn Leitzell (Co. M), and Freeman Hogan (Co. M) were captured by the Bolsheviks near Bolshie Ozerki (Kenneth Steuer, *Pursuit of an Unparalleled Opportunity*, 1919; Passport Application, 1919; National Archives).

bound for Plesetskaya. Leitzell, Hogan, Laursen, and Ryall were cold, hungry, and miserable. Later, Joel Moore would write of their experience: "Imagine the three American soldiers and the 'Y' man … sitting disconsolately in a filthy *taplooshka* [boxcar], hands and faces with three days and nights of grime and dirt, scratching themselves under their dirty rags [and] cussing the active cooties that had come with the shirts."[16]

The Americans demanded a bath when their train reached Plesetskaya. The Bolos were surprised by this demand but in the end acceded to it. Glenn Leitzell remarked, "After our bath we felt better as we were able to shake a few cooties." The men were fed some barley soup and rye bread but then lined up in front of their boxcar and informed that they were going to be executed. Leitzell stated, "I am thankful to say this never happened."[17] The men were loaded back into the boxcar and their train chugged further south, reaching Naundom early the next morning. Their train continued southward, reaching Vologda on April 7, 1919. The Americans were unloaded from their boxcar and shoved into a crowded cell filled with Russian prisoners. Glenn Leitzell grumbled, "[We] were fed with black bread loaded with sand, [and] some sour cabbage soup." He noted, "About 25 [prisoners] had to eat out of one bucket."[18]

Meanwhile, American military and civilian contacts with Bolshevik officials confirmed that Leitzell, Hogan, Laursen, and Ryall had all been captured during the past battle near Bolshie Ozerki. Ryall's wife, Catherine, was notified at this time that her husband was a prisoner and was being taken to Moscow. She recalled, "I did not hear from Mr. Ryall for days; and on [April 8, 1919] a messenger came to the boxcar with word that he had been captured by the Bolsheviks."[19]

On April 10, 1919, the Yank prisoners were transported to Moscow, arriving there the next day. They gawked at the Russian capital city, stunned by what they saw. Leitzell recalled, "On our arrival we found the city streets muddy, [with] heaps of snow and dead horses among the rubbish, no business places open, all stores having been looted, here and there a stand with horse meat, salt fish, carrots or turnips, and sour milk could be bought."[20] The Americans were met by a Russian who spoke English. The man welcomed them to Moscow and led them to a building where they joined other prisoners—English, French, and Scots. They also met their fellow 339th comrade, Pvt. George Albers (Co. I).

George Albers, who had been in Moscow since his capture in November 1918, introduced the Americans to the city. The newcomers learned to their surprise that they could move about Moscow as they pleased. Rations were served at 10:00 a.m., usually consisting of cabbage soup plus either some salt fish or horsemeat and a 12-ounce chunk of black bread. They were free until 5:00 p.m., when the same type of food was served again. Leitzell observed, "Conditions were very bad: no way of getting food in the city and many people [were] starving. All were rationed.... Those that did strenuous work got a half pound of bread a day; those who did light work got one-fourth pound." Jens Laursen remarked, "Liberty is unknown in Russia. Their motto from my point of view was; 'what is yours is mine.'"[21]

April's remaining days went quickly, the five Americans doing what they could to get by. Amazingly, they were able to find work, earning 25 rubles a day. George Albers recalled, "Sometimes [the work] was carrying out furniture seized by the government in the homes of the wealthy, sometimes it was digging graves for the people who had died of starvation ... the frozen bodies laid out in a row while we blasted through four feet of frozen earth."[22] They were fortunate to meet a British Red Cross worker who looked out for them. She found ways to get them extra morsels of bacon and bread as well as to supply them with tea and tobacco. They also met an American woman, the wife of a Bolshevik government official, who did what she could to provide extra food and other items. Joel Moore recorded, "How good it was one day to meet an American woman who had eighteen years before married a Russian in Chicago and come to Moscow to live. Her husband was a grain buyer for the Bolshevik government but she was a hater of the Red Rule and gave the boys all the comfort she could."[23]

The Bolsheviks allowed the five Americans freedom to move about the city, as it was important to the fledging Red government to show the world that it was not at war with the United States. Glenn Leitzell remarked, "The Red fanatics really thought we were converted to the silly stuff called Bolshevikism.... It was plain to us also that they were playing for recognition of their government by the United States."[24] The Americans took advantage of this situation to the point of wiggling their way into a private club only open to Bolshevik officials. Here, among the Reds' high-ranking statesmen, the American prisoners found books and newspapers to read, and for a few rubles they could purchase bowls of hot soup and roasted horsemeat.[25] Bryant Ryall wrote letters to his wife and, remarkably, Catherine received them. Catherine Ryall stated, "Father Roach, a British chaplain ... brought letters to me from my captive husband."[26]

This Irish clergyman, only identified as Father Roach, had also been captured on March 31, 1919, but was able to convince his captors that it was more important to them that he be released and sent back to the Allies as a gesture of good will. Father Roach, as one American newspaper reported, "brought the first direct word regarding the safety of any Americans captured by the Bolsheviks."[27] Father Roach's efforts to publicize the prisoners' plights, both British and Yank, spurred movements to free the soldiers. The American Red Cross, with offices in Archangel and in Moscow, was able to establish relationships between the Allies and the Bolsheviks. Joel Moore wrote, "The Red Cross was instrumental in prevailing upon the military authorities to open white flag conversations at the front lines in regard to a possible exchange of prisoners." He noted the difficulties that occurred: "Two meetings [had problems]: At one time the excited Bolos forgot their own men and the enemy who were parlaying in the middle of No Man's Land and started a lively artillery duel with the French artillery.... Another time the Americans' Russian Archangel Allies got excited and fired upon the Bolshevik soldiers who were sitting under a white flag on the railroad tracks watching the American captain come towards them."[28]

The prisoners, though, were unaware of efforts to gain their release. They remained in Moscow, free to move about at will, with only one major obligation they were required to fulfill. Glenn Leitzell noted, "Each Sunday the Bolsheviks would come and take us to their Bolshevik meetings and tried to teach us the Bolshevik doctrine, and made us promise when we reached the States to preach and practice and promote Bolshevism at home (which we promised just then to get along)."[29] Leitzell remembered, "The Bolsheviks did their best to convert [us] Yankees [but we] kept [our] peace and expressed no opinions.... [We] were supposed to be 'ripe' for bolshevism when [we] left Russia."[30]

On April 20, 1919—Easter Sunday—the Bolsheviks held a massive parade through the main streets of Moscow that eventually ended up at Red Square. Here, Lenin gave a speech. Joel Moore described the event: "[Lenin] told the people that the United States was sending food to their country. That was about the only way they could keep the people encouraged. And the Moscow papers also stated that they had great victor[ies] on all the various fronts."[31] Sergeant Leitzell remembered, "[We] nearly lost [our] membership in the club, along with its soup and horse-steak privileges because [we] would not march in the Red parade."[32]

Senior YMCA officials intensified their attempts to free the American prisoners. One of these executives, Louis Penningroth, who had been working in central Europe doing prisoners' relief work, traveled to Moscow and began talks with the Bolsheviks. In one such meeting Penningroth suggested that, according to the journalist Frazier Hunt, "There could not be any harm in letting him have six American prisoners of war." The Red bureaucrats considered Penningroth's request and decided to allow the prisoners' release. After all, as Penningroth noted, "[the prisoners] had been petted, pampered, propagandized, lectured, taken to dances, plays, and feeds."[33] The Bolsheviks anticipated these Americans would be ready to share good tidings about their new revolutionary government.

Louis Penningroth met with the American prisoners. He reported, "We talked with the boys awhile, then [I] said, 'well, how'd you fellows like to go home?' 'Home! Say, can a duck swim?' [George Albers] replied. 'Well, you might as well start getting ready. You are going with me at 1:30 this afternoon.'" Penningroth continued, "Then George Albers ... said, 'Say what'cha kidding us this way? This going home ain't no joke to us.'" It took Penningroth several minutes to convince the distrusting soldiers that he was telling the truth; when the prisoners understood they could go home, they filled the room with howls. Penningroth noted, "One slender young Scotch boy asked, 'How about us Tommies? We're going to stay while the Yanks go home.'" Penningroth then explained that he could also take six Brits with him.[34]

Jens Laursen recalled, "We were held in Moscow [until] we obtained our release, which came on May 18 ... We left Moscow at 7 o'clock and arrived in Petrograd at 10 o'clock A.M., where we were taken to the Hotel Astoria and from there went to the International Red Cross of Petrograd. We were treated very good there. At 6:30 o'clock [we were] taken to the depot in an automobile and left there for Finland, where we had a long wait and a hard time before the Bolos would let us cross the line."[35] Glenn Leitzell said, "We were not delayed until we reached the Finnish border. Here a young sailor who was in command refused to permit us to cross the station, our papers did not satisfy him. The train [did not] pull out from Petrograd carrying 400 women, children and babies, penniless, weeping and starving because a Bolsheviki whim prevented them going. Under the influence of flattery he softened a little and agreed to let us go." Leitzell continued, "We were then stripped and searched inch by inch, all money and credentials, letters, propaganda and wireless proposals to our government sealed by the Bolsheviki foreign office were taken. As we left the office the soldiers in command were eagerly grabbing for [our] American money—all they left us was Russian rubles which are of no value." Jens Laursen added, "After a two kilometer walk carrying a sick English soldier, we reached the little bridge which gave us freedom.... We were a happy bunch when we got over the Finnish Front lines to a little station.... There we had a little lunch, the first real food we had tasted since we left the company. About 7 o'clock P.M. a special train came for us and brought us to a little town called Terijoka, about 50 kilometers from Petrograd."[36]

The American newspapers were quick to announce the Americans' release. Once paper proclaimed, "Detroiter is Released.... Bryant R. Ryall ... Glen Leitzell ... Freeman Hogan ... and Jens Laursen ... have been released and are proceeding to Copenhagen."[37] The jubilant Americans proceeded homeward; however, in a quirk of fate, these men had penetrated far deeper into Russia than any Allied armed soldier or combat unit ever would. Glenn Leitzell's feelings toward Russia were summed up when he announced, "They're not making any Bolsheviks of American prisoners. They preach bolshevikism to us, but it doesn't go.... The leaders are preaching that every one ought to have the same amount of money, but every leader has a pile of rubles stuck away."[38] Leitzell's feelings were seconded by Jens Laursen, who said, "I figure they're [all] crooked and deceitful and are a bunch of cut-throats. All the honest ones want to get out of Russia as soon as possible. They all want to go to America."[39] And Freeman Hogan's feelings were not much different; he stated, "If America ever went Bolshevik, like Moscow.... I'd make myself a lone hand to stand out against them."[40]

Chapter 18

Spring 1919

April 17, 1919: Brigadier General Wilds P. Richardson took one last look at the icebreaker *Kanada* and then, with chest out and shoulders back, paraded off the ship and onto an Archangel wharf. The general led his staff to waiting transportation, and not long after this, he stood before the steps of the 339th Infantry Regiment's headquarters. General Richardson marched into the building, surprising the headquarters orderlies, and demanded, "Where is Colonel Stewart? I want to see him now." Moments later, the general was escorted into the office of the 339th's senior officer. Brigadier General Richardson faced the astounded Col. Stewart and declared, "I am now in charge of all American troops in northern Russia…. You are relieved of your command."[1]

Wilds P. Richardson was born March 20, 1861, after the move of his parents, Oliver and Hester Wingo Richardson, to Ladonia, Hunt County, Texas. Oliver, a 32-year-old teacher, then left his 24-year-old wife and traveled to Spartanburg, South Carolina, where he volunteered to join the 36th South Carolina Militia regiment.[2] Hester Richardson was left to raise her newborn baby as well as a three-year-old daughter, Lula. Unfortunately, Hester was not healthy, and she died in July 1862, leaving her two small children to a sister. Oliver Richardson returned to take charge of his children in early 1864 and quickly married Susan Nielson, a 21-year-old teacher from the nearby town of Paris, Texas. Together, the couple taught school and raised Wilds and Lula.

Wilds Richardson attended

Brig. Gen. Wilds "Dick" Richardson had been in Alaska for nearly 25 years before being ordered to France in 1918 (U.S. Army Signal Corps).

schools in Paris, Texas, but he much preferred the world outside of the classroom. His parents allowed the boy his freedom, but they made sure "Dick," as he was called, was well schooled. Thus, Dick grew up loving the challenges of Texas' frontier culture, while at the same time being solidly grounded in academics. The young man attended West Point, graduating in 1884, ranking 22nd out of 37 graduates.[3]

Second Lieutenant Dick Richardson was assigned to the garrison at Angel Island in California, a post involved in subduing the Modoc tribe in northern California. Following this, in December 1885, he was ordered to Fort Bowie, Arizona, a station for United States troops trying to subjugate the Apaches.[4] This role lasted until in November 1886, when Richardson was reassigned to Fort Niobrara, Nebraska, a post tasked with reining in the last elements of the Sioux Nation still roaming the west. Here, his promotion to first lieutenant came December 16, 1889.[5] First Lieutenant Richardson eventually was sent to Alaska, a posting he relished. He declared, "In Alaska, [I] found [my] niche."[6]

Richardson was promoted to captain, and in Alaska he made his mark. He directed the construction of Fort William H. Seward as well as a system of trails and roads. One of these trails he took part in creating would eventually become a section of what is now the Iditarod.[7] In April 1904, promoted to the rank of major, he was assigned to a role as Alaska's road commissioner. Major Richardson worked feverishly and later his efforts were recognized by some of Alaska's citizens; the 365-mile highway between Valdez and Fairbanks became known as the Richardson Highway.

Wilds Richardson, with the rank of major and his assortment of official positions, was a huge man. In 1907, at his routine military physical, his weight was recorded at over 280 pounds, and his body was compared to that of William Taft, the prospective United States presidential candidate. The physician who examined him remarked, "[He had] a little more fat than is necessary."[8] Fortunately for Richardson, he passed his physical, enabling him to launch his next series of expansions: more road improvements, bridge construction, and a system of taxation plans to fund these public works. His promotion to lieutenant colonel came in March 1911 and to colonel in April 1914.

Wilds "Dick" Richardson earned his brigadier general's star on August 5, 1917, and with the American military ramping up for the nation's entry into the Great War, he was relieved of his duties in Alaska and sent to Camp Lee, Virginia. From there, he was sent to Camp Beauregard, Louisiana, where he was given command of the 78th Brigade, 39th Infantry Division. Richardson's brigade landed at Brest, France, on September 3, 1918, and from there, his doughboys went to the 39th Division's staging area near St. Florent, France.[9] The brigade did nothing. Richardson was exasperated as he watched his men sit idly. He complained, "The men [had] begun to learn how to loaf and avoid doing things, and to neglect instructions."[10] Brigadier General Richardson was also aggravated by the army's decision to remove officers and men from his brigade, as these troops were being sent off to replace losses in other American combat units.

By mid–October 1918, his brigade had been stripped of so many of its soldiers it was but a shell of a combat formation. On October 14, 1918, Brig. Gen. Richardson was given orders to proceed to the 7th Brigade, 4th Infantry Division, a unit involved in the fighting around St. Mihiel. A week later, Richardson reached Bois d'Rappes, where after thirty-four years in the military he heard shots fired by an enemy's weapon. Wilds Richardson recorded, "[I] was close enough to the Germans that the 'cook house' near [my] quarters was hit by a shell." Sadly for the ambitious general, he never got closer to the war. He wrote, "[I] missed the greatest battle yet fought by the United States Army [the Champagne-Marne offensive]."[11]

General Richardson did not have a command on November 11, 1918, when the Armistice was signed. Instead, he existed as nothing more than a name on a roster sheet of officers slated for return to the United States. He languished in this perplexing position until March 10, 1919, when General Pershing informed Richardson he had been selected to take over the American command in northern Russia; Richardson's vast experiences in the wilds of Alaska had earned him a job while other officers were being sent home. Richardson traveled to Paris, where he met President Woodrow Wilson, who was there as part of the Paris Peace Conference. President Wilson told Richardson his mission would be to act independently of the British high command, get the American troops out of Russia, and to do so with as few casualties as possible.[12]

Brigadier General Dick Richardson arrived in Murmansk on April 8, 1919, and almost immediately was informed of Company I's mutiny. Richardson, who had brought along an entire staff of experienced assistants, had them investigate this incident. His staff, which included "an acting general staff officer, chief of staff, adjutant, and inspector, his aide, and staff officers assigned to operations, intelligence, personnel, and supply," efficiently presented him with their findings.[13] General Richardson stated, "This incident was given wide circulation in the States, and I am satisfied from my investigation that an exaggerated impression was created as to its seriousness." He added, "The so-called mutiny [was] a temporary disaffection of one of the companies.... Every soldier connected with the incident performed his duty as a soldier. And as far as I think the matter should be closed." However, he did believe "the noncommissioned officers could have handled the affair more forcefully."[14]

Richardson and his staff climbed aboard the ice breaker *Kanada*, which arrived in Archangel on April 17, 1919. Richardson's first impression of Stewart was striking. He recalled, "[Stewart] was a tired officer ... in bad health ... [and] rather beaten down by the British leaders."[15] And Richardson's intuition was correct; 1st Lt. Albert May (Co. I) noted, "[Stewart] told me that he was beset with stomach ulcers, [and] that he should have been hospitalized."[16] The general moved his staff into a suite of nearby rooms and assumed control of the regiment. General Richardson did not spend much time with the 339th's colonel and ultimately decided "he would not recommend Stewart for meritorious service in the Russian campaign."[17]

General William Ironside heard of Wilds Richardson's presence and sent a colonel to greet him as well as convey a set of orders for Richardson to carry out.

An American staff worker reported, "[Gen. Richardson] picked up the telephone [and] called Ironside. He said, 'General, I'm telling you, my men ain't going out.'" The staffer recorded Ironside's response: "'Well General, I am higher in command than you.'" Wilds Richardson's reply was "Yeah, I know ... but ... [the] war is over. I don't have to take orders from you." Richardson then continued, "[General] Ironside ... I am going to give you an order. I give you three weeks' time to ... relieve my men.... If my men don't get relief by [the] fifth of May, I'm pulling out!"[18]

The two generals, both men with bear-sized bodies and mammoth-sized egos, soon met face to face. Though Ironside towered over Richardson, the American outweighed him by forty or more pounds and had vast experience in dealing with Alaska's wild and wooly miners, cheats, and ruffians. The American military publication *The Sentinel* noted, "Richardson met with Ironside in the afternoon, and said he had nothing more to say than what was sent by Pershing."[19] The two senior officers would work together for the next six months, but their relationship was purely professional and Siberian-like frosty.

Brigadier General Richardson did not trust the intelligence that Col. Stewart's staff had assembled; he preferred to develop his own. The general boarded a train and on April 21, 1919, arrived at Third Battalion headquarters in Obozerskaya. Major J. Brooks Nichols met him at the train station and the two conversed for hours. Much had happened on the Railroad front since the fight near Bolshie Ozerki, including on April 1, 1919, a massive Bolo assault on the Americans' positions at verst 445 and 446. Lieutenant Clarence Primm summed up this attack, writing, "Bolsheviks with artillery, machine guns and Lewis guns galore, attacked a position held by a battery of Russian artillery, two Russian machine guns, and 24 Americans, and got licked."[20]

That morning, the Bolsheviks advanced upon several blockhouses manned by riflemen and machine gunners from Company I. One of these men, Cpl. Cleo Colburn (Co. I), reported, "We were quartered in Number One Blockhouse on the left flank of Verst 446, when on April 1, at 7:40 AM we were attacked by what we [from prisoners] found out to be 200 fresh troops.... There were eight men besides myself in the blockhouse: Harvey Minteer with a Lewis gun and three helpers; Tony Cialkowski, Alfred Becker, and Frank McCauley. I with a Vickers gun and four helpers, Richard Kleiber, Howard Kroenski, Louis Stemptzyk, and [Joseph] Ustarboski." Colburn continued, "We thought when we saw them coming we would be overcome, but we kept coverage with rifle fire and we got word back to the French artillery of our predicament.... With the two machine guns and the rifles using rifle grenades, we were able to hold them off ... [for] an hour and a quarter.... Then the French opened up with their artillery, and they covered our area with shellfire. That drove the Bolos back."[21] Corporal Colburn added, "During our firing, Pvt. Becker and I about kissed ourselves goodbye. Becker's pill passed just over his head and went through our backdoor, and mine hit my tripod directly in front of me."[22] Later, a supply sergeant recorded, "Corp. Colburn, with a Vickers machine gun, fired 2,700 cartridges. Private Harvey Minteer, with a Lewis gun, fired 1,900 rounds. In the morning the Bolsheviki retired and eighteen dead lay where they fell, and a wide trail of blood left by the retreating forces in the snow showed evidence of many more casualties."[23] Later, when Gen. Richardson arrived at Obozerskaya, Cpl. Colburn wrote, "Major Nichols and Gen. Richardson visited our post, [shook] hands, [and] congratulated Minteer and I for our good work."[24]

The Bolsheviks retreated southward, both from verst 445 and Bolshie Ozerki, creating a buffer zone between them and the American positions. Then, a period of relatively quiet peace settled in on the Railroad front, lessening the tension in the region, enabling one American soldier to write home, "I am well as could be expected in this cold country and I guess it will never start to get warm here." He added, "They say that we will get out of here by June first but I don't know whether we will or not as there are so many stories going around."[25] Another noted, "Captain Winslow and two British officers [took] a white flag and [went] to [the] Bolos' lines, trying to exchange prisoners. [They] stayed about an hour, then returned, having to make another trip [the] next day."[26]

General Richardson's brief visit also gave the Americans some comforting encouragement. Corporal Colburn recorded, "[We heard] the official news that three cruisers and seven destroyers were on the way from [the] U.S. direct to Archangel."[27] This information allowed the doughboys to speculate about when they would be going home. Lieutenant Wesley Wright (Co. M) mused, "We of the 4th platoon have had a few disagreeable times together, a few pleasant, and a whole heap of ordinary ones. And isn't it strange how we always think back to the pleasant ones."[28] Even though the dream of going home might have been closer to happening, nothing had changed; the Yanks were still in northern Russia, guarding their posts, watching the Bolos, and wondering when the Reds would attack.

The next few days brought changes that buoyed the Americans' spirits: letters from home and a weather transformation. Corporal Clem Grobbel (Co. I), on April 13, 1919, reacted to messages from home, writing, "So mother is going to 'vote.' I will be darned. I hope she votes it wet [meaning against Prohibition]." He then added, "The weather is warming up a bit now, makes a fellow think of spring. The snow is melting fast."[29] Lieutenant Primm, also responding to American news, remarked, "I hear ... there have been ... mass meetings held in Detroit to get the 339th out of Russia ... the men are proud to be called 'Detroit's Own.'" He continued, "We are now resting and working, but not fighting. We do not expect to fight unless attacked, and then we always expect to 'clean up' on the poor troops of the enemy."[30] A third, Cpl. Norbert Schillinger (Co. M), hoping for a swift return to the States, reminisced, "They say we are going to be relieved, but they have been telling us that for so long it is nothing new."[31]

Major Nichols refused to allow his riflemen to grow lax, and one way of keeping the men sharp was to send patrols out to check on the Bolsheviks. On April 14, 1919, 1st Sgt. Walter Dundon recorded, "[Our patrol sighted] a patrol of Bolsheviks ... [near] Valsheniza."[32] These brushes with Bolo troops became more common as the temperatures climbed; however, both sides' veteran riflemen preferred to keep calm when these incidents occurred. One doughboy admitted, "When you stay steady in one place ... you keep sending out patrols. We sent out a patrol; they sent out a patrol. Finally you got to where you begin to meet their patrol in the woods someplace. And you get to be, not enemies, but kind of friends." He continued, "We wouldn't just actually see them, but they'd put things in a tree ... like a mailbox out there in the woods. And we would exchange notices: they'd say, 'you join us,' and then we'd tell them to come and join us, so we wouldn't have to fight."[33] Another Yank added, "The Bolos couldn't understand what the Americans were doing in Russia. They could understand why the British were there, but what the Americans were doing, they wanted to know why we were fighting."[34] This period of relative peace allowed men to dream about home, and in doing so, some grew pensive. One homesick fellow recalled, "Being alone was bad. And, oh, it was like a prison—nature's prison that you couldn't get away from." He added, "The strain was beginning to tell. I think the thing was mainly the repetition of the same routine day after day after day."[35]

This tranquility weakened the soldiers' vigilance, and this flaw in discipline resulted in calamity. First Sergeant Walter Dundon recorded, "April 19— Cpl. [William H.] Russell accidentally killed by hand grenade. Cpls. [Walter] Picard, [Frank] Romanski and Pvt. [Norman] Miller wounded by same grenade."[36] William Russell, a 23-year-old from Detroit, had been one of the men honored by Gen. Ironside for his action on April 1, 1919, when the general pinned a Distinguished Service Cross medal to his chest. Russell had been an accountant/clerk for Packard Motors before the war. His draft registration card described him as of medium height, with gray eyes and brown hair.[37] Company M, which had been preparing for an Easter celebration, buried Cpl. William Russell and passed on Easter festivities. Walter Dundon wrote, "[British] Chaplain Watkins was with us but the anticipated gladness of [Easter] had been blasted."

The next day, April 20, 1919, a force of White Russian soldiers arrived at Obozerskaya to be apportioned to each of Moore's and Winslow's platoons. The Americans began training the Russians in how to man the blockhouses, carry out patrols, and ultimately assume the Yanks' responsibilities. Captain Joel Moore remarked, "Each platoon has a platoon of Russian Archangel troops to break in at the posts of 448, 446, and two at 445."[38] April 21, 1919, remained quiet, but the next day was not. By this time, Brig. Gen. Dick Richardson had arrived at Obozerskaya and made his way to verst 455. Captains Moore and Winslow mustered the platoons for the general to inspect. Moore wrote, "General Richardson ... assembled [the troops] at Verst 455." The general spoke to the troops, saying, "He regretted not being with them during the winter combat. This brought quite a shout of laughter."[39] Richardson ignored the laughter and plowed on with more to say. Moore noted Richardson's speech: "Remember, you are Americans in a foreign country taking part in a great game, making history which will be written and talked of for generations.... Your people are pleased and proud of you. They have not forgotten you.... They want to see you come home as soon as you can."[40] The veteran riflemen studied their new commander. One private mused, "[Richardson was] inclined to obesity, and of medium height. His long pointed nose, red, flushed face, mustache, and brutal mouth were outstanding. He was neatly dressed, and as he faced us, I saw a silver star on each shoulder."[41] Captain Moore and Winslow's soldiers did like one of the last things said by Richardson: "The

339th infantry would be the first of all the troops to be evacuated, and that he expected 12,000 British troops to reoccupy the Allied positions to support the Russians ... [and] he would see that our British allies put nothing further on us."[42]

General Richardson returned to Archangel, leaving the men of the Third Battalion centered on Obozerskaya and positions south of there, the soldiers now believing the end to their travails was near. The Bolsheviks got word of Richardson's speech, and they too felt optimism knowing the Americans would soon be abandoning their defenses and returning home. Cpt. Joel Moore wrote, "There was a suspicion that the Reds were content to merely harry the Americans, but not to take any more losses going against them, preferring to wait till [we] had gone."[43] The next week went by quietly. Lieutenant Clarence Primm, on April 26, 1919, wrote, "[I] am now living in a blockhouse about 15 feet square.... There are nine of us, but we are never all inside at once. Our men are looking forward to going home. Our new American General commander has been down to the front, looked us over, and given us a short talk. We like him."[44]

The expectant Americans continued protecting their blockhouses, trenches, and defensive positions as well as training their White Russian counterparts. But the Yanks' alertness was easing, and accidents continued to happen. On April 26, 1919, Cpl. Frank Sawickis (Co. I) was "seriously wounded by an accidental explosion of a Bolshevik grenade."[45] Sawickis, a 25-year-old who had come to the United States in 1912 from Lithuania (then part of Russia), died three days later. His draft registration card listed him as tall with blue eyes and brown hair.[46] Months later, when the army was returning the remains of the American soldiers who had died in Russia, his family objected. Sawickis' brother, John, commented, "I [would] have preferred to allow my brother's body to remain in Russia."[47]

Lieutenant Clarence Primm, unaware that Cpl. Sawickis had been mortally injured and knowing his men were anxious to be removed from the front, wrote, "We expect a general inspector here tomorrow, so we have cleaned up around the post. [I] have even shaved and washed [my] hands." He added, "Our artillery and the Bolos' indulged in a little duel for two hours yesterday.... That happens every once in a while."[48] Lieutenant Primm's riflemen, just as their leader, ignored the artillery; they were much more concerned about the coming inspection. Rumors abounded, includng the most important one they hoped to be true—their removal from the area of combat would begin following this inspection. Therefore, when Maj. Howard Scales, the inspector general for Gen. Richardson, arrived, the doughboys greeted his scrutiny with excitement. Major Scales arrived on April 30, 1919, and he examined Companies I and M.[49] The first sergeants of those units turned in their muster reports to Maj. Scales' team, recording all unit losses. Company I had suffered four killed in action, one accidental death, and seven dead from disease. Company M listed five killed in action, two accidental deaths, two dead from disease, and one dead from wounds.[50] Major Howard Scales took the reports and returned to Archangel. He reported to Gen. Richardson, stating, "The rumors of poor morale has no basis ... [and] troop conduct was remarkably good."[51]

On the next day, May 1, 1919, the doughboys received the first proof that they would be leaving; Cpt. Joel Moore was given orders to stand down one of his platoons and replace them with White Russian soldiers. Walter Dundon duly recorded this feat, noting, "Part of the 2nd platoon outposted at 455 relieved by the Russians."[52] The Bolsheviks soon learned of the Yanks' Russian replacements and began shelling those positions. Lieutenant George Stoner, his troops happy to be out of the line of fire, recorded, "Heavy artillery fire on both sides [for] four hours. Light infantry action on front. No casualties."[53] The Bolo artillery increased its shelling of White Russian positions and added to this bombardment on May 4, 1919, by sending an airplane over the lines to drop bombs on them.[54] One American doughboy wrote, "I think that the [Bolsheviks], if they had really wanted to, they could have probably cut us off and captured the entire force.... If they really wanted to.... But there was actually no purpose for them in doing so."[55]

On May 5, 1919, Gen. Wilds Richardson returned to Obozerskaya and verst 455, called for the Americans to form again for inspection, and handed out medals. First Sergeant Walter Dundon wrote, "Decorations bestowed on the men today in the presence of General Richardson."[56] One recipient of these awards, 1st Lt. George Stoner, noted in his diary, "To [verst] 455 to receive [a] French medal."[57] Richardson did not stay long, but this second appearance in such a short time buoyed the soldiers' morale—they figured they were to leave very soon!

The Bolsheviks added more bombing flights as the weather grew warmer, routinely dropping explosives on the White Russian defenses, while avoiding positions known to be manned by the Americans. The Yanks were almost giddy in their expectations of leaving, and many celebrated on May 7, 1919, when Col. P.T. Akutin (Cpt. Joel Moore's counterpart and friend from the Pinega campaign) was officially given command of the defenses at Obozerskaya. Joel Moore recorded the event, writing, "Major Nichols was relieved at Verst 455 ... by Col. Akutin, whose Russian troops took over the active defense of the front, with the Americans at Obozerskaya in reserve. At this place and at Bolsheozerki, G, L, M, I, and E Companies in the order named ... together with Machine Gun company platoons, were relieved by British and Russian troops. American Engineers also withdrew from this front at the same time."[58] The next day, May 8, 1919, the last of the doughboys were pulled from their front-line positions, leaving all the military responsibilities to the White Russians and the British. Walter Dundon watched as his entire company was consolidated in Obozerskaya and recorded, "Co. relieved from front lines and entrained at verst 455 for Obozerskaya, arriving Obozerskaya 2:00 A.M."[59] Company M had become officially relieved of duty.

The next four days went by quickly, Cpt. Moore's riflemen taking baths, cleaning their equipment, and turning in all their winter gear. The only break in the routine came when Gen. Richardson made a third trip to Obozerskaya. The general, accompanied by Maj. Nichols, along with a small security contingent, traveled south as far as the American defenses had been extended. There, at verst 445, Gen. Richardson walked among the trenches and blockhouses and studied the Bolo defenses with binoculars. Richardson also inspected the White Russians who had replaced the Americans. He shook his head in dismay and recorded, "If anyone suspected [the White Russians] lacked proficiency, the morning's performance proved it."[60]

May 15 and 16, 1919, were highlighted by inspections of equipment by Maj. Nichols, and on the 17th, the companies received their departure date. Lieutenant George Stoner happily wrote, "Received date of our departure from Obozerskaya and name of ship we are to sail on." He added the next day, "Bob [Wieczorek], Sgts. [Charles] Hebner and [Ralph] Walker and I went fishing with rifles—caught 6."[61] Then, on May 20, 1919, Company M's exuberant riflemen and officers boarded a train for Archangel, and finally, after an agonizing wait, it headed north, taking these embattled Americans away from danger. One officer, glancing back at the place the Americans had fought over since last September, stated, "It was one long nightmare."[62]

Chapter 19

Homeward Bound

May 12, 1919: First Lieutenant Charles E. Lewis rolled the sheet of paper from the typewriter and studied it briefly; the 339th Infantry's muster totaled 122 officers and 3,739 men. Lewis handed the report to an enlisted man. "This goes to the General," he said. The soldier took the report and left Lewis' office.[1] Lieutenant Lewis was the 339th's regimental intelligence officer and the assistant regimental adjutant; completing timely muster rolls for Gen. Richardson was one of his ongoing responsibilities. He had been carrying out this task for some time now, and he was good at it.

Charles Lewis was born June 12, 1889, in Manchester, Michigan. Lewis' parents, Charles Sr. and Francis "Fanny" Lewis, lived on a large farmstead near Manchester, courtesy of Fanny's wealthy family. Fanny's assets (her family was known for its highly successful farms and orchards), combined with her husband's railroad construction inheritance, enabled the couple to manage their large estate as well as establish a successful boot and shoe mercantile business.[2] Their son Charles attended schools in Manchester, excelling in academics, plus doing just as well in athletics, to the point of earning a leadership role on his high school's football team. Charles graduated from Manchester High School in 1907 as class valedictorian.

Charles Lewis attended the University of Michigan, acquiring a bachelor of arts in 1912 and a bachelor of law in 1913. He took a position as an attorney with the Detroit law firm Warren, Cady, and Ladd, and during the next four years of

First Lieutenant Charles E. Lewis was a lawyer before joining the Army in 1917. (Bentley Historical Library, University of Michigan).

practicing law, he earned a reputation as "a man of integrity and habits beyond reproach ... [with] splendid ability and the best of character." When he applied for the army's Officer Candidate School, his boss, Sanford Ladd, wrote, "What we are going to do to fill the gap [of his being gone] ... we do not know."[3] Lewis went into the army's R.O.T.C program at Ft. Sheridan, Illinois, and pinned on his second lieutenant's bars on August 15, 1917. He was sent to Camp Custer and assigned to the 339th Infantry as the assistant regimental adjutant.

Lieutenant Lewis fulfilled this role as the 339th's recruits rolled into Camp Custer. His promotion to first lieutenant on December 31, 1917, did not change his assignment, though his responsibilities increased; he also became the Second Battalion's acting adjutant.[4] Here, he met Major J. Brooks Nichols, the battalion commander. The two officers, both who believed in honesty, integrity, and hard work, discovered they worked well together.

The Second Battalion, composed of companies E, F, G, and 'H, totaling 637 officers and men, loaded onto the S.S. *Nagoya* on August 27, 1918, and the ship joined the convoy heading to Archangel. Four days later, Lt. Lewis briefed Maj. Nichols, stating, "Health of the troops good." This report changed dramatically; on September 2, 1918, Lewis' account noted, "Epidemic of Spanish influenza spreading ... [and] unchecked."[5] The S.S. *Nagoya* arrived in Archangel on September 5, 1918, with the flu raging; sixty men were critically ill. The battalion's medical personnel struggled to find a place for these patients, especially when their designated barracks housed over one hundred Russian civilian refugees. The refugees were moved, and by September 7, 1918, Lt. Lewis was able to inform Maj. Nichols that the epidemic was checked; there were only thirty-three men in the hospital, and the battalion now numbered 997 officers and men present for duty.[6]

Lieutenant Charles Lewis watched with great respect as Maj. J. Brooks Nichols handled the streetcar workers' strike; however, on September 28, 1918, Lt. Lewis sadly wrote into his journal, "Major Nichols, Commander of 2nd Bn. ordered to Obozerskaya for duty with 3rd Bn., relieved Major Young, who is to command 2nd Bn."[7] Major Charles Young arrived at battalion headquarters three days later and moved into Nichols' vacated office. Lieutenant Lewis soon understood the nature of his new boss; Maj. Young relished pomp and glittery and toadying up to the British high command. Lewis wrote, on October 12, 1918, "Furnished detail of 50 men to take part in ceremony in honor of Maj. Gen. Poole, Commander in Chief who is to leave for England." Not long after this entry, Lewis recorded, "Furnished 10 squads in command of Major Young to take part in Parade past Embassy."[8]

Charles Lewis was shifted from the Second Battalion adjutant to regimental assistant adjutant, and from his new office in the 339th's headquarters building, he worked for Col. George Stewart, providing reviews and reports. Lewis recalled, "I compiled a sort of regimental diary for Colonel Stewart.... This comprised information received weekly from Company Commanders and other officers in the field."[9] Charles Lewis also worked as an intelligence officer, a job he disliked. He remarked, "All military intelligence work was in charge of British headquarters and ... the American Infantry regiment were so stripped of centralized command and authority that any regimental intelligence work was futile."[10] Then, Lt. Lewis was burdened with an additional role; Maj. Charles Young had assumed the position of chief of court martial trials, and remembering his ex-adjutant had been a lawyer, he snatched the lieutenant up and made him a trial judge advocate at these court martials.

General Dick Richardson's arrival in Archangel changed the Yanks' relationship with the British, a liaison between the two Allies that completely frustrated Lewis. He recorded, "Our relations with the English were, in general, rather strained. The exercise of command within our own American regiment was seriously stifled by reason of the fact ... that American Companies ... were in most instances placed under the command of British ... officers." Lewis added, "This led ... in the minds of many of the American Unit Commanders to be an abuse of American Troops."[11] But now, with Gen. Richardson in charge, and with the American rifle companies rolling into Bakharitza and Archangel, 1st Lt. Charles Lewis was able to relax and think about an end to his Russian experience.

The officers and men of Company M felt the same way—they were glad to be away from the battle front and excited by the news they were going home. Captain Moore's company arrived at Bakharitza on May 21, 1919. Then, the men were ferried to a permanent-looking campsite on a nearby island. This site, Camp Economie, was composed of a large number of tents, roughly thrown together wooden buildings, and a smattering of warehouses and supply stations. The riflemen were surprised that they were not billeting in the barracks at Smolny, and one soldier recalled, "We were sent to Economy Island. It was quite a big island ... [we] are living in board-floored tents stained a dark color—I suppose to keep out the continual sun, so that the men may sleep. We get fish to eat at times, and had eggs for breakfast."[12] The food may have been better than at the front, but all the soldiers quickly discovered Camp Economie came with a troubling malady—swarms of bloodthirsty mosquitoes. One rifleman voiced the complaint of many, grumbling, "Mosquitoes nearly ate us up last night," and medic Godfrey Anderson, who tried to help the frequently bitten doughboys, added, "The mosquitoes were legion, large, and aggressive. Some of our company would appear in the morning with eyes swollen shut as if they had been stung by bees."[13]

The Yanks dealt with the mosquitoes, preferring them to the dangers of the front, with one doughboy announcing, "Arrived at Economie.... Seems too good to be true."[14] The riflemen cleaned themselves up, took care of their weapons, reported for health inspections, and began close-order drill. One writer recalled, "the men were reintroduced to the military life: saluting, policing the area, venereal inspections, drills, and kitchen duty."[15] The riflemen in Company M, relieved of war's stress, took this return to rear-echelon life in stride. Many, though, had arrived at Camp Economie exhausted and in poor health. Dysentery ran rampant through the men. Company M's 1st Sgt. Walter Dundon recorded numerous times in his journal, "Many sick with dysentery."[16]

In time, though, the young Americans regained their health, and by May 26, 1919, 1st Sgt. Dundon no longer made note of "men with dysentery." Instead, the energetic Yanks were up to the antics engaged in by all robust young Americans.

In Company M, the men gathered together and presented an award to one of their company cooks, 25-year-old Roy Fisher. The young cook, who had been transferred from the 338th Infantry, had done the best he could with the substandard rations they had been issued; his meals were adequate, but certainly not great. Captain Joel Moore, who observed the enlisted men's ceremony, wrote, "Cook Roy Fisher was presented with the big lead M. & V. [meat and vegetables] medal. The boys at 445 had made it of shrapnel balls picked up on the field. That red-headed cook sure found out he was popular with the men."[17] In another, a doughboy, his reputation built upon entertaining his comrades, suffered an embarrassing mishap. His lieutenant, Clarence Primm, noted, "A tub of grease for trading purposes was set to one side of the field kitchen and covered with an immense barrel. At the jubilee bonfire, the company minstrel mounted the barrel, the better to please his audience. In the ardor of his song he teetered on his toes. The barrelhead did not hold up [and he fell into the grease]."[18]

Lieutenant Clarence Primm also found himself in a new situation. On May 27, 1919, he wrote in a letter to his parents, "I have been handed a new job. [I hope] it may be temporary.... I cannot foresee how long I shall be busy with it."[19] Primm had impressed Brig. Gen. Richardson on those occasions when the general traveled to Obozerskaya. General Richardson, once Company M was safely housed at Economie, called Lt. Primm to headquarters and informed the young officer that he was being detached from his company. Clarence Primm would now be working directly with Richardson. Little did Primm know, he would never rejoin Company M.

The troopers in Company M did not have time to consider the loss of one of their lieutenants. On May 28, 1919, they readied themselves for the "big baseball game." Baseball had become the doughboys' greatest entertainment, and games were played on every open space on Economie's island. Private James Siplon recalled, "We had baseball teams and everything. We would start a baseball game at 10:00 PM and end it at midnight."[20] General Richardson, striving to improve the men's morale, encouraged the baseball games and soon a tournament was organized pitting each of the companies' best teams against each other. By May 28, 1919, Company M's team and the Headquarters Company's team were the last two remaining. They were to play for the "Championship of North Russia," and the betting on the two teams was heavy. Joel Moore noted, "It was a fat pot—more than 20,000 rubles in the purse."[21]

General Richardson declared the afternoon of the twenty-eighth of May to be a half-holiday, and nearly all who could attend, including the general and Col. Stewart, showed up at the main ball field to watch. The game turned out to be close, but with Company M's star, Cpl. Harry Bissonette, leading their team in hitting, Company M went on to win, 5 to 2. Joel Moore recorded, "It was a pitchers' battle most of the time. 'M' Co. bunched hits in the 4th inning, scoring two runs, [while] the HQ Co. made a pair of errors, piling up three more runs." Moore boasted, "We took ten thousand rubles from HQ Co."[22] Unexpectedly, though, during the avidly watched game, Maj. Charles Young suffered a suspicious injury. A 339th rifleman wrote, "[Maj. Young] was sitting over at the ballgame; somebody

The Polar Bear patch and the NR patch were worn by the men who served in the 339th Infantry (Carol Primm and Peter Stuntz Collection).

hit him right in the head with a half brick. They knocked him out!"[23] A search was made for the culprit but none was ever found. An officer did remember, though, "the men had little respect for Col. Stewart [and Maj. Young]."[24]

The next day, May 29, 1919, Company M was reviewed, inspected, and informed they would represent the 339th Infantry in the upcoming Memorial Day Parade. Lieutenant Clarence Primm wrote, "'M' Company of the 339th Infantry and a platoon of sailors from the *U.S.S. Des Moines* constituted the uniformed American forces in the parade. These detachments ... had been selected as the smartest appearing and best-drilled men available in the North."[25] A number of dignitaries and high-ranking officers gave speeches, including Gen. Richardson, who said, "We are assembled here on the soil of a great Ally and a traditional friend of our country, to do what honor we may to the memory of America's dead buried here, who responded to their country's call in the time of her need and have laid down their lives."[26] Once the speeches ended, Lt. Primm noted, "A heart-breaking call of the trumpet over the graves of the fallen sounded the mourning notes.... The signal, as it broke forth, filled the air with sorrow and grief, as if it called the whole world to bow before those who ... gave their lives."[27]

Later, Lt. George Stoner recalled, "General Richardson ... and even Col. Stewart praised [Company M] for its fine appearance that day."[28]

Captain Moore's riflemen returned to Camp Economie, but not before one of their enlisted men, Pvt. John Vrahoritis, married a Russian woman in a Greek Orthodox wedding. The 27-year-old Vrahoritis, a Greek immigrant to the United States, had settled in Detroit and worked at a Ford factory before being drafted. He had met Maria Esyevileva in Archangel at a restaurant, where she worked as a cook. The two completed the paperwork enabling the young bride to immigrate to America, and though they understood she could not travel with her husband when the 339th left Russia, she did have the proper documentation for a successful immigration.[29]

The riflemen, now with some time on their hands, got together and came up with the idea for a way to distinguish themselves from all other military units. Eventually a decision was reached; they would call themselves the "Polar Bears," and they believed a patch displaying a walking polar bear on a blue background seemed most appropriate. A delegation took this proposal to Gen. Richardson, who approved it, and sent the petition to Gen. Pershing, the U.S. Army commander in chief. General Pershing approved the request and forwarded it to Gen. Richardson, Pershing's General Order No. 5 stating, "A white Polar Bear on a blue field has been authorized by G.H.Q. This insignia will be made of cloth and sewn on the left sleeve of the blouse and overcoat one inch below the shoulder seam."[30]

On May 31, 1919, the doughboys received word that they would be leaving Russia in the next forty-eight hours. The jubilant young men scrambled to get into Archangel for a last visit to places of interest and to say their good-byes. One wrote, "A lot of the women [of Archangel] were crying."[31] Generals Richardson and Ironside conducted a final inspection and review. On June 2, 1919, the euphoric Americans of Companies I and M, as well as A, E, G, L, and the Machine Gun Company, followed Maj. J. Brooks Nichols out of Camp Economie and up the gangplank onto the transport ship *Czar*.[32] One rifleman, Pvt. Floyd Lewis, recalled, "We eagerly clambered aboard to leave. I recall that I hung on the stern railing to shout, 'Goodbye Russia! Goodbye Archangel'!"[33] Captain Joel Moore recorded, "We left with 192 men.... Twenty of the men were so hard hit by camp sickness that they had to be left behind when the company boarded the *Czar*."[34] These men who remained at Camp Economie, along with the soldiers from the remaining companies, were scheduled to board the transport ship, the *Menominee*, which would leave a few days later. Another soldier left behind, Lt. Clarence Primm, watched as the *Czar* pulled out of the harbor on June 3, 1919, its sirens screeching loudly. He wrote, "My old company left yesterday for Brest, France.... In my new work on the staff I have something to do with reports on personnel ... [I] surely have had a necklace of horseshoes to play with this year."[35]

The *Czar* did not get far before it ran into problems; however, this did not bother the high-spirited Americans. Lieutenant George Stoner remarked, "Last line cast off at 7:40 A.M. Ran aground, but was pulled off—A wonderful day, and one we have been looking forward to for a long time." He added, "Going northward it began to get colder. 4 P.M. we began to pass through ice fields."[36] The lieutenant recorded on June 4, 1919, "Awakened at 4:20 by ship bumping into ice. At 8:15 had breakfast, went on deck to watch ice and seals. Passed through the neck of White Sea into the Arctic Ocean."[37] George Stoner's riflemen, who also were watching for floating ice, soon found themselves saddled by an unexpected privation; Maj. Charles Young decided it was time to confiscate all illegal items that the men had brought on board. An exasperated private recalled, "Coming back on the boat, we're [ordered] to have a pack inspection. We get the packs laid out there, and [the] captain of the boat comes down. 'What's all this?' [he asked]." The soldier continued, "Major Young said, 'We're going to have pack inspection.' 'Not on my boat, you're not!' [the Captain said] ... 'I'm Major Young!' [said Young] ...'I'm the captain of this ship,' [said the Captain.] 'If you want to have pack inspection, you go in the brig! Boys, pick up your packs, put them in the bunk.... You're going home. You're not doing any more soldiering.'"[38]

Major J. Brooks Nichols, commanding the 339th's men aboard the *Czar*, received word that the authorization for the Polar Bear patch had been approved after his half of the regiment pulled out of port. He passed the news to his company commanders, who informed their men. First Sergeant Whitney McQuire (Co. I) led a delegation organized to design the Polar Bear patch. He asked Cpl. Henry Duff (Co. I), a rifleman with noted artistic abilities, to draw a polar bear that could be used as a pattern. First Sergeant Whitney took that pattern to some sailors aboard the *Czar* and they made up a patch, using materials from the ship's sail locker. Corporal Henry Duff recalled, "When Whit brought the finished product back from the sailors it looked like an egg or a blob. It sure was no Polar Bear. We were getting desperate, almost to France and no insignia."[39] Duff added, "Someone came up with the idea of just a simple NR for North Russia. At that time there was a patent medicine on the market called 'Natures Remedy' ... there was an NR on the box and that was the design we used for the patch." Corporal Duff continued, "Sgt. McQuire had the sailors make up a few of them ... from old Navy uniforms—and he distributed them."[40]

On June 5, 1919, the convoy reached the coast of Scandinavia, and Lt. Stoner recorded, "Off coast of Norway. Fine scenery—mountains are covered with snow. Weather is fine."[41] The temperatures increased each day as the route took the Americans southward. Their ship anchored briefly in a Shetland harbor, giving Lt. Stoner time to write, "Entered harbor of Lerwick Shetland Islands. ... Very pretty and a good harbor. First signs of civilization since last August."[42] From there, they entered the Irish Sea and on June 11, 1919, landed at Brest, France. The Americans disembarked onto French soil, formed into column and marched three miles to Camp Pontanezen. This hike proved to be taxing; the Polar Bears, veterans of a rough Russian winter, were now experiencing France's summer temperatures. One overheated rifleman exclaimed, "Ahead of them lay a three-mile march uphill to Pontanezen camp. It was no joke. Before the men got in[to camp] they were sighing for Russia's wintry cold!"[43]

Camp Pontanezen was a massive facility, responsible for processing the Yank soldiers going back to the United States. The camp's daily newspaper, *The Pontanezen Duckboard*, boasted that more than half a million men had been billeted

More than 500,000 soldiers passed through Camp Pontanezen in the first six months of 1919 (U.S. Army Signal Corps).

there since the start of 1919. The post sprawled out over hundreds of acres and included well-built mess halls, warehouses, offices, and hospitals, as well as hundreds of large tents, all linked together by miles of boardwalks the resident soldiers called "duckboards." One American, surveying the site and all its activities, wrote, "Pontanezen consists of tents laid out in parallel rows, with boardwalks between.... The camp is quite extensive. There [are] trucks to pick up the garbage cans, which were handled by German prisoners."[44] Lieutenant Stoner added, "Tents—condition of camp good.... To bed early."[45] Another 339th soldier agreed with the lieutenant, remarking, "Slept on iron bed—first one for a year."[46] However, before the Yanks succumbed to sleep, they all approved of what they found in Pontanezen's mess halls, and many exclaimed, "much ... was forgotten when they sat down to a real hot American dinner." And Company M's 1st Sgt. Walter Dundon also was happy to announce, "REAL EATS. 'Bokoo seconds.'"[47]

The next day, June 12, 1919, the men of the 339th began turning in their Russian clothing and putting on fresh and clean American uniforms. They showered and shaved and got haircuts, and following an exchange of gear, looked much like they had when they left the United States in July 1918. Sergeant Matthew

19. Homeward Bound

Grahek (Co. M) admitted, "We were a hard looking outfit, so they sent us to get de-loused [and] new uniforms, so we'd look halfway decent when we got back to the States."[48] The soldiers then posed for company and battalion photographs, and following that, they returned to their mess halls and tented billets. Unknown to most of the men, a transport ship, the U.S.S. *Von Steuben*, had arrived at Brest, bringing in a new supply of soldiers. The *Pontanezen Duckboard* reported, "Replacement troops arrived on *Von Steuben*—the Sixth replacement Unit ... reporting 26 officers and 980 enlisted men [arrived] for replacements in the army of occupation."[49] This ship soon would be their ride home!

The next few days went by quickly, the Polar Bears relaxing and taking in the sights. Corporal Clement Grobbel wrote his parents, "Brest, France.... This is a far better country than Russia will ever be. You can see some fine buildings, roads and layouts of the country here. In Russia nothing but woods."[50] Other Yanks, mostly those who had been stationed in Archangel and had accumulated bundles of rubles, scrambled to sell their piles of cash. One such rifleman, Pvt. Rudolph Marxer (Co. B), recalled, "I had a bunch of rubles, and [when] we got ready to leave [Russia]. I didn't know what the devil I was going to do with them. [We] couldn't take them to the bank. The [military police] would investigate you if you did." He continued, "When we got in to Brest, France.... I happened to see a Salvation Army hut. I went in there and there was a woman sitting there and I said, 'We've got a bunch of rubles.' She said, 'Yes, I hear you just came in today' ... I said, 'The boys ... they got a lot of rubles and we can't—we don't know what to do with them.'" Marxer added, "She said, 'Have the boys figure out how much they have, and put them in envelopes, and I'll go to the bank and get them exchanged. And she got them for us."[51]

The Polar Bears formed for a last inspection on June 20, 1919, with all the men of the 339th now uniformed and outfitted with proper American clothing and equipment. The only obvious difference between the various companies was seen by the distinctiveness of their Polar Bear patches. Most of the men from the *Czar* wore the "NR" patch on their left shoulder. However, the companies that had remained at Camp Economie and had been issued the rapidly-made "polar bear on blue" patches all wore a "Polar Bear" patch, though of different styles; Companies F, H, K, and Supply wore a silkscreen version of the Polar Bear patch, while Companies C, D, and HQ sported a two-piece, die-cut Polar Bear patch.[52]

The Polar Bears, following this final formation, loaded their baggage onto trucks. Then, work details loaded this gear onto their transport ship, the U.S.S. *Von Steuben*. The next day, led by Maj. J. Brooks Nichols, six companies of the 339th Infantry, Companies I and M, plus A, E, G, and L, marched to the wharf and aboard the *Von Steuben*. Captain Horatio Winslow's Company I mustered five officers and 196 enlisted men, while Cpt. Joel Moore's Company M totaled five officers and 189.[53] Both captains had had to strike from their company rolls at least three dozen men due to illness. Joel Moore sadly had to exclude two more soldiers, Cpl. Walter Rosenau and Cpl. Eugene Merwin, who had been injured on June 16, 1919, when Camp Pontanezen's Knights of Columbus building collapsed.[54]

The *Von Steuben* pulled out of port at 10:00 a.m. on June 22, 1919, an event that Lt. Stoner cheerfully announced, "[A] fine day."[55] Another Yank, Sgt. John Crissman (Co. A), added, "This is a very large boat with four stacks. Eats are good and have cots to sleep on."[56] The next several days were uneventful, with 1st Sgt. Walter Dundon recording the same entry each day: "Fine voyage."[57] The soldiers, though, were not satisfied with their "NR" patches. Corporal Henry Duff (Co. I) reminisced, "We ... were proud of our new insignia [but] ... it wasn't enough.... We were issued new helmets after our arrival in Brest ... so we decided to paint our helmets white." Duff continued, "We went all over the ship collecting the helmets and took them to a central part of the ship ... and we slopped white paint on them. We ... had a stencil made by the sailors on their stencil machine in the bosom locker, and we daubed RUSSIA across the top [of the helmets] in blue paint."[58]

On June 30, 1919, the *Von Steuben* entered Hoboken, New Jersey's harbor, to the cheers of the happy Polar Bears. Major J. Brooks Nichols, commanding the men from the six 339th Infantry companies, signed the *Von Steuben*'s "Landing Return" transport forms and summed up the trip, "Food very good. Sanitation excellent, accommodations good. No serious sickness—No men for hospital—No deaths—Splendid weather during trip."[59] A *Detroit Free Press* reporter, who had accompanied a reception delegation from Detroit, wrote, "The welcoming committee hoisted an enormous sign ... [and] yelled they wanted the boys back in the city, 'where life is worth living' as soon as possible, while the returning cries from the 339th boys were, 'No more Bolos for us' and 'What we want is some real blown-in-the-bottle American grub'!"[60]

The Polar Bears marched off the *Von Steuben*, "bringing with them strapped to their army packs ... [their] white enameled helmets, and wearing on their right coast sleeves a queer looking black 'NR'... and were taken to Camp Merritt, NJ."[61] They were in-processed at Camp Merritt and billeted for the night. That evening, recruiters moved through the soldiers, trying to get these veterans to re-enlist—they met with little success. Members of the American Legion, a service organization that had been established to support American veterans, as well as advocating patriotism and promoting national security, did much better because one of the organization's policies included suppressing bolshevism in the United States. A *Detroit Free Press* reporter recorded, "Having had plenty of experience with the Russian type of Reds, these veterans of the 339th infantry have decided to join the American Legion en masse.... Major J. Brooks Nichols ... explained to all the American veterans, by platoons, that one of the platforms of the American Legion was to stamp out bolshevism in America. They vociferously informed him they wanted to join."[62]

The Polar Bears loaded onto trains on July 2, 1919, knowing their next stop would be Detroit. They arrived early on July 4, 1919, and Detroit's mayor, Frank Couzens, climbed aboard the train and informed Maj. Nichols that the state of Michigan had voted to give all of her soldiers a cash bonus of $15 for each month they had served.[63] He planned to escort the Polar Bears to Belle Isle, where a tremendous welcome home celebration was planned, but a large crowd had assembled at the Michigan Central Station. A Detroit reporter noted, "Michigan

19. Homeward Bound 173

The Polar Bears celebrated with their families at Belle Isle on July 4, 1919 (*The Detroit Free Press*, July 4, 1919).

Central Station is packed with relatives, [and] friends of Detroit's Own.... Refreshments are overlooked by the boys as they rush to outstretched arms of loved ones."[64] Eventually, though, the 339th did make its way to Belle Isle and the celebrations commenced. What followed next was pandemonium: joy, elation, and jubilation as loved ones hugged and kissed, as families clutched their returning boys, amid screams of pleasure and floods of blissful tears. One rifleman, overcome by all the emotion, merely remembered, "The first of the Polar Bears to return to Detroit were welcomed on Belle Isle with a parade and a chicken dinner."[65]

Sadly, not all of the tears were joyous; in a few cases, tragedy cut deeply among the waiting families. The *Detroit Free Press* covered one such family: "At 7 o'clock Wednesday morning, Mr. and Mrs. Collins rode to Roosevelt park and found the tent marked 'Company H.' Their son, Corporal Earl W. Collins ... was coming home. They sat side by side upon a bench and just waited. Earl would find them all right, and then they would all go home and mother would get a fine dinner, such as Earl hadn't eaten in months. And so, they waited. Hours went by and no trains came. Then finally a train came in and soldiers began to appear. The Collins' saw the frantic hugging, and the tears of happy women. Earl was not in that group." The article continued, "Another train came, more greetings, more soldiers, but no Earl. Still the couple waited for they heard there was another train and surely he was on that. They had heard he was wounded ... they heard he was coming in the last contingent of the 339th, so they waited. More soldiers came, big, brown boys like their Earl, met their folks and went away. Something was wrong. Somebody said the last train had come." The *Detroit Free Press* story added, "They timidly asked a question. This question traveled from mouth to mouth, and reached a Red Cross worker. The worker went away to find out about Earl. He asked a member of Company 'H' if Corporal Earl W. Collins had come with the outfit. The private looked surprised, 'Why no,' he said hesitating, 'he didn't come. He was captured by the Bolos and died in a hospital in Moscow.' 'The parents are waiting in the tent for him. Will you tell them please?' asked the Red Cross worker. 'Gosh Lady, I hate to do it,' the soldier said, 'but I will.' He broke the news as gently as he could. Mr. Collins half rose from his seat and, with a gasp, toppled over unconscious. Mother Collins was the stronger. She cried piteously, the stifling, heart-breaking sobs of a broken mother. Mr. Collins revived quickly and together they rode in a Red Cross car back [to a] home that would never be the same again."[66]

The soldiers were eventually rounded up and herded back onto the trains—their next destination, Camp Custer. Here, they handed in their equipment, received their final pay, and on July 7, 1919, were discharged. The Polar Bears were once again civilians, and all agreed with Pvt. Fred Kooyers (Co. E), who stated, "[I was] just glad to get home."[67] However, when the veterans did return to their homes, their Russian experiences stayed with them. One soldier remarked, "The first thing my mother said to me, 'Where'd you get your white hair?'" and another noted, "When I came out of the army, Jean, my wife, said to me, 'Mike, you're entirely different than when you went in the service.'"[68]

The Polar Bears, once returned to their families, began to consider their past year's experience. Many, when they compared their happenings against what their neighbors had experienced, they came away wondering if they had been short-changed. James Siplon remarked, "I wouldn't take a million dollars for the experience that I had, but I wouldn't take a million dollars to go over it again." He also grumbled, "We had no business [being] over there."[69] Floyd Lewis stated, "It's certainly sorry that we got involved in something that was more or less on the side, and still lost a lot of good men."[70] Harry Costello's comment may have summed up what many felt when he said, "Officers and men returning to the United States from their campaign in Russia against Bolsheviki [sic] have been forced to the conclusion ... that they did not receive a square deal."[71] And finally, Rudolph Marxer, and other Polar Bears returning to work, encountered people who did not understand their northern Russian circumstance. Marxer complained, "[People would ask,] 'what the hell was you doing up there?' Everybody wanted to know. And they're still asking.... I didn't know what to tell them.... It made [me] feel that, God, [I'd] wasted a couple years of [my] life." He continued, "When I got home ... looking for a job ... they said, 'Well, you must have been in prison. Everybody's been home here a year now.' I got that thrown in my face more than once—'Where the hell was you?' ... I says, 'I was up in Russia.' What the hell did [I] do wrong?"[72]

Chapter 20

Bringing Home the Fallen

June 14, 1919: First Lieutenant Clarence "C.J." Primm watched as two transport ships steamed out of the harbor and headed away from Archangel. The transport ships, the *Porto* and the *Menominee,* held the remaining soldiers of the 339th Infantry, nearly 2,300 troops, plus Red Cross workers, YMCA personnel, and, finally, the man who said he would be the last American to leave Russia, Col. George E. Stewart.[1] Lieutenant Primm had talked with some of the 339th's captains and lieutenants the night before, and these departing officers, knowing Primm would actually be one of the last to leave, wished him well. They also let Primm know their troops were still puzzled by this entire northern Russian experience. One officer had remarked, "Not a soldier knew, not even vaguely, why he had fought or why he was going now, and why his comrades were left behind."[2]

C.J. Primm was not the last American remaining in Archangel; there were nearly 1,500 Americans still in the area. But he was the lone

First Lieutenant Clarence "C.J." Primm was one of the last Americans to leave North Russia (Carol Primm and Peter Stuntz Collection).

member of the 339th. Primm, who had acquired fluency in speaking Russian, was now overseeing the removal of the regiment's dead. The lieutenant did not know how to dig up the fallen soldiers' remains, nor did he know what to do with the bodies once they had been exhumed. But Gen. Richardson had informed him a Graves Registration Service unit would soon be arriving. Primm's job would be to liaison between the G.R.S. team and the Russians. The G.R.S. group had not arrived as of yet; thus, in the meantime, Primm was helping Gen. Richardson and his staff pack up their records in preparation for their departure. Primm wrote, "The General and reduced Staff will remain here a short time at least, the last of the much besobbed troops being on their way this week."[3]

More Americans left in the next few days, a small collection of headquarters staff members aboard the *Quilpue* on June 25, 1919, and a large group of nearly 750 American soldiers, this batch mainly troops from the 310th Engineers, who left Archangel aboard the *Steigerwald* on June 27.[4] Primm longingly watched each ship leave, but for now, he was at the beck and call of Gen. Richardson, and he had been given a job to complete. Primm noted, "The General said yesterday ... he wants the officers to take little trips out among the villages when possible.... I expect to have quite a bit of that in connection with the collection of our dead." The lieutenant added, "The General's plan ... [is to] help maintain local Russian morale, as well as give some of the officers who came with him a chance to see what sort of country is tributary to [Archangel]."[5]

The Allies' withdrawal depended upon their White Russian allies being able to take over the responsibility of defending themselves. The British high command believed it had bolstered the Whites enough to enable them to assume all military operations, with one officer declaring, "There is therefore reasonable hope that the whole of this North Russian situation may be placed upon a purely Russian basis."[6] General Richardson, though, had little faith in the Whites, and was doing all he could to extract every American from North Russia while British soldiers still held the battle lines.

General Ironside concluded the best way to bolster the Allies' position involved knocking the Bolsheviks backward and forcing them onto the defensive. He mustered British troops and White Russian forces on three fronts: on the left flank—to clear the Bolos from Pinega; in the center—a major assault to capture the Dvina River city of Kotlas; and on the right (the Archangel-Vologda RR)—for a strike southward to take the Bolshevik base of operations at Plesetskaya. General Ironside believed if these three objectives could be obtained, the British would be able to withdraw from Russia without problems. He expected this plan to work, as he had at his command Scottish troops who had just arrived to reinforce the British forces, and by the end of June 1919, nearly 22,000 British-trained White Russian soldiers. The British/White Russian campaign began at that time, and for the first week, all three fronts realized some success. Unfortunately, not long after that, the advances bogged down, far from their objectives. Then, the situation crumbled. On July 7, 1919, two companies of a Slavo-British Legion positioned on the Dvina River mutinied. They murdered three British officers and wounded two more. The mutiny was suppressed by nearby British forces and, following a court martial, the leaders of the mutiny were executed.[7] Nonetheless, this mutiny foretold of more problems to come.

The American Graves Registration Service team arrived on July 12, 1919, causing Lt. Primm to write, "The Graves Registration Service, from France ... consisted of one officer and seven men to be able to collect the bodies of all American dead in North Russia, prepare them for transportation in metallic caskets hermetically sealed, and have all this done in a few weeks." Primm, in frustration, also added, "The little G.R.S. detachment arrived in Archangel with no supplies or equipment for their job except a typewriter and a box of blank forms to be filled in. No spades or shovels, no embalming facilities or materials, coffins, [and] no transport. [They had] no knowledge of Russian, Russians, or Russia! And a majority of our dead were scattered out over 1,200 miles of lines of communication, some of which had been seized by enemy forces after the withdrawal of the Americans."[8]

However, when Primm met the lieutenant in charge of the G.R.S. team, he was impressed. He recorded in a letter home, "Lt. Conway of the Graves Registration Service arrived from France ... and so the prospects of my leaving here in a few weeks are brightening."[9] Second Lieutenant Michael V. Conway was a talented officer who led an experienced group of NCOs and enlisted men. The American Graves Registration Service had become efficient at locating America's dead, identifying the fallen, and processing the bodies for shipment back to the United States. The G.R.S., by mid–1919, had 318,000 men employed in this grim duty, dealing with America's 117,000 dead.[10] These troops worked fastidiously at their task, and, as their orders detailed, "no grave was considered fully reported until the G.R.S. officer ... had visited the grave [and] was reasonably satisfied to the [dead soldier's] identity, and had affixed a plate bearing the letters 'GRS' [on it] ... thereby indicating acceptance."[11] This was a gruesome mission, but made easier than in past wars because, by March 1918, American soldiers were required to wear "two aluminum identification tags, each the size of a silver Half dollar, and of suitable thickness, stamped with [the soldier's] name, rank, regiment ... and serial number."[12]

Lieutenant Conway assembled his team, which began work at Archangel's Allied Cemetery. He also assigned a small team to accompany Clarence Primm, who volunteered to guide them to the American dead buried near Chekuevo. Primm's little group took the train to Obozerskaya and from there hiked the forty miles to Chekuevo. They arrived in Chekuevo and found the British and White Russian soldiers in turmoil. Lieutenant Primm, on July 19, 1919, recorded, "I went to the office of Col. Andrews [British] in Chekuevo at 9:45 o'clock to arrange matters.... The Colonel ... appeared more excited and nervous than I had ever seen him ... [because] a small town had just been taken [from] our troops. He then pointed out to us on the large campaign map the situation of this town, and then in anger ... exclaim[ed], 'There's where that damned company was.'" Primm continued, "This was the first intimation I had that anything was wrong. I do not know what Col. Andrews knew or suspected concerning the mutiny at Eusolia, or its effect at Chekuevo. Certainly he must have thought it grave."[13]

Primm's team discovered conditions were such they would not be able to retrieve their American dead. He wrote, "My billet was in Pyantino, about half a verst across the field from Chekuevo. My assistant asked permission to see a friend in a neighboring house for a moment, and returned directly somewhat excited, to inform me that it was impossible to go to Chekuevo.... He indicated to me the troops collected in the street ... were on their way to Chekuevo to arrest the Russian and British staffs, having already arrested their own officers." Primm added, "I believe the few troops in Chekuevo were in cooperation with the mutineers.... I ventured out a moment later.... One of my best Russian friends, a Sergeant Major ... advised me to return to my room at once, which I did."[14] The Yanks remained in their quarters for the rest of the day; meanwhile the mutineers consolidated their power over the troops loyal to the Allies. Lieutenant Primm, the next morning, recorded, "I was awakened about five o'clock by the sound of firing ... when the executions occurred ... ten Russian officers, two soldiers, and the regimental priest."[15]

These executions ended any resistance by the White Russians, and with that, Bolshevik soldiers moved into Chekuevo. A few White Russian soldiers fled, but, for the most part, their troops were not troubled by the incoming Bolos. Lieutenant Primm wrote, "Bolo Commissars, with [a] few troops, arrived on horseback early.... All through the day detachments of Bolos, with baggage on *telyegas* (four-wheeled carts) kept streaming by.... They fraternized very freely with the North Russian troops."[16] The Americans were trapped inside their houses; they did not venture outside as they watched the Reds rounding up Allied soldiers. Lieutenant Primm met with the Bolo Commissars, trying to convince them the Yanks were neutral and needed to leave. On July 23, 1919, he noted, "At four o'clock I was told I could go to Onega [and take] a boat sailing in an hour ... on which I could go to Archangel."[17]

The Americans were not granted permission to leave, and the frustrated Lt. Primm scribbled into his journal, "We are still here, and stirring times are here too.... All I can say is that if the Allies do not get in with both feet and stamp out armed Bolshevism soon, the peril of 'German Kultur' will fade into insignificance beside the world menace that is now crystallizing." He continued, grumbling about the Allies' stance, "Politicians may tell you that we are not at war with the Bolos ... but I say that [the Bolos] are at war against all law and order except the law of rape and plunder at the will of the lowest class, backed by arms and enforced against a great unarmed populace."[18] Indeed, Clarence Primm had little respect for the common Bolshevik soldier. He described their barbarities in a letter: "A village that I know was occupied by the Bolos. They raped all the women, killed some inhabitants, and carried away thirty of the women with them ... and as per usual, everything of use was taken if wanted, and much was broken and befouled." The lieutenant summed up his criticisms of the situation, writing, "Any action whatsoever that even implies the right of the Bolshevik movement to exist, as it now constitutes itself, is an insult to civilization and a direct blow at its fundamentals."[19]

Eventually the Americans were granted permission to leave Chekuevo, and they hustled down the river to Onega. Unfortunately, they arrived to discover the steamboat bound for Archangel was already gone. Primm resolutely applied for permission to march back to Obozerskaya, and after a lengthy meeting, received approval to return to Chekuevo. The Americans arrived back at Chekuevo just in time to witness further Bolo depravations. Primm observed, "[I] returned to Chekuevo just too late to see Col. Andrews, before his removal, with all other

British personnel to the south."[20] The doughboys retreated to their billets, seeking shelter from the calamities taking place. But again, the lieutenant braved the hazards to pester the Red leadership, demanding a route back to Archangel. He growled, "[I] besieged the various Bolo authorities for permission to get through to Archangel [and was] always met with the same suave excuse that some other authority who would come in a day or two [who] would have to pass on that."[21] He eventually wrote in anger, "Circumstances are such that I cannot even guess when I shall leave here."[22]

Finally, on August 2, 1919, the stubborn officer's badgering of the Bolshevik leadership worked; they granted him his wish. He wrote, "[I] finally secured permission to make the trip to Archangel ... [I was] escorted blindfolded through the Bolshevik lines."[23] He and his team hustled east to Obozerskaya, arriving just as this city was being turned over to the Bolos. Primm learned the Allies' push to take positions south of verst 445 had met with failure. The Bolsheviks counterattacked and rolled over all of the blockhouse defensive systems the American engineers and riflemen of Companies I and M had constructed, and now, in early August 1919, the Reds were mopping up the final White Russian units around Obozerskaya. General William Ironside was forced to write, "It was clear that we had failed to create a reliable Russian Army."[24]

Two days later, August 4, 1919, and safely back in Archangel, Lt. Primm evaluated the G.R.S.'s progress. He shook his head in dismay, especially when he learned the Russian prisoners who were being used to dig up the graves in Archangel had revolted. Primm wrote, "About my work there is little to be said. Owing to some conditions that have intervened, there may be much time lost in getting our dead out of North Russia."[25] Lieutenant Primm was informed that the teams sent to the Pinega area had returned, bringing with them only a few coffins. He remarked, "I sent the Graves Registration Unit out for what should [have been] a three-week trip.... Already I have a wire that indicates that their inexperience with this style of country and people is causing (to them) discouraging difficulty."[26] The young officer groused, "I shall be assisting at [this] job until all are removed or until General Pershing decides that the work shall be abandoned."[27]

Meanwhile, the Americans continued to prepare for final withdrawal. General Wilds Richardson closed down the American Expedition's headquarters and turned it over to the British. Clarence Primm wrote, "We moved our office into another building not far from the former headquarters. Less rent, and a British General wanted our larger place anyway. We only use three rooms now for office space, instead of a whole floor."[28] General Richardson called Lt. Primm into his office and praised the young officer, saying, "I wish to express to you my appreciation of the efficient services rendered ... by you ... [and] your voluntary offer to remain behind to assist in completing the work of transfer of the American soldier and sailor dead from North Russian soil to their home country."[29] C.J. Primm came away from the meeting, recalling, "he asked me to stick around town because of the numerous little things that I have to look out for—not that any one or all of them are especially hard, but because I have the details ready in my noodle and delays might occur in some matters if I were away."[30]

Caskets containing American soldiers who died in Russia, arrayed in Hoboken (*New York Tribune*, November 23, 1919).

General Wilds Richardson and his staff boarded the transport ship *Kalyan* and on August 23, 1919, left Archangel. Lieutenant Primm, Lt. Conway, his team, and a small group of other Americans were all that remained in Archangel.[31] A few days later, the group from the United States Embassy, consisting of eight officers and forty-eight enlisted men, left on the transport ship *Kildoman Castle*, forcing Primm to say, "there [are] only two officers of the A.E.F. here—Lt. Conway and myself."[32] The two lieutenants worked feverishly, trying to get as many caskets prepared for travel. They also made alternate plans for escape, should Archangel fall before they had completed their mission. Lieutenant Primm recorded, "[I] filled out papers applying for an emergency passport.... This is in case I get hung up here after all the State Department officials are gone, and [I] have to go out by some roundabout route."[33]

Finally, by late September 1919, there was nothing else Primm and Conway could accomplish. They knew there were over a hundred American dead buried in locations now controlled by the Bolsheviks. Primm had attempted to gain permission to repatriate the 339th's dead, but the Bolsheviks refused his petitions for entry into their areas. Lieutenant Primm and Conway also watched as more and more White Russian defenses collapsed, further endangering Archangel's existence as a free city. It was time to leave. After receiving permission from the American high command, they loaded over one hundred American dead aboard the transport ship *Czar* and on September 30, 1919, left Archangel, heading for Antwerp, Belgium.[34] On October 10, 1919, the last remaining Americans left Archangel, ending America's presence in the northern Russian region.[35]

The *Czar* landed in Antwerp, and here Lt. Primm and Conway turned the coffins over to the Graves Registration Service for final processing. Clarence Primm rested, turned in his Russian wardrobe and equipment, put on a fine dress uniform, and enjoyed the comforts that Europe had to offer. On October 15, 1919, he oversaw the loading of the caskets onto the U.S.S. *Pocahontas*, and the next day, the ship steamed away, heading for Brest, France. The caskets were unloaded at Brest, with Lt. Primm remaining with the Polar Bear dead as their escort. He stayed in France until the caskets could be loaded aboard the funeral ship the *Lake Drago*. This solemn ship left Brest in mid–November 1919, heading for Hoboken, New Jersey. The *Manitowoc Herald*, on November 18, 1919, announced, "[Lt.] C.J. Primm, of this city, who is on his way home from Russia where he was stationed with the American forces, will land at Hoboken on Thursday of this week … [aboard] the [funeral ship, *Lake Drago*] … Primm is in charge of 139 bodies of American soldiers who lost their lives in Russia and whose remains are being sent home."[36] The *Lake Drago* arrived in Hoboken on November 20, 1919. The *New York Herald* reported, "The coffins were removed from the ship as soon as she had been made fast and were then arranged on the pier, each coffin draped with an American flag."[37]

The families of the dead soldiers had been notified of their arrival in Hoboken and were given the choice of determining their final destinations. Some families opted to immediately pick up their fallen sons. Thus, on November 26, 1919, seventy caskets were put aboard a train heading for Detroit. The Michigan Central Railroad delivered the caskets to Detroit two days later, where, in a somber ceremony, the honored dead were received. Then, following the military rites, the soldiers' remains were conveyed to their families, who took them home to local cemeteries. One such casket, the one bearing Pvt. Homer Wing (Co. A, 310th Engineers), was taken to his home in Rochester, Michigan. The Rochester newspaper reported, "Schools and businesses were closed as the American Legion, the Red Cross, and 225 school children led a solemn funeral procession through town to Mount Avon Cemetery, where Homer Wing was, at last, laid to rest."[38]

Clarence Primm returned to his wife and family but did not seek a discharge. Instead, he remained in the military as a reserve officer and was eventually stationed at Camp Custer and Fort Sheridan, where he worked as a publicity officer. Primm's duties kept him involved in communications, and by 1929 (and now a captain), he was in charge of publishing the military's newspaper, *The Soldier*. By now, the veterans of the 339th Infantry, and the other units that had been sent to Russia, had banded together and formed the Polar Bear Association. The men in this organization had voted J. Brooks Nichols as their first president. Nichols was followed by John Cudahy and Joel Moore as presidents, and then, in 1928, Company M's old first sergeant, Walter Dundon, was elected.

Walter Dundon, now thirty-nine years old and a division manager for a real estate/financing company, along with four other veterans of North Russia, had gathered funding, permissions, and travel documents to enter Soviet Russia to retrieve their missing comrades. This had been a monumental task, as described by Dundon: "Through contacts with the Federal Government, the State of Michigan and the city of Detroit, I raised about a quarter of a million dollars.... I was advised that these funds could not be used until diplomatic relations were established with Russia." He continued, "No diplomatic relations existed between the United States and Russia at that time. [I] was able to get the necessary visas through the unofficial Russian ambassador to Washington whose life had been saved by a member of the American forces in Siberia during the fighting there in 1918–19."[39]

Though the legal and financial technicalities were difficult, the actual finding of the buried soldiers was going to be even more challenging. A Michigan newspaper recorded, "Most of the Polar Bears sleep singly or in small groups—one here, a pair in the next town and perhaps four or five in the edge of the forest five miles away."[40] Polar Bear Association President Dundon remarked, "I had contacted a number of former members of the American North Russian Expedition seeking information as to burial locations. Many responded with maps and rough drawings of the various locations. The information differed widely because of the trying conditions under which the burials were made and the time that had elapsed."[41]

The five-man commission left Detroit on July 17, 1929, and arrived in Berlin eleven days later. From here, the group broke up into two teams, with Dundon traveling with Michael J. McCulla (Co. G veteran), the two going by airplane, while the other three were to take trains to Russia. Walter Dundon and Michael McCulla left Berlin, their flight heading for Moscow. However, severe weather forced the plane to consume all of its fuel, requiring the pilot to make an emergency landing at a Soviet military base. Dundon recalled, "We were immediately surrounded by Russian soldiers with fixed bayonets and forbidden to either look out the windows or leave the plane. Later they ordered us out of the plane, lined us up, searched us, and had us stand ... [near] the plane, with their fixed bayonets too close to our stomachs for comfort. Finally a horse drawn tank came out, fueled the plane, and we took off for [Moscow]." The second team also arrived in Moscow, and on August 9, 1929, they all boarded a train for Archangel. Dundon noted, "The weather was hot and the smoke from the wood burning locomotive rolled into the open windows. After an all night ride we looked like black-faced comedians."[42]

Once in Archangel, the commission met up with a small group from the Veterans of Foreign Wars as well as a Graves Registration Service team. Then, they began their search for American graves. Walter Dundon wrote, "We were required to get permission for each trip from the base and to register in and out of towns. Food was scarce, especially away from our base, and we tried to pack all [our] food with us."[43] The Soviets, not wanting people to know there were Americans roaming their country, required them to "pack away their good clothes ...

and outfit themselves in Russian peasant garb." One of the team members wrote, "When outfitted in the native costumes [we] resembled Bolshevik soldiers ... attired in baggy pants and blouses, long coats with a belt around the middle, calf-length boots and fur caps."[44]

The team traveled by train, riverboat, horseback, cart, or hiking long distances, moving from location to location, searching out the ten-year-old grave sites. For the forty-year-old veterans, these conditions were expected, though trying. For the G.R.S. team, which was composed of young soldiers, the experience was completely new. One remarked, "We climbed cliffs, scrambled over sand dunes and waded knee-deep through marshes and swamps."[45] Walter Dundon, his experiences bringing back old memories, recalled, "The Russian officials and the populace were very cooperative, though one had to get used to their slow way of doing business.... [We discovered] Tea was a good barter item and would often be accepted rather than cash for help in searching for the bodies." He also noted, "[The] Natives often remarked, 'What a wonderful place America must be to send men away over here for dead people.'" Their accommodations were rough; they stayed in peasant homes, sleeping on the floor, and sharing their rations with the homeowners. Dundon wrote, "The most difficult part of more than two months in the woods and villages was lack of transportation, food, and sanitation. Accommodations away from the base were poor. Sleeping on the floors of peasant homes, waking up dirty and hungry is difficult to get used to." He added, "The Russian peasants were very friendly and cooperative and willing to share whatever they could."[46]

The Americans located the graves, one by one, with a G.R.S. soldier stating, "We found remains in swamps, in deserted cemeteries along the line of our trenches that still remained, in front yards of peasant houses, along the sides of cliffs, and some whose graves were covered with a forest of underbrush."[47] Another noted, "We had been searching vainly for the graves ... after searching for days I found a row of twenty-three graves, all bearing small crude wooden crosses." The searcher continued, "Only one still bore the name of the veteran buried beneath, and this one was located at the very edge of the cemetery. I examined the cross and read the name of Herbert S. Kistler [Co. I]. I then knew that the twenty-three graves were the graves of Americans."[48]

The Americans hired locals to exhume the bodies. This activity always proved to be a source of great interest for the Russia peasants. Dundon remarked, "When digging for bodies, people seemed to come from nowhere." He did confess, "On one occasion a body was not where my information said it should be, and one man in the crowd of onlookers volunteers to show me where the body was. The next day he unearthed the body about a mile from where my information said it was."[49] Sadly, the remains being exhumed were usually in poor condition. A soldier exclaimed, "Ten years of alternating heat, rain, and deep freeze left very little of the men underground. Nothing remained ... but skeleton bones and the skull, with here and there small pieces of decayed flesh attached to joints."[50] Another team member exclaimed, "Oh, it was a hell of a job."[51]

Ultimately, the commission located, exhumed and identified, by dog tags, dental records, or location, eighty-six American soldiers, including five from Company I and three from Company M. A Michigan newspaper summed up their experience, reporting, "Guided by their faded recollections of a ... pine covered country and maps sketched 10 years ago by cold-stiffened fingers, five Michigan men ... seek the scatter resting places of.... American soldiers who were killed there a decade ago."[52]

Each set of remains was washed in Lysol, wrapped in linen and placed within zinc boxes, a circumstance hampered by the fact the Soviets did not have the proper materials for these constructions. The Americans, knowing they did not have much time before the northern Russian winter set in, cobbled together their own boxes. One team member recorded, "Time was so short that we had to buy metal and construct the zinc coffins [ourselves]."[53] The zinc boxes were built and filled with the identified remains, then loaded aboard a train bound for Leningrad, and from there, on October 27, 1929, a Soviet steamer pulled out of port, heading for Le Havre, France. Here, the remains were put inside regulation military caskets, the zinc boxes being wrapped in layers of wool blankets. A joint American-French memorial service was held November 18, 1929, before eleven of the caskets were interred in a U.S. military cemetery in France, an action done at the request of the dead soldiers' family members.

The remaining caskets were loaded onto the S.S. *President Roosevelt*, which left Le Havre in late November 1929 and arrived in Hoboken, New Jersey, on November 28, 1929. The *Indianapolis News* proclaimed, "The bodies of seventy-[four] United States soldiers ... came back to the homeland today—to half-staffed flags, a seventeen gun salute and funeral music."[54] Seventeen remains were immediately shipped to relatives in various states for private burial, and three sent to Arlington National Cemetery. The final fifty-six were put aboard a special nine-coach funeral train draped with black crepe to make the journey to Detroit. The train stopped in every city and town of any size along the way, where "Taps" was played at each station, as nothing like this had ever been done since the train bearing President Lincoln's body made its journey from Washington, D.C., to Illinois in 1865.

The funeral train reached Detroit December 1, 1929, to be met by thousands of mourners who had gathered in front of Detroit's Union Station, their coats white from falling snow. The *New York Times* reported, "Crowds lined Ford Street, braving the snow and cold to pay tribute to the last remnants of the [339th Infantry]."[55] It was an experience some never forgot. One VFW team member who had gone to Russia to help retrieve the fallen recalled, "As the mothers and fathers of these heroes stood silently in the bleak snow-driven cold at Detroit, our responsibilities in discharging a most arduous task were again emphasized with a deeper and more penetrating significance."[56] Once the city hall ceremony ended, 3,500 members of the VFW and allied organizations accompanied the flag-covered hearses as they slowly worked their way to the White Chapel Cemetery. Here, the caskets were placed within the Temple of Memories, to await Memorial Day 1930.

Finally, on May 30, 1930, Memorial Day, these fifty-six Polar Bears were finally laid to rest in plots surrounding a newly chiseled, marble polar bear. This

The ceremony on May 30, 1930, formally interred 56 members of the Polar Bear Regiment (Michigan Heroes' Museum).

Polar Bear memorial was described by a reporter: "[It was of] black Swedish granite supporting a large white Georgia marble Polar Bear. Under the front paws of the bear lies a cross and a helmet." The inscription contains the words of Stephen Decatur: "Our Country, in her intercourse with foreign nations, may she always be in the right; but our Country, right or wrong."[57] Following the solemn ceremony, Walter Dundon recalled, "I was approached by a small, elderly lady, who asked if I was the man who recovered her son's body. I told her I had recovered all the bodies. She asked me to accompany her to a certain casket and asked, 'Can you tell me for sure that my son's body lies inside?' I said, 'Lady, I do not know your name but I can tell you that the name on that box is the name of the person who lies inside it.' She pulled my head down and kissed me through her tears and said, 'This is the first time in thirteen years my heart is at rest.'"[58]

Chapter Notes

Chapter 1

1. Primm, Carol, and Stuntz, Pete (ed.), *Polar Bear Tales*, 2009.
2. *Alumni Directory: The University of Chicago*, 1919, 65.
3. Jones, Frank, et al., *Souvenir: Camp Custer*, 1918, 3.
4. Jones, Frank, et al., *Souvenir: Camp Custer*, 1918, 4.
5. Lewis, Charles E., "Strength of Regiment," Historical File of the U.S. Expeditionary Force, North Russia, 1918–19. National Archives, 30 April 1919.
6. Petropoulos, George, Polar Bear Oral History Project (PBOHP), 1978.
7. Kemperman, Radus, PBOHP, 23 June 1977.
8. Grahek, Matthew, in Ward, William, *A Well Kept Secret*, 2010.
9. Hershberger, Russell, PBOHP, 6 June 1977. Siplon, James, PBOHP, 6 July 1977.
10. Holmes-Greeley, Paula. "After 100 Years, CWC Remains Critical to Muskegon's Manufacturing Base," www.mlive.com, 22 August 2008.
11. Siplon, James F., PBOHP, 6 July 1977.
12. Siplon, James F., WWI Draft Registration Card, 5 June 1917.
13. Grobbel, Clement, "Letters," 27 June 1918.
14. Anderson, Godfrey, *A Michigan Polar Bear Confronts the Bolsheviks: A War Memoir*, 2010, 28.
15. Kooyers, Fred, *Diary*, George Albers Papers, 1918–19, University of Michigan Bentley Historical Library (UMBHL), 27 May 1918.
16. Anderson Godfrey, *A Michigan Polar Bear*, 2010, 28–9.
17. Lewis, Alfred, PBOHP, 29 June 1977.
18. Grace, Charles, PBOHP, 14 June 1977.
19. Kooyers, Fred, *Diary*, 30 May 1918.
20. Kooyers, Fred, *Diary*, 1 June 1918.
21. Kooyers, Fred, *Diary*, 2 June 1918.
22. Lewis, Alfred, PBOHP, 29 June 1977.
23. Salchow, Hugo, PBOHP, n.d.
24. Marxer, Rudolph, PBOHP, 16 June 1977.
25. Anderson, Godfrey, *A Michigan Polar Bear*, 2010, 31.
26. Grace, Charles, PBOHP, 14 June 1977.
27. Kooyers, Fred, *Diary*, 30 May 1918.
28. Batz, Robert A. "Flint Man Fought Bolsheviks," *The Flint Journal*, 11 December 1966.
29. Zank, Richard, in Ward, William, *A Well Kept Secret*, 2010.
30. Lewis, Alfred, PBOHP, 29 June 1977.
31. Kooyers, Fred, *Diary*, 17–18 June 1918.
32. Kooyers, Fred, *Diary*, 18 June 1918.
33. Yohey, George, in Ward, William, *A Well Kept Secret*, 2010.
34. Willett, Robert L., *Russian Sideshow: America's Undeclared War, 1918–1920*, 2003, 121.
35. Siplon, James F. PBOHP, 6 July 1977. Willett, Robert L., *Russian Sideshow*, 2003, 60. U.S. 1920 Census. Primm, Carol, and Stuntz, Pete, *Polar Bear Tales*, 2009.
36. "Bulletins," U.S. Army in the World War, 1917–1919, Center of Military History, U.S. Army, 1992.
37. Kooyers, Fred, *Diary*, 31 May 1918.
38. Anderson Godfrey, *A Michigan Polar Bear*, 2010, 30.
39. Moore, Joel, et al., *The History of the American Expedition Fighting the Bolsheviks: Campaigning in North Russia*, 1920, 217.
40. Tremaine, Roy, Michigan Heroes Museum, 2018.
41. Carey, Donald, in Nelson, James C., *The Polar Bear Expedition*, 2019, 17.
42. Siplon, James F. PBOHP, 6 July 1977.
43. Lewis, Alfred, PBOHP, 29 June 1977.
44. Kooyers, Fred, *Diary*, 14 July 1918.

Chapter 2

1. "Lists of Outgoing Passengers, 1917–1938," U.S. Army World War I Transport Service, National Archives, 1918.
2. *The University of Wisconsin Alumni Directory*, 1849–1911, 1912.
3. Winslow, Horatio, *Rhymes and Meters: A Practical Guide for Versifiers*, 1909.
4. "The Pulp Magazine Project," www.pulpmags.org.

5. "The Pulp Magazine Project," www.pulpmags.org.
6. "Jane Burr (1882–1957)," www.laborarts.org.
7. Lewis, Floyd, PBOHP, 29 June 1977.
8. Anderson, Godfrey, *A Michigan Polar Bear*, 2010, 41.
9. Safer, Samuel, *The Flint Journal*, 11 December 1966.
10. Anderson, Godfrey, *A Michigan Polar Bear*, 2010, 41.
11. Dundon, Walter, in Moore, Joel, et al., *The History of the American Expedition*, 1920.
12. Kooyers, Fred, *Diary*, 16 July 1918.
13. Kooyers, Fred, *Diary*, 20 July 1918.
14. "Lists of Outgoing Passengers," U.S. Army WWI Transportation Service, 1918.
15. Dundon, Walter, in Moore, Joel, et al., *The History of the American Expedition*, 1920.
16. Kooyers, Fred, *Diary*, 20 July 1918.
17. Siplon, James F., PBOHP, 6 July 1977.
18. Anderson, Godfrey, *A Michigan Polar Bear*, 2010, 51.
19. Douma, Frank, *Diary*, Frank W. Douma Papers, UMBHL, 3 August 1918.
20. Anderson, Godfrey, *A Michigan Polar Bear*, 2010, 51.
21. Douma, Frank, *Diary*, 3 August 1918.
22. Dundon, Walter, in Moore, Joel, et al., *The History of the American Expedition*, 1920.
23. Dundon, Walter, in Moore, Joel, et al., *The History of the American Expedition*, 1920.
24. Willett, Robert L., *Russian Sideshow*, 2003, 19.
25. Anderson, Godfrey, *A Michigan Polar Bear*, 2010, 53.
26. Stoner, George, *The Diary of 1st Lt. George W. Stoner, Jr., Company M, 339th Infantry Regiment, 85th Division, U.S. Army*, 3 August 1918.
27. Douma, Frank, *Diary*, 4 August 1918.
28. Kooyers, Fred, *Diary*, 3 August 1918.
29. Douma, Frank, *Diary*, 4 August 1918.
30. Anderson, Godfrey, *A Michigan Polar Bear*, 2010, 53.
31. Dundon, Walter, in Moore, Joel, et al., *The History of the American Expedition*, 1920.
32. Douma, Frank, *Diary*, 6 August 1918.
33. Chambers, J.A., "Operations of the 339th Infantry Regiment in Russia," Historical Files of the U.S. Expeditionary Force, North Russia, 1918–19, 6 August 1918.
34. Siplon, James F., PBOHP, 6 Juyl 1977.
35. Anderson, Godfrey, *A Michigan Polar Bear*, 2010, 53.
36. Douma, Frank, *Diary*, 15 August 1918.
37. Kooyers, Fred, *Diary*, 15 August 1918.
38. Stoner, George, "The Diary of 1st Lt. George W. Stoner, Jr.," 8 August 1918.
39. "Chu Chin Chow," www.wikiwand.com, 3 May 1920.
40. Lewis, Floyd, PBOHP, 29 June 1977.
41. Colburn, Cleo, PBOHP, 17 June 1977.
42. Marxer, Rudolph, PBOHP, 16 June 1977. Douma, Frank, *Diary*, 12 August 1918.
43. Robbins, William B., "Letter," 7 October 1918.
44. Primm, Carol, and Stuntz, Pete, *Polar Bear Tales*, 2009.
45. Sarosiek, Jan, in Ward, William, *A Well Kept Secret*, 2010.
46. Dundon, Walter, in Moore, Joel, et al., *The History of the American Expedition*, 1920.
47. Costello, Harry, in Nelson, James C., *Polar Bear Expedition*, 2019.
48. Cudahy, John, in Nelson, James C., *Polar Bear Expedition*, 2019.
49. Peatling, John, in Ward, William, *A Well Kept Secret*, 2010.
50. Simmons, Christopher, "The Alleged Mutiny of Company 'I,'" Norwich University, 20 May 2010.
51. Carey, Donald, in Willett, Robert L., *Russian Sideshow*, 2003, 21.
52. Costello, Harry J., *Why Did We Go to Russia?* 1920, 13.
53. Moore, Joel R., et al., *The History of the American Expedition*, 1920, 218.
54. Bartels, Levi, PBOHP, 1978.
55. Slaugh, Albert, PBOHP, 12 June 1978.
56. Dundon, Walter, in Moore, Joel, et al., *The History of the American Expedition*, 1920.
57. Kooyers, Fred, *Diary*, 25 August 1918.
58. Barrett, Andrea, "Traveling Corpse: How an American Sergeant's Journey Through Frigid North Russia Inspired a Work of Historical Fiction," *The American Scholar*, Winter 2015.
59. Kooyers, Fred, *Diary*, 25 August 1918.
60. Stoner, George, "The Diary of 1st Lt. George W. Stoner, Jr.," 28 August 1918.

Chapter 3

1. "Stewart, George E.," *Registers of Officers Who Served in the U.S. Army*, 1918.
2. U.S. Census, 1940.
3. "Stewart, George E.," *Registers of Officers Who Served in the U.S. Army*, 1918.
4. Visher, Stephen S., "Noted on Typhoons," *Monthly Weather Review*, November 1922, 583–89.
5. "Stories of Sacrifice," Congressional Medal of Honor Society, www.cmohs.org, 2021.
6. Beers, Henry P., "U.S. Naval Forces in Northern Russia," November 1943.
7. Beers, Henry P., "U.S. Naval Forces in Northern Russia," November 1943.
8. Francis, David R., *Foreign Relations*, 12 March 1918.
9. Sauter, Joseph, in Ward, William, *A Well Kept Secret*, 2010.
10. Rowers, Will, *Detroit Free Press*, 12 February 1919.
11. Francis, David R., *Foreign Relations*, 7 July 1918.
12. "War Diary of the 16th Canadian Field,

Artillery," www.canadiangreatwarproject.com, 2010.
13. Siplon, James, PBOHP, 19776 July 1977.
14. Francis, David R., *Foreign Relations*, 7 July 1918.
15. Primm, Carol, and Stuntz, Pete, *Polar Bear Tales*, 2009, 6.
16. Cudahy, John, *Archangel: The American War with Russia*, 1924.
17. Moore, Joel, et al., *The History of the American Expedition*, 1920, 48.
18. Primm, Carol, and Stuntz, Pete, *Polar Bear Tales*, 2009, 6–7.
19. Lewis, Floyd, PBOHP, 29 June 1977.
20. Larsen, Alfred, PBOHP, 13 June 1977.
21. Moore, Joel, et al., *The History of the American Expedition*, 1920, 48, 51–2.
22. Moore, Joel, et al., *The History of the American Expedition*, 1920, 52.
23. Francis, David R., *Foreign Relations*, 5 August 1918.
24. Primm, Clarence, "Letters," in Primm, Carol, and Stuntz, Pete, *Polar Bear Tales*, 30 August 1918.
25. Larsen, Alfred, PBOHP, 13 June 1977.
26. Rudolph, Marxer, PBOHP, 16 June 1977.
27. Neft, Davis S., et al., *The Sports Encyclopedia: Baseball 2001*, 2001.
28. Anderson, Godfrey, *A Michigan Polar Bear*, 2010, 65.
29. Lewis, Floyd, PBOHP, 29 June 1977.
30. Kooyers, Fred, PBOHP, 13 June 1977.
31. Moore, Joel, et al., *The History of the American Expedition*, 1920, 15.
32. Rudolph, Marxer, PBOHP, 16 June 1977.
33. Lewis, Floyd, PBOHP, 29 June 1977.
34. Larsen, Alfred, PBOHP, 13 June 1977.
35. Slagh, Albert, PBOHP, 12 June 1978. Bartels, Levi, PBOHP, 1978.
36. Simpson, Charles, in Willett, Robert L., *Russian Sideshow*, 2003.
37. "New Archangel Plans Bring Up Fiasco of 1918," *Detroit News*, 1941.
38. Anderson, Godfrey, *A Michigan Polar Bear*, 2010, 65.

Chapter 4

1. Moore, Joel R., "Application for Examination." Polar Bear Stories: "Detroit's Own" Polar Bear Memorial Association, 2 May 1917.
2. *Great Falls Tribune*, Great Falls, MT, 26 September 1947.
3. Moore, Joel R., "Application for Examination," 2 May 1917. Moore, Joel, "HQ Citizens' Training Camp Notice," 7 May 1917. Moore, Joel R. "Appointments in Training Camp," 6 August 1917, Joel R. Moore Papers, UMBHL.
4. Primm, Carol, and Stuntz, Pete, *Polar Bear Tales*, 2009, 13.
5. Moore, Joel, et al., *The History of the American Expedition*, 1920, 53.
6. Baldwin, Robert C. "The Allied Military Expedition to North Russia: 1918–1919," June 1969.
7. David R. Francis, *Russia from the American Embassy, April 1916–November 1918*, 1921, 271.
8. "War Diary of Allied General Headquarters," Historical Files, 12 February 1919.
9. Willett, Robert L., *Russian Sideshow*, 2003, 13–14.
10. Baldwin, Robert C. "The Allied Military Expedition to North Russia: 1918–1919," June 1969.
11. Nelson, James C. *The Polar Bear Expedition*, 2019, 34–37.
12. Moore, Joel, et al., *The History of the American Expedition*, 1920, 53.
13. Anderson, Godfrey, *A Michigan Polar Bear*, 2010, 66.
14. Anderson, Godfrey, *A Michigan Polar Bear*, 2010, 69.
15. "U.S. Army Rifle Company (1917–1921)," www.battleorder.org, 2019.
16. Costello, Harry J., *Why Did We Go to Russia*, 1920, 15–16.
17. Primm, Carol, and Stuntz, Pete, *Polar Bear Tales*, 2009, 16.
18. Colburn, Cleo, "Letters from the Yanks," *Ann Arbor Observer*, 1918.
19. Dundon, Walter, in Moore, Joel, et al., *The History of the American Expedition*, 1920.
20. Batz, Robert L., "Flint Man Fought Bolsheviks," *The Flint Journal*, 11 December 1966.
21. Cudahy, John, *Archangel: The American War with Russia*, 1924.
22. Siplon, James, PBOHP, 6 July 1977.
23. Ryan, Charles, in Moore, Joel, et al., *The History of the American Expedition*, 1920, 42.
24. Cudahy, John, *Archangel: The American War with Russia*, 1924.
25. Colburn, Cleo, PBOHP, 17 June 1977.
26. Moore, Joel, et al., *The History of the American Expedition*, 1920, 19.
27. Willett, Robert L., *Russian Sideshow*, 2003, 32.
28. Siplon, James, PBOHP, 6 July 1977.
29. Cudahy, John, *Archangel: The American War with Russia*, 1924.
30. Colburn, Cleo, "Letters from the Yanks," n.d. Colburn, Cleo, PBOHP, 17 June 1977.
31. "Cows Milked Between Fires," *The Detroit Free Press*, 14 March 1919.
32. Moore, Joel, et al., *The History of the American Expedition*, 1920, 20.
33. Dundon, Walter, in Moore, Joel, et al., *The History of the American Expedition*, 1920.
34. Dundon, Walter, in Moore, Joel, et al., *The History of the American Expedition*, 1920.
35. Cudahy, John, *Archangel: The American War with Russia*, 1924, 87.
36. Willett, Robert L., *Russian Sideshow*, 2003, 33. Nelson, James C., *The Polar Bear Expedition*, 2019, 43.

37. Dundon, Walter, in Moore, Joel, et al., *The History of the American Expedition*, 1920.
38. Moore, Joel, *"M" Company: 339th Infantry in North Russia*, 1920.
39. Dundon, Walter, in Moore, Joel, et al., *The History of the American Expedition*, 1920.
40. Dundon, Walter, in Moore, Joel, et al., *The History of the American Expedition*, 1920.
41. Dundon, Walter, in Moore, Joel, et al., *The History of the American Expedition*, 1920.
42. Nelson, James C., *The Polar Bear Expedition*, 2019, 43.
43. Primm, Clarence, Letters, 8 September 1918.

Chapter 5

1. Dundon, Walter, in Moore, Joel, *"M" Company*, 1920.
2. Bolander, Andy, "A Polar Bear's Return to Russia," www.recordpatriot.com.
3. Dundon, Walter F., WWI Draft Registration Card, 5 June 1917.
4. "Mrs. Cecile Hager Dundun," *The Battle Creek Enquirer*, 9 May 1919.
5. Moore, Joel, *"M" Company*, 1920.
6. Salchow, Hugo, Oral History, UMBHL, n.d.
7. Siplon, James, PBOHP, 6 July 1977.
8. Hershberger, Russell, PBOHP, 20 June 1977.
9. Nelson, James C., *The Polar Bear Expedition*, 2019, 43.
10. Dundon, Walter, in Moore, Joel, *"M" Company*, 1920.
11. Colburn, Cleo, "Letters from the Yanks," 1918.
12. Colburn, Cleo, "Letters from the Yanks," 1918.
13. Moore, Joel, et al., *The History of the American Expedition*, 1920, 21.
14. Colburn, Cleo, "Letters from the Yanks," 1918.
15. Moore, Joel, et al., *The History of the American Expedition*, 1920, 21.
16. Colburn, Cleo, "Letters from the Yanks," 1918.
17. Dundon, Walter, in Moore, Joel, *"M" Company*, 1920.
18. Rotman, Martin, PBOHP, Project, 13 June 1978.
19. Moore, Joel, *"M" Company*, 1920.
20. Colburn, Cleo, "Letters from the Yanks," 1918.
21. Moore, Joel, *"M" Company*, 1920.
22. Stoner, George, "The Diary of 1st Lt. George W. Stoner, Jr.," 11 September 1918.
23. Colburn, Cleo, "Letters from the Yanks," 1918.
24. Moore, Joel, *"M" Company*, 1920.
25. Dundon, Walter, in Moore, Joel, *"M" Company*, 1920.
26. Dundon, Walter, in Moore, Joel, *"M" Company*, 1920.
27. May, Albert, in Gordon, Dennis, *Quartered in Hell: The Story of the American North Russian Expeditionary Force, 1918–1919*, 1982, 170.
28. Moore, Joel, et al., *The History of the American Expedition*, 1920, 22.
29. Moore, Joel, et al., *The History of the American Expedition*, 1920, 22.
30. May, Albert, in Gordon, Dennis, *Quartered in Hell*, 1982, 170.
31. May, Albert, in Gordon, Dennis, *Quartered in Hell*, 1982, 170.
32. Dundon, Walter, in Moore, Joel, *"M" Company*, 1920.
33. "The Wall of Valor Project," www.valor.militarytimes.com.
34. Colburn, Cleo, *Diary*, 16 September 1918.
35. Moore, Joel, et al., *The History of the American Expedition*, 1920, 299–300.
36. Jahns, Lewis E., "Field Order No. 1," 18 September 1918.
37. Moore, Joel, et al., *The History of the American Expedition*, 1920, 22.
38. Dundon, Walter, in Moore, Joel, *"M" Company*, 1920.
39. Moore, Joel, et al., *The History of the American Expedition*, 1920, 246.
40. Willett, Robert L., *Russian Sideshow*, 2003, 34.
41. Dundon, Walter, in Moore, Joel, *"M" Company*, 1920.

Chapter 6

1. "Large Industry Survived Years of Depression," *The Buffalo Courier*, 17 September 1905.
2. *The Railway Age*, 18 October 1901.
3. *New York Supplement Vol. 95*, 5 February 1906, 298–9.
4. *New York Supplement Vol. 95*, 5 February 1906, 300.
5. *New York Supplement Vol. 95*, 5 February 1906, 298.
6. Marquis, Albert N. (ed.), *Book of Detroiters*, 1914, 369.
7. Moran, Darby, "Historical Architecture of Grosse Point," www.highbiemaxon.com, 10 April 2018.
8. Costello, Harry J., "Why Did We Go to Russia?" *Detroit Free Press*, 27 July 1919.
9. *Detroit Free Press*, 27 July 1919.
10. Nelson, James C. *The Polar Bear Expedition*, 2019, 50.
11. Ironside, William, "Signal Platoon Wins Commendation," www.worldwar1gallery.com, 23 May 1919.
12. Cudahy, John, *Archangel: The American War with Russia*, 1924.
13. Dundon, Walter, in Moore, et al., *History of the American Expedition*, 1920.
14. Stoner, George, "The Diary of 1st Lt. George W. Stoner, Jr.," 24 September 1918.

15. Dundon, Walter, in Moore, et al., *History of the American Expedition*, 1920.
16. Moore, Joel, et al., *The History of the American Expedition*, 1920, 23.
17. Blackington, George, "History of the 339th Regiment of Infantry, 1917–1919," *The Polar Bear Club*, April 1926, 64.
18. Moore, Joel, et al., *The History of the American Expedition*, 1920, 23.
19. Young, Charles, "Report of Engagement," Historical Files of the U.S. Expeditionary Force, North Russia, 12 October 1918.
20. Nichols, J. Brooks, "Report of Engagement," Historical Files of the U.S. Expeditionary Force, North Russia, 30 September 1918.
21. Young, Charles, "Report of Engagement," Historical Files, 12 October 1918.
22. Moore, Joel, et al., *The History of the American Expedition*, 1920, 23.
23. May, Albert, in Gordon, Dennis, *Quartered in Hell*, 1982, 171.
24. Moore, Joel, et al., *The History of the American Expedition*, 1920, 23.
25. May, Albert, in Gordon, Dennis, *Quartered in Hell*, 1982, 171.
26. Cudahy, John, *Archangel: The American War with Russia*, 1924.
27. Moore, Joel, et al., *The History of the American Expedition*, 1920, 23.
28. Cudahy, John, *Archangel: The American War with Russia*, 1924, 90.
29. Siplon, James, PBOHP, 6 July 1977.
30. Moore, Joel, et al., *The History of the American Expedition*, 1920, 23.
31. Primm, Clarence, Letters, 2 October 1918.
32. Siplon, James, PBOHP, 6 July 1977.
33. Moore, Joel, et al., *The History of the American Expedition*, 1920, 24.
34. Colburn, Cleo, PBOHP, 17 June 1977.
35. Bonnell, Jay, "A Reminiscence of the Polar Bear Expedition," n.d.
36. May, Albert, in Gordon, Dennis, *Quartered in Hell*, 1982, 174.
37. Keith, Lawrence P. "Report of Engagement," Historical Files of the U.S. Expeditionary Force, North Russia, 1 October 1918.
38. Moore, Joel, et al., *The History of the American Expedition*, 1920, 24.
39. Cudahy, John, *Archangel: The American War with Russia*, 1924, 91.
40. Keith, Lawrence P. "Report of Engagement," Historical Files, 1 October 1918.
41. Young, Charles, "Report of Engagement," Historical Files, 12 October 1918.
42. Nichols, J. Brooks, "Report of Engagement," Historical Files, 30 September 1918.
43. Young, Charles, "Report of Engagement," Historical Files, 12 October 1918.
44. Young, Charles, "Report of Engagement," Historical Files, 12 October 1918.
45. Moore, Joel, et al., *The History of the American Expedition*, 1920, 24.
46. Keith, Lawrence P. "Report of Engagement," Historical Files, 1 October 1918.
47. Siplon, James, PBOHP, 6 July 1977.
48. Moore, Joel, *"M" Company*, 1920.
49. Moore, Joel, et al., *The History of the American Expedition*, 1920, 25.
50. Moore, Joel, et al., *The History of the American Expedition*, 1920, 25.
51. Moore, Joel, *"M" Company*, 1920.
52. Moore, Joel, *"M" Company*, 1920.
53. Moore, Joel, *"M" Company*, 1920.
54. Young, Charles, "Report of Engagement," Historical Files, 12 October 1918.
55. Moore, Joel, *"M" Company*, 1920.
56. Moore, Joel, *"M" Company*, 1920.
57. Murchie, Guy, Jr., "Tragedy at Archangel," *Chicago Sunday Times*, 26 February 1939.
58. Moore, Joel, et al., *The History of the American Expedition*, 1920, 25.
59. Moore, Joel, *"M" Company*, 1920.
60. Blackington, George, *The Polar Bear Club*, April 1926, 64.
61. Moore, Joel, et al., *The History of the American Expedition*, 1920, 25.
62. "Members of 339th Bitter at Britons," *Detroit Free Press*, 25 February 1919.

Chapter 7

1. Yopp, Herman, WWI Draft Registration Card, June 1917.
2. *Brief History of Divisions, U.S. Army, 1917–1918*, June 1912.
3. "Privates Designated for Transfer to the 339th Infantry," List of Outgoing Passengers, November 1918.
4. "Ship Transport," U.S. Army World War I Transport Service, 7 September 1918.
5. Snow, David B., "Men from Paducah Battled Against Red Army in Russia," *The Paducah Sun*, 20 October 2019.
6. Lewis, Charles, "Replacement Troops, 339th Infantry," 30 April 1919.
7. Yopp, Herman, in Moore, Joel, *"M" Company*, 1924.
8. Larsen, Alfred, PBOHP, 13 June 1977.
9. Siplon, James, PBOHP, 7 June 1977.
10. Dundon, Walter, in Moore, Joel, *"M" Company*, 1920.
11. Primm, Clarence, Letters, 8 October 1918.
12. Grobbel, Clement, Letters, "The WWI Correspondence of Cpl. Clement Grobbel, 339th Inf., 85th Div., U.S. Army," Detroit's Own Polar Bear Memorial Association, 10 October 1918.
13. Dundon, Walter, in Moore, Joel, *"M" Company*, 1920.
14. Primm, Clarence, Letters, 8 October 1918.
15. Siplon, James, PBOHP, 1977.
16. Dundon, Walter, in Moore, Joel, *"M" Company*, 1920.
17. Moore, Joel, *"M" Company*, 1920, 8.

18. Nichols, J. Brooks, "Report of Engagement," 23 October 1918.
19. Stringham, Charles, in Moore, Joel, *"M" Company*, 1924.
20. Moore, Joel, *"M" Company*, 1920, 8.
21. Stoner, George, "The Diary of 1st Lt. George W. Stoner, Jr.," 13 October 1918.
22. Moore, Joel, *"M" Company*, 1920, 8.
23. Moore, Joel, *"M" Company*, 1920, 8.
24. Dundon, Walter, in Moore, Joel, *"M" Company*, 1920.
25. Starr, Stephen, in Moore, Joel, *"M" Company*, 1924.
26. Primm, Clarence, Letters, 23 October 1918.
27. Moore, Joel, *"M" Company*, 1920, 9.
28. Moore, Joel, *"M" Company*, 1920, 9.
29. Cudahy, John, *Archangel: The American War with Russia*, 1924.
30. Moore, Joel, *"M" Company*, 1920, 9.
31. Moore, Joel, *"M" Company*, 1920, 9.
32. Stoner, George, "The Diary of 1st Lt. George W. Stoner, Jr.," 14 October 1918.
33. Moore, Joel, *"M" Company*, 1920, 9.
34. Dundon, Walter, in Moore, Joel, *"M" Company*, 1920.
35. Nichols, J. Brooks, "Report of Engagement," 23 October 1918.
36. Moore, Joel, *"M" Company*, 1920, 9.
37. Nichols, J. Brooks, "Report of Engagement," 23 October 1918.
38. Willett, Robert L., *Russian Sideshow*, 2003, 38.
39. Moore, Joel, et al., *History of the American Expedition*, 1920, 27.
40. Nelson, James C., *The Polar Bear Expedition*, 2019, 104.
41. Grobbel, Clement, Letters, 20 October 1918.
42. Siplon, James, PBOHP, 1977.
43. Moore, et al., *History of the American Expedition*, 1920, 27.
44. "Signal Platoon Wins Commendation," www.worldwar1gallery.com, 23 May 1919.
45. "War Diary," 14 October 1918.
46. May, Albert, in Gordon, Dennis, *Quartered in Hell*, 1982, 175–6.
47. Moore, et al., *History of the American Expedition*, 1920, 28.
48. Rasmussen, Roy, in Roy Paul Rasmussen Papers, UMBHL.
49. Dundon, Walter, in Moore, Joel, *"M" Company*, 1920.
50. Stoner, George, "The Diary of 1st Lt. George W. Stoner, Jr.," 16 October 1918.
51. Moore, Joel, *"M" Company*, 1920, 10.
52. Moore, Joel, *"M" Company*, 1920, 10.
53. Moore, Joel, *"M" Company*, 1920, 10.
54. Moore, Joel, *"M" Company*, 1920, 10.
55. Moore, Joel, *"M" Company*, 1920, 11.
56. Moore, Joel, *"M" Company*, 1920, 11.
57. Barrett, Andrea, "Traveling Corpse: How an American Sergeant's Journey Through Frigid North Russia Inspired a Work of Historical Fiction," *The American Scholar*, Winter 2015.
58. Dundon, Walter, in Moore, Joel, *"M" Company*, 1920.
59. Moore, Joel, *"M" Company*, 1920, 11.
60. Dundon, Walter, in Moore, Joel, *"M" Company*, 1920.
61. "War Diary," 20 October 1918.
62. Grobbel, Clement, Letters, 20 October 1918.
63. Dundon, Walter, in Moore, Joel, *"M" Company*, 1920.
64. Dundon, Walter, in Moore, Joel, *"M" Company*, 1920.

Chapter 8

1. Nelson, James, *The Polar Bear Expedition*, 2019, 90.
2. Ironside, Edmund, *Ironside: The Authorized Biography of Field Marshall Lord Ironside*, 2018.
3. Ironside, Edmund, *Ironside: The Authorized Biography*, 2018.
4. Ironside, Edmund, *Ironside: The Authorized Biography*, 2018.
5. Ironside, Edmund, *Ironside: The Authorized Biography*, 2018.
6. Ironside, Edmund, *Ironside: The Authorized Biography*, 2018.
7. Francis, David, *Foreign Relations*, 14 October 1918.
8. Blackington, George, *The Polar Bear Club*, April 1926.
9. Nelson, James C., *The Polar Bear Expedition*, 2019, 92.
10. Moore, Joel, et al., *The History of the American Expedition*, 1920, 29.
11. Kooyers, Frederick, PBOHP, 13 June 1977. Hershberger, Russell, PBOHP, 20 June 1977.
12. Primm, Clarence, Letters, 23 October 1918.
13. Siplon, James, PBOHP, 7 June 1977.
14. Primm, Clarence, Letters, 23 October 1918.
15. Dundon, Walter, in Moore, Joel, *"M" Company*, 1920.
16. Siplon, James, PBOHP, 6 June 1977.
17. Colburn, Cleo, PBOHP, 17 June 1977.
18. Moore, Joel, et al., *The History of the American Expedition*, 1920, 205.
19. Siplon, James, PBOHP, 6 June 1977.
20. Hershberger, Russell, PBOHP, 20 June 1977.
21. Grobbel, Clement, Letters, 29 October 1918.
22. Barrett, Andrea, "Traveling Corpse: How an American Sergeant's Journey Through Frigid North Russia Inspired a Work of Historical Fiction," *The American Scholar*, Winter 2015.
23. Moore, Joel, *"M" Company*, 1920, 12.
24. Stoner, George, *Diary*, 30 October 1918.

25. Dundon, Walter, in Moore, Joel, *"M" Company*, 1920.
26. Siplon, James, PBOHP, 6 June 1977.
27. Albers, George, WWI Draft Registration Card, 5 June 1917.
28. Nelson, James C., *The Polar Bear Expedition*, 1920, 260–61.

Chapter 9

1. Grobbel, Mike, Personal Communication, 27 May 2021.
2. Grobbel, Mike, Personal Communication, 27 May 2021.
3. Grobbel, Clement, Letters, 13 April 1919.
4. Grobbel, Mike, "Outnumbered on the Vologda Railroad Front," 2007.
5. "1,500 Reds Attack 87 Men," *The Detroit Free Press*, 15 April 1919. Winslow, Horatio, "Report of Engagement," 7 November 1918.
6. Dundon, Walter, in Moore, Joel, *"M" Company*, 1920.
7. Nichols, J. Brooks, "Report of Engagement," 5 November 1918.
8. Winslow, Horatio, "Report of Engagement," 7 November 1918.
9. Winslow, Horatio, "Report of Engagement," 7 November 1918.
10. "1,500 Reds Attack 87 Men," *The Detroit Free Press*, 15 April 1919.
11. Moore, Joel, et al., *The History of the American Expedition*, 1920, 29–30.
12. "Paid with Life for Bravery," *Brooklyn Daily Eagle*, 20 February 1919.
13. Sieloff, Theodore, "The Wall of Valor Project," www.militarytimes.com.
14. Moore, Joel, et al., *The History of the American Expedition*, 1920, 29–30.
15. Grobbel, Clement, "The Wall of Valor Project," www.militarytimes.com.
16. Moore, Joel, et al., *The History of the American Expedition*, 1920, 29–30.
17. Winslow, Horatio, "Report of Engagement," 7 November 1918.
18. Nichols, J. Brooks, "Report of Engagement," 5 November 1918.
19. Moore, Joel, et al., *The History of the American Expedition*, 1920, 29–30.
20. Winslow, Horatio, "Report of Engagement," 7 November 1918.
21. Dundon, Walter, in Moore, Joel, *"M" Company*, 1920.
22. "War Diary of the 16th Brigade Canadian Field Artillery," 8 November 1918.
23. Lewis, Floyd, PBOHP, 29 June 1977.
24. Siplon, James, PBOHP, 6 June 1977.
25. Slagh, Albert, PBOHP, 12 June 1978.
26. Francis, David, *Foreign Relations*, 13 November 1918.
27. Siplon, James, PBOHP, 6 June 1977.
28. Safer, Sam, "Flint Man Fought Bolsheviks," *The Flint Journal*, 11 December 1966.
29. Siplon, James, PBOHP, 6 June 1977.
30. Larsen, Alfred, PBOHP 13 June 1977.
31. Siplon, James, PBOHP, 6 June 1977.

Chapter 10

1. U.S. Census, 1900.
2. Maitland, James, WWI Draft Registration Card, 5 June 1917.
3. Ramsey, Leon, "Two Points of View," Newspaper Clippings, Leon Ramsey Papers, 1917–1919, UMBHL.
4. Moore, Joel, *"M" Company*, 1920, 14.
5. Moore, Joel, et al., *The History of the American Expedition*, 1920.
6. Dundon, Walter, in Moore, Joel, *"M" Company*, 1920, 12 November 1918.
7. Colburn, Cleo, PBOHP, 1977.
8. Primm, Carol, and Stuntz, Pete, *Polar Bear Tales*, 2009, 42.
9. Beers, Henry, "U.S. Naval Forces in Northern Russia," 1943, 15.
10. Moore, Joel, et al., *The History of the American Expedition*, 1920, 45.
11. Moore, Joel, *"M" Company*, 1920, 14.
12. Kooyers, Fred, *Diary*, UMBHL, 19 November 1918.
13. Moore, Joel, *"M" Company*, 1920, 14. Dundon, Walter, in Moore, Joel, *"M" Company*, 1920.
14. Primm, Carol, and Stuntz, Pete, *Polar Bear Tales*, 2009, 36.
15. Colburn, Cleo, PBOHP, 1977.
16. Willett, Robert L., *Russian Sideshow*, 2003, 26.
17. Lewis, Floyd, PBOHP, 29 June 1977.
18. Sauter, Joseph, in Ward, William, *Well Kept Secret*, 2010.
19. Primm, Carol, and Stuntz, Pete, *Polar Bear Tales*, 2009, 44–5.
20. Moore, Joel, *"M" Company*, 1920, 14.
21. Lewis, Floyd, PBOHP, 29 June 1977.
22. Moore, Joel, *"M" Company*, 1920, 14.
23. Lewis, Floyd, PBOHP, 29 June 1977.
24. Kooyers, Frederick, PBOHP, 13 June 1977.
25. Willett, Robert L., *Russian Sideshow*, 2003, 128.
26. Willett, Robert L., *Russian Sideshow*, 2003, 129.
27. Kooyers, Fred, *Diary*, UMBHL, 19 September 1918.
28. Willett, Robert L., *Russian Sideshow*, 2003, 128.
29. Willett, Robert L., *Russian Sideshow*, 2003, 129.
30. Batz, Robert L., "Flint Man Fought Bolsheviks," *The Flint Journal*, 11 December 1966.
31. Primm, Carol, and Stuntz, Pete, *Polar Bear Tales*, 2009, 37.
32. Larsen, Alfred. PBOHP, 13 June 1977.
33. Siplon, James, PBOHP, 7 June 1977.
34. Larsen, Alfred, PBOHP, 13 June 1977.

35. Cudahy, John, *Archangel: The American War with Russia*, 1924.
36. Primm, Carol, and Stuntz, Pete, *Polar Bear Tales*, 2009, 107.
37. Siplon, James, PBOHP, 7 June 1977.
38. Willett, Robert L., *Russian Sideshow*, 2003, 128.
39. Cudahy, John, *Archangel: The American War with Russia*, 1924.
40. Hershberger, Russell, PBOHP, 20 June 1977.
41. Rotman, Martin. PBOHP, 13 June 1977.
42. Gordon, Dennis, *Quartered in Hell*, 1982, 166.
43. Bartels, Levi, PBOHP, 1978.
44. Czerwinski, John, "Member of 339th Bitter at Britons," *Detroit Free Press*, 25 February 1919.
45. Grobbel, Clement, Letters, 20 November 1918.
46. Batz, Robert L., "Flint Man Fought Bolsheviks," *The Flint Journal*, 11 December 1966.
47. Toornman, John, in Ward, William, *Well Kept Secret*, 2010.
48. Dundon, Walter, in Moore, Joel, *"M" Company*, 1920.
49. Moore, Joel, *"M" Company*, 1920, 14.
50. Dundon, Walter, in Moore, Joel, *"M" Company*, 1920.
51. Lewis, Floyd, PBOHP, 29 June 1977.
52. Dundon, Walter, in Moore, Joel, *"M" Company*, 1920.
53. Stoner, George, *Diary*, 23 November 1918.

Chapter 11

1. U.S. *Census*, 1900, 1910.
2. Sickles, Floyd A., WWI Draft Registration Card, 5 June 1917.
3. Moore, Joel, et al., *The History of the American Expedition*, 1920, 184.
4. "War Diary of the 16th Brigade, Canadian Field Artillery," 27 November 1918.
5. Primm, Clarence, Letters, 28 November 1918.
6. Dundon, Walter, in Moore, Joel, *"M" Company*, 1920. "War Diary of the 16th Brigade, Canadian Field Artillery," 28 November 1918.
7. Stoner, George, *Toledo Blade*, 22 January 1919.
8. Stoner, George, *Diary*, 29 November 1918.
9. Marxer, Rudolph, PBOHP, 16 June 1977.
10. Moore, Joel, et al., *The History of the American Expedition*, 1920, 218.
11. Moore, Joel, et al., *The History of the American Expedition*, 1920, 219.
12. "War Diary of the 16th Brigade, Canadian Field Artillery," 29 November 1918.
13. Dundon, Walter, in Moore, Joel, *"M" Company*, 1920.
14. "War Diary of the 16th Brigade, Canadian Field Artillery," 30 November 1918.
15. "War Diary of the 16th Brigade, Canadian Field Artillery," 1 December 1918.
16. Dundon, Walter, in Moore, Joel, *"M" Company*, 1920.
17. Moore, Joel, et al., *The History of the American Expedition*, 1920, 113.
18. Riordan, C.E. Letters, 20 March 1919.
19. Primm, Clarence, Letters, 5 December 1918.
20. Dundon, Walter, in Moore, Joel, *"M" Company*, 1920.
21. Murchie, Guy, Jr., "Tragedy at Archangel," *Chicago Sunday Tribune*, 26 February 1919.
22. Primm, Clarence, Letters, 21 November 1918.
23. Stoner, George, *Toledo Blade*, 22 January 1919.
24. Marxer, Rudolph, PBOHP, 16 June 1977
25. Primm, Clarence, Letters, 5 December 1918.
26. "War Diary of the 16th Brigade, Canadian Field Artillery," 5 December 1918.
27. Riordan, C.E., Letters, 30 September 1919.
28. Dundon, Walter, in Moore, Joel, *"M" Company*, 1920.
29. "War Diary of the 16th Brigade, Canadian Field Artillery," 6 December 1918.
30. Moore, Joel, "Letter," in *"M" Company*, 11 December 1918.
31. "War Diary of the 16th Brigade, Canadian Field Artillery," 6 December 1918.
32. Moore, Joel, et al., *The History of the American Expedition*, 1920, 185.
33. Primm, Clarence, Letters, 28 November 1918.
34. Moore, Joel, et al., *The History of the American Expedition*, 1920, 185.
35. "War Diary of the 16th Brigade, Canadian Field Artillery," 7 December 1918.
36. "War Diary of the 16th Brigade, Canadian Field Artillery," 11 December 1918.
37. Colburn, Cleo, *Diary*, 9 December 1918.
38. Dundon, Walter, in Moore, Joel, *"M" Company*, 1920.

Chapter 12

1. "Legionnaire Dies of Heart Attack," *Monroe News*, 29 January 1950.
2. Stoner, George W., "Extract From Discharge Certificate," 19 October 1920. Stoner, George, *Diary*, 6 September 1917.
3. Stoner, George, *Diary*, 20 November 1917.
4. Dundon, Walter, in Moore, Joel, *"M" Company*, 1920.
5. Cudahy, John, *Archangel: The American War with Russia*, 1924.
6. Blackington, George, "The Bayonet Decides," *The Polar Bear Club*, April 1926.
7. Dundon, Walter, in Moore, Joel, *"M" Company*, 1920.
8. Moore, Joel, *"M" Company*, 1920, 16.

9. Moore, Joel, *"M" Company,* 1920, 16.
10. Stoner, George, *Diary,* 18 December 1918.
11. Moore, Joel, et al., *The History of the American Expedition,* 1920, 118–9.
12. Dundon, Walter, in Moore, Joel, *"M" Company,* 1920.
13. Moore, Joel, et al., *The History of the American Expedition,* 1920, 119.
14. Moore, Joel, et al., *The History of the American Expedition,* 1920, 120.
15. Stoner, George, *Diary,* 20 December 1918.
16. Moore, Joel, *"M" Company,* 1920, 17.
17. Sukhanovsky, Alexey, "Rescue Private Yopp," *Homeland Magazine,* 1 October 2018.
18. Sukhanovsky, Alexey, "Rescue Private Yopp," *Homeland Magazine,* 1 October 2018.
19. Dundon, Walter, in Moore, Joel, *"M" Company,* 1921.
20. Moore, Joel, *"M" Company,* 1920, 17–8.
21. Dundon, Walter, in Moore, Joel, *"M" Company,* 1921.
22. Stoner, George, *Diary,* 21 December 1918.
23. Moore, Joel, et al., *The History of the American Expedition,* 1920, 122.
24. Geltz, Albert, in Albert E. Geltz Papers, UMBHL.
25. Primm, Carol, and Stuntz, Pete, *Polar Bear Tales,* 2009, 88.
26. Sauter, Joseph, in Ward, William, *Well Kept Secret,* 2010.
27. Moore, Joel, *"M" Company,* 1920, 18.
28. Moore, Joel, *"M" Company,* 1920, 18.
29. Moore, Joel, *"M" Company,* 1920, 18.
30. Moore, Joel, et al., *The History of the American Expedition,* 1920, 122.
31. Stoner, George, *Diary,* 25 December 1918.
32. Moore, Joel, *"M" Company,* 1920, 18. Moore, Joel, et al., *The History of the American Expedition,* 1920, 122.
33. Moore, Joel, et al., *The History of the American Expedition,* 1920, 122.
34. Moore, Joel, *"M" Company,* 1920, 18.
35. Stoner, George, *Diary,* 26 December 1918.
36. Dundon, Walter, in Moore, Joel, *"M" Company,* 1920.
37. Stoner, George, *Diary,* 27 December 1918.
38. Moore, Joel, et al., *The History of the American Expedition,* 1920, 125. Moore, Joel, *"M" Company,* 1920, 18–19.
39. Stoner, George, *Diary,* 27 December 1918.

Chapter 13

1. Grahek, Matthew, Michigan Heroes Museum, 14 April 2021.
2. U.S. *Census,* 1910.
3. Grahek, Matthew, WWI Draft Registration Card, June 1917.
4. Grahek, Matthew, in Ward, William, *A Well Kept Secret,* 2016, 29.
5. Grahek, Matthew, in Ward, William, *A Well Kept Secret,* 2016, 29.
6. Grahek, Matthew, in Ward, William, *A Well Kept Secret,* 2016, 32.
7. Grahek, Matthew, in Ward, William, *A Well Kept Secret,* 2016, 34.
8. Grahek, Matthew, in Ward, William, *A Well Kept Secret,* 2016, 34.
9. Baldwin, Robert C., "The Allied Military Expedition to North Russia," June 1969.
10. Willett, Robert L., *Russian Sideshow,* 2003, 105.
11. Lewis, Charles, "Report of Dec. 7, 1918," Operations of the 339th Infantry.
12. Stoner, George, *Diary,* 29 December 1918.
13. Dundon, Walter, in Moore, Joel, *"M" Company,* 1920.
14. Moore, Joel, et al., *The History of the American Expedition,* 1920.
15. Dundon, Walter, in Moore, Joel, *"M" Company,* 1920.
16. Dundon, Walter, in Moore, Joel, *"M" Company,* 1920.
17. Moore, Joel, et al., *History of the American Expedition,* 1920, 76.
18. Larsen, Alfred, PBOHP, 13 June 1977
19. Cudahy, John, *Archangel: The American War with Russia,* 1924, 194.
20. Blackington, George, "The Bayonet Decides," *The Polar Bear Club,* April 1926.
21. Dundon, Walter, in Moore, Joel, *"M" Company,* 1920.
22. Williams, Charles T., in Moore, Joel, *"M" Company,* 1920.
23. Stoner, George, *Diary,* 4 January 1919.
24. Moore, Joel, et al., *The History of the American Expedition,* 1920, 152.
25. Stoner, George, *Diary,* 8 January 1919.
26. Stoner, George, *Diary,* 5 January 1919.
27. Larsen, Alfred, PBOHP, 13 June 1977
28. Rotman, Martin, PBOHP, 13 June 1977
29. Stoner, George, *Diary,* 8 January 1919.
30. Stoner, George, *Diary,* 12–13 January 1919.
31. Moore, Joel, "Record of Events," *War Diary, Company 'M,' 339th Infantry,* 12 January 1919.
32. Dundon, Walter, in Moore, Joel, *"M" Company,* 1920.
33. Cudahy, John, *Archangel: The American War with Russia,* 1924, 195.
34. Stoner, George, *Diary,* 15 January 1919.
35. Moore, Joel, "Report of Jan. 15, 1919," Operations of the 339th Infantry, 15 January 1919.
36. Murchie, Guy, Jr., "Tragedy at Archangel," *Chicago Sunday Tribune,* 26 February 1919.
37. Primm, Carol, and Stuntz, Pete, *Polar Bear Tales,* 2009.
38. Dundon, Walter, in Moore, Joel, *"M" Company,* 1920.
39. Primm, Clarence, "Letters," 26 January 1919
40. Dundon, Walter, in Moore, Joel, *"M" Company,* 1920.

41. Moore, Joel, "Operations of the 339th Infantry," 8 February 1919.
42. Dundon, Walter, in Moore, Joel, *"M" Company*, 1920.
43. Moore, Joel, et al., *History of the American Expedition*, 1920, 153.
44. Moore, Joel, "Record of Events," *War Diary, Company 'M,' 339th Infantry*, 31 January 1919. Moore, Joel, et al., *History of the American Expedition*, 1920, 209.
45. Moore, Joel, et al., *History of the American Expedition*, 1920, 153.
46. Stoner, George, *Diary*, 4 February 1919.
47. Moore, Joel, "Operations of the 339th Infantry," 8 February 1919.
48. Moore, Joel, et al., *History of the American Expedition*, 1920, 154.
49. Dundon, Walter, in Moore, Joel, *"M" Company*, 1920.
50. Moore, Joel, et al., *History of the American Expedition*, 1920, 154.
51. Dundon, Walter, in Moore, Joel, *"M" Company*, 1920.
52. Nelson, James C., *The Polar Bear Expedition*, 2019, 177.
53. Stoner, George, *Diary*, 15, 18,19 February 1919.
54. Dundon, Walter, in Moore, Joel, *"M" Company*, 1920.
55. Larsen, Alfred, PBOHP, 13 June 1977.
56. Moore, Joel, "Operations of the 339th Infantry," 20 February 1919.
57. Dundon, Walter, in Moore, Joel, *"M" Company*, 1920.
58. Stoner, George, *Diary*, 25 February 1919.
59. Primm, Carol, and Stuntz, Pete, *Polar Bear Tales*, 2009, 77.
60. Stoner, George, *Diary*, 6 March 1919.
61. Moore, Joel, et al., *History of the American Expedition*, 1920, 155.
62. Dundon, Walter, in Moore, Joel, *"M" Company*, 1920.
63. Costello, Harry J., *Why Did We Go to Russia?* 1920, 68.

Chapter 14

1. *U.S. Census*, 1900.
2. *U.S. Census*, 1910.
3. Reese, Gordon B., WWI Draft Registration Card, 5 June 1917.
4. Bartels, Levi, PBOHP, 1978.
5. Grobbel, Clement, Letters, 14 February 1919.
6. Cudahy, John, *Archangel: The American War with Russia*, 1924.
7. Hershberger, Russell, PBOHP, 20 June 1977.
8. Colburn, Cleo, "Oral History," 1977.
9. Moore, Joel, et al., *History of the American Expedition*, 1920, 257.
10. Moore, Joel, et al., *History of the American Expedition*, 1920, 256.
11. Cudahy, John, *Archangel: The American War with Russia*, 1924.
12. Primm, Clarence, Letters, 17 February 1919.
13. Moore, Joel, et al., *History of the American Expedition*, 1920, 80.
14. Cudahy, John, *Archangel: The American War with Russia*, 1924, 196.
15. Grace, Charles, PBOHP, 14 June 1977.
16. Moore, Joel, et al., *History of the American Expedition*, 1920, 163.
17. Larsen, Alfred, PBOHP, 13 June 1977.
18. "Flint Man Fought Bolsheviks," *The Flint Journal*, 11 December 1966.
19. Hershberger, Russell, PBOHP, 20 June 1977.
20. Kooyers, Frederick, PBOHP, 13 June 1977.
21. Hershberger, Russell, PBOHP, 20 June 1977. Moore, Joel, et al., *History of the American Expedition*, 1920, 103.
22. Moore, Joel, et al., *History of the American Expedition*, 1920, 221.
23. Cudahy, John, *Archangel: The American War with Russia*, 1924.
24. Willett, Robert L., *Russian Sideshow*, 2003, 44.
25. Willett, Robert L., *Russian Sideshow*, 2003, 140.
26. Cudahy, John, *Archangel: The American War with Russia*, 1924.
27. "Wants Our Troops Taken from Russia," *New York Times*, 8 January 1919.
28. Willett, Robert L., *Russian Sideshow*, 2003, 139.
29. "New Archangel Plans Bring Up Fiasco of 1918," *Detroit News*, 1941.
30. Primm, Clarence, Letters, 19 February 1919.
31. Willett, Robert L., *Russian Sideshow*, 2003, 43.
32. Moore, Joel, et al., *History of the American Expedition*, 1920, 180.
33. Sarosiek, Jan, in Ward, William, *Well Kept Secret*, 2010.
34. Gibbs, Ivan, in Ward, William, *Well Kept Secret*, 2010.
35. Moore, Joel, et al., *History of the American Expedition*, 1920, 59.
36. Bartels, Levi, PBOHP, 1978.
37. Kooyers, Frederick, PBOHP, 13 June 1977.
38. "339th Men Forced to Bury the Dead," *Detroit Free Press*, 5 May 1919.
39. "Confirmation of the Report that George Albers, captured," *Leelanau Enterprise*, 10 April 1919.
40. Hershberger, Russell, PBOHP, 20 June 1977.
41. Moore, Joel, et al., *History of the American Expedition*, 1920, 256.
42. Robbins, Miriam, "William Bryan 'Bill' Robbins," *Backgrounds By Marie*, 29 December 2003.

Chapter 15

1. Siplon, James, "Interview, 7 June 1977.
2. Emery, Mike, "Retro Richmond: Once Known as the Lawn Mower Capital," *The Palladium*, 24 September 2018.
3. McGuire, Whitney, WWI Draft Registration Card, September 6, 1917.
4. Primm, Clarence, Letters, 5 March 1919.
5. Primm, Clarence, Letters, 3 March 1919.
6. Moore, Joel, et al., *The History of the American Expedition*, 1920, 257.
7. Primm, Clarence, Letters, 14 March 1919.
8. Grobbel, Clement, Letters, 10 March 1919.
9. Primm, Clarence, Letters, 8 March 1919.
10. Abel, Henry, "Letter from Henry Abel," Newspaper Clippings and Ephemera, Henry Abel Papers, UMBHL.
11. Moore, Joel, *"M" Company*, 1920.
12. Cudahy, John, *Archangel: The American War with Russia*, 1924, 76.
13. Grahek, Matthew, in Ward, William, *A Well Kept Secret*, 2010, 30.
14. Moore, Joel, et al., *The History of the American Expedition*, 1920, 239.
15. Colburn, Cleo, *Diary*, 16 March 1919.
16. Moore, Joel, *"M" Company*, 1920.
17. Taylor, Joseph, "Report of Engagement on Dec. 11, 1918," Historical Files of the U.S. Expeditionary Force, 13 December 1918.
18. Taylor, Joseph, "Report of Engagement on Dec. 11, 1918," Historical Files of the U.S. Expeditionary Force, 13 December 1918.
19. Martin, Hugh, "Mutinies in North Russia," Historical Files of the U.S. Expeditionary Force, 1 July 1919.
20. Martin, Hugh, "Mutinies in North Russia," Historical Files of the U.S. Expeditionary Force, 1 July 1919.
21. Simmons, Christopher, "The Alleged Mutiny of Company I," Norwich University, 20 May 2011.
22. Simmons, Christopher, "The Alleged Mutiny of Company I," Norwich University, 20 May 2011.
23. Willett, Robert L., *Russian Sideshow*, 2003, 120.
24. Phillips, Michael, "The One Time American Troops Fought Russians," *The Wall Street Journal*, 9 November 2018.
25. Simmons, Christopher, "The Alleged Mutiny of Company I," Norwich University, 20 May 2011.
26. Primm, Clarence, Letters, 15 March 1919.
27. Weatherson, Michael, and Bochin, Hal, *Hiram Johnson: Political Revivalist*, 1995, 86.
28. "Part of 339th Out of Russia," Newspaper Clippings and Ephemera, Henry Abel Papers, UMBHL. Scales, Howard, "Alleged Mutiny of Company I, 339th Infantry," Washington, D.C., 25 June 1920.
29. Moore, Joel, "Record of Events," *War Diary, Company 'M,' 339th Infantry*, 1919.
30. Moore, Joel, et al., *The History of the American Expedition*, 1920, 228.
31. Moore, Joel, et al., *The History of the American Expedition*, 1920, 228. Moore, Joel, "Record of Events," *War Diary, Company 'M,' 339th Infantry*, 1919.
32. Costello, Harry, "The 'Mutiny' in Russia of the American Troops Was One in Name Only," *St. Louis Post-Dispatch*, 3 August 1919.
33. Siplon, James, "Interview, 7 June 1977.
34. Simmons, Christopher, "The Alleged Mutiny of Company I," Norwich University, 20 May 2011.
35. "Part of 339th Out of Russia," Newspaper Clippings and Ephemera, Henry Abel Papers, UMBHL.
36. "Reinforce U.S., Is 339th Plea," *Detroit Free Press*, 7 March 1919.
37. Simmons, Christopher, "The Alleged Mutiny of Company I," Norwich University, 20 May 2011.
38. Simmons, Christopher, "The Alleged Mutiny of Company I," Norwich University, 20 May 2011.
39. Simmons, Christopher, "The Alleged Mutiny of Company I," Norwich University, 20 May 2011.
40. Siplon, James, "Interview, 7 June 1977.
41. Costello, Harry, "The 'Mutiny' in Russia of the American Troops Was One in Name Only," *St. Louis Post-Dispatch*, 3 August 1919.
42. Martin, Hugh, "Mutinies in North Russia," Historical Files of the U.S. Expeditionary Force, 1 July 1919.
43. Siplon, James, "Interview, 7 June 1977.
44. Costello, Harry, "The 'Mutiny' in Russia of the American Troops Was One in Name Only," *St. Louis Post-Dispatch*, 3 August 1919.
45. May, Albert, in Gordon, Dennis, *Quartered in Hell*, 1981, 177. Costello, Harry, "The 'Mutiny' in Russia of the American Troops Was One in Name Only," *St. Louis Post-Dispatch*, 3 August 1919.
46. Siplon, James, "Interview, 7 June 1977.
47. Colburn, Cleo, *Diary*, 30 March 1919.
48. Siplon, James, "Interview, 7 June 1977.
49. Simmons, Christopher, "The Alleged Mutiny of Company I," Norwich University, 20 May 2011.
50. Costello, Harry, "The 'Mutiny' in Russia of the American Troops Was One in Name Only," *St. Louis Post-Dispatch*, 3 August 1919.
51. Costello, Harry, "The 'Mutiny' in Russia of the American Troops Was One in Name Only," *St. Louis Post-Dispatch*, 3 August 1919.
52. Moore, Joel, et al., *The History of the American Expedition*, 1920, 229–30.
53. Moore, Joel, et al., *The History of the American Expedition*, 1920, 229–30.
54. Scales, Howard, "Alleged Mutiny of Company I, 339th Infantry," Washington, D.C., 25 June 1920.
55. Zacharias, Patricia, "Detroit's Polar Bears

and Their Confusing War," *The Detroit News*, Nov. 1998.

Chapter 16

1. Fulcher, Earl, "A Prisoner of War," 339th Infantry, 7 May 1919.
2. Collins, Earl, WWI Draft Registration Card, 5 June 1917.
3. Collins, Earl, WWI Draft Registration Card, 5 June 1917.
4. Fulcher, Earl, "A Prisoner of War," 339th Infantry, 7 May 1919.
5. Fulcher, Earl, "A Prisoner of War," 339th Infantry, 7 May 1919.
6. Fulcher, Earl, "A Prisoner of War," 339th Infantry, 7 May 1919.
7. Fulcher, Earl, "A Prisoner of War," 339th Infantry, 7 May 1919.
8. Cudahy, John, *Archangel: The American War with Russia*, 1924, 107.
9. Willett, Robert L., *Russian Sideshow*, 2003, 53.
10. Moore, Joel, et al., *The History of the American Expedition*, 1920, 169.
11. Page, D.C.M., "A Chat with Ironside," 19 March 1919.
12. Page, D.C.M., "A Chat with Ironside," 19 March 1919.
13. Nelson, James C., *The Polar Bear Expedition*, 2019, 238.
14. Nelson, James C., *The Polar Bear Expedition*, 2019, 237.
15. Cudahy, John, *Archangel: The American War with Russia*, 1924, 108.
16. Nelson, James C., *The Polar Bear Expedition*, 2019, 237.
17. Nelson, James C., *The Polar Bear Expedition*, 2019, 238.
18. Nelson, James C., *The Polar Bear Expedition*, 2019, 239.
19. Nelson, James C., *The Polar Bear Expedition*, 2019, 239.
20. Nelson, James C., *The Polar Bear Expedition*, 2019, 239.
21. Nelson, James C., *The Polar Bear Expedition*, 2019, 239.
22. Kooyers, Fred, PBOHP, 13 June 1977.
23. Martin, Hugh, "Mutinies in North Russia," Historical Files of the U.S. Expeditionary Force, 1 July 1919.
24. Martin, Hugh, "Mutinies in North Russia," 1 July 1919.
25. Nelson, James C., *The Polar Bear Expedition*, 2019, 240–1.
26. Dundon, Walter, in Moore, Joel, *"M" Company*, 1920.
27. Nelson, James C., *The Polar Bear Expedition*, 2019, 241.
28. Moore, Joel, "Record of Events," 28 March 1919.
29. Moore, Joel, *"M" Company*, 1920. Moore, Joel, et al., *The History of the American Expedition*, 1920, 190.
30. Dundon, Walter, in Moore, Joel, *"M" Company*, 1920.
31. Primm, Carol, and Stuntz, Pete, *Polar Bear Tales*, 2009.
32. Primm, Clarence, Letters, 29 March 1919.
33. Zank, Richard, in Ward, William, *A Well Kept Secret*, 2010.
34. Cudahy, John, *Archangel: The American War with Russia*, 1924, 111.
35. Primm, Carol, and Stuntz, Pete, *Polar Bear Tales*, 2009.
36. Moore, Joel. "Record of Events," 30 March 1919.
37. Primm, Clarence, Letters, 29 March 1919.
38. Dundon, Walter, in Moore, Joel, *"M" Company*, 1920.
39. Moore, Joel, et al., *The History of the American Expedition*, 1920, 192.
40. Moore, Joel. "Record of Events," 31 March 1919.
41. Moore, Joel. "Record of Events," 31 March 1919. Moore, Joel, et al., *The History of the American Expedition*, 1920, 191.
42. Moore, Joel. "Record of Events," 31 March 1919.
43. Moore, Joel, et al., *The History of the American Expedition*, 1920, 191.
44. "Wolverine Held by Reds 6 Weeks," *Detroit Free Press*, 19 July 1919. Moore, Joel, *"M" Company*, 1920.
45. Cudahy, John *Archangel: The American War with Russia*, 1924, 113.
46. Moore, Joel, et al., *The History of the American Expedition*, 1920, 300.
47. Moore, Joel, et al., *The History of the American Expedition*, 1920, 191.
48. The Wall of Valor Project, www.militarytimes.com.
49. Moore, Joel, *"M" Company*, 1920.
50. Moore, Joel, et al., *The History of the American Expedition*, 1920, 191.
51. Cudahy, John, *Archangel: The American War with Russia*, 1924, 112.
52. Moore, Joel, et al., *The History of the American Expedition*, 1920, 191.
53. Stoner, George, *Diary*, 2 April 1919.
54. Moore, Joel, "Record of Events," 2 April 1919.
55. Cudahy, John, *Archangel: The American War with Russia*, 1924, 109.
56. Moore, Joel, "Record of Events," 2 April 1919.
57. Chew, Allen F., "Fighting the Russians: Three Case Studies," *Leavenworth Papers*, December 1981.
58. Chew, Allen F., "Fighting the Russians: Three Case Studies," *Leavenworth Papers*, December 1981.
59. Cudahy, John, *Archangel: The American War with Russia*, 1924, 114–5.

60. Chew, Allen F., "Fighting the Russians," December 1981.
61. Cudahy, John, *Archangel: The American War with Russia*, 1924, 114–5.
62. Ballensinger, Richard, "Operations Report," 7 April 1919.
63. Detroit's Own, "Polar Bear Memorial Association—Military Decorations."
64. Moore, Joel, et al., *The History of the American Expedition*, 1920, 301.
65. Moore, Joel, "Record of Events," 3 April 1919.
66. Moore, Joel, "Record of Events," 3 April 1919.
67. Stoner, George, *Diary*, 4 April 1919.
68. Moore, Joel, "Record of Events," 4 April 1919.
69. Baldwin, Robert L., "The Allied Military Expedition to North Russia, 1918–1919," June 1969, 159.
70. Moore, Joel, et al., *The History of the American Expedition*, 1920, 192.
71. Chew, Allen F., "Fighting the Russians," December 1981.
72. Moore, Joel, et al., *The History of the American Expedition*, 1920, 192.

Chapter 17

1. "Wolverine Held by Reds 6 Weeks," *Detroit Free Press*, 18 July 1919.
2. U.S. *Census*, 1940.
3. Laursen Jens C., WWI Draft Registration Card, 5 June 1917.
4. Moore, Joel, *"M" Company*, 1920.
5. "War Work Bulletin," YMCA, 29 August 1919.
6. "Wolverine Held by Reds 6 Weeks," *Detroit Free Press*, 18 July 1919.
7. Moore, Joel, *"M" Company*, 1920. Moore, et al., *The History of the American Expedition*, 1920, 275.
8. Moore, Joel, *"M" Company*, 1920.
9. Nelson, James C., *The Polar Bear Expedition*, 2019, 260.
10. "Mifflinburg Boy, a Russian Captive, Tells Adventures," *Sunbury Daily*, Sunbury, PA, 7 July 1919.
11. Moore, Joel, *"M" Company*, 1920.
12. Moore, Joel, *"M" Company*, 1920.
13. Moore, et al., *The History of the American Expedition*, 1920, 276.
14. Moore, et al., *The History of the American Expedition*, 1920, 276. Moore, Joel, *"M" Company*, 1920.
15. Moore, Joel, *"M" Company*, 1920.
16. Moore, et al., *The History of the American Expedition*, 1920, 278.
17. Moore, Joel, *"M" Company*, 1920.
18. Moore, Joel, *"M" Company*, 1920.
19. "War Work Bulletin," YMCA, 29 April 1919.
20. Moore, Joel, *"M" Company*, 1920.
21. Moore, Joel, *"M" Company*, 1920. Moore, et al., *The History of the American Expedition*, 1920, 278.
22. Nelson, James C., *The Polar Bear Expedition*, 2019, 263.
23. Moore, et al., *The History of the American Expedition*, 1920, 279.
24. Nelson, James C., *The Polar Bear Expedition*, 2019, 263.
25. Nelson, James C., *The Polar Bear Expedition*, 2019, 263.
26. "War Work Bulletin," YMCA, 29 April 1919.
27. "Reds Fall in Battle: U.S. Soldiers Are Safe," *Morgan County Republican*, 11 April 1919.
28. Moore, Joel, et al., *The History of the American Expedition*, 1920, 273.
29. Moore, Joel, *"M" Company*, 1920.
30. "Mifflinburg Boy, a Russian Captive, Tells Adventures," *Sunbury Daily*, Sunbury, PA, 7 July 1919.
31. Moore, Joel, *"M" Company*, 1920.
32. Moore, et al., *The History of the American Expedition*, 1920, 280.
33. Hunt, Frazier, "Iowa Man Gets Russ Reds to Let 6 Yanks Go Home," *Chicago Daily Tribune*, 14 May 1919.
34. Hunt, Frazier, "Iowa Man," *Chicago Daily Tribune*, 14 May 1919.
35. Moore, Joel, *"M" Company*, 1920.
36. Moore, Joel, *"M" Company*, 1920.
37. "Detroiter Is Released," *Detroit Free Press*, 23 May 1919.
38. "Mifflinburg Boy, a Russian Captive, Tells Adventures," *Sunbury Daily*, Sunbury, PA, 7 July 1919.
39. "Mifflinburg Boy, a Russian Captive," *Sunbury Daily*, Sunbury, PA, 7 July 1919.
40. "Mifflinburg Boy, a Russian Captive," *Sunbury Daily*, Sunbury, PA, 7 July 1919.

Chapter 18

1. Steely, Skipper, *Allied Intervention in Russia, 1918–1920: General Richardson and His Role in the Withdrawal of American Troops from Northern Russia*, 2013.
2. 1860 U.S. *Census*.
3. Steely, Skipper, *General Richardson*, 2013.
4. Williamson, William H. (ed.), *Biographical Register of the Officers and Graduates of the United States Military Academy*, Vol. VIII, 1920.
5. Williamson, William H. (ed.), *Biographical Register*, 1920.
6. Steely, Skipper, *General Richardson*, 2013.
7. Steely, Skipper, *General Richardson*, 2013.
8. Steely, Skipper, *General Richardson*, 2013.
9. Williamson, William H. (ed.), *Biographical Register*, 1920.
10. Steely, Skipper, *General Richardson*, 2013.
11. Steely, Skipper, *General Richardson*, 2013.

12. Nelson, James C., *The Polar Bear Expedition*, 2019, 231.
13. Willett, Robert L., *Russian Sideshow*, 2003, 127.
14. Nelson, James C., *The Polar Bear Expedition*, 2019, 233. Steely, Skipper, *General Richardson*, 2013.
15. Steely, Skipper, *General Richardson*, 2013.
16. May, Albert, in Gordon, Dennis, *Quartered in Hell*, 1982, 173.
17. Steely, Skipper, *General Richardson*, 2013.
18. Sarosiek, Jan, in Ward, William, *Well Kept Secret*, 2010.
19. *The Sentinel*, 19 April 1919.
20. Primm, Clarence, Letters, 12 April 1919.
21. Colburn, Cleo, PBOHP, 17 June 77.
22. Colburn, Cleo, *Diary*, 1 April 1919.
23. "Personal Glimpses," *Literary Digest Magazine*, 12 July 1919.
24. Colburn, Cleo, *Diary*, 6 April 1919.
25. Chriswell, Keith, Letters, 1 April 1919.
26. Colburn, Cleo, *Diary*, 7 April 1919.
27. Colburn, Cleo, *Diary*, 5 April 1919.
28. Wright, Wesley, in Moore, Joel, *"M" Company*, 1920.
29. Grobbel, Clement, Letters, 13 April 1919.
30. Primm, Clarence, Letters, 12 April 1919.
31. Schillinger, Norbert, in Moore, Joel, *"M" Company*, 1920.
32. Dundon, Walter, in Moore, Joel, *"M" Company*, 1920.
33. Larsen, Alfred, PBOHP, 13 June 1977.
34. Rotman, Martin, PBOHP, 13 June 1978.
35. Salchow, Hugo, PBOHP, n.d.
36. Dundon, Walter, in Moore, Joel, *"M" Company*, 1920.
37. Russell, William H., WWI Draft Registration Form, 5 June 1917.
38. Moore, Joel, *"M" Company*, 1920. Dundon, Walter, in Moore, Joel, *"M" Company*, 1920.
39. Steely, Skipper, *General Richardson*, 2013.
40. Moore, Joel, et al., *History of the American Expedition*, 1920, 199.
41. Carey, Donald, in Steely, Skipper, *General Richardson*, 2013.
42. Steely, Skipper. *General Richardson*, 2013.
43. Moore, Joel, et al., *History of the American Expedition*, 1920, 199.
44. Primm, Clarence, Letters, 26 April 1919.
45. Bricker, Roy, "Daily Changes," Historical Files of the U.S. Expeditionary Force, 2 May 1919.
46. Sawickis, Frank, WWI Draft Registration Form, 5 June 1917.
47. "Dead Soldier Not a Racine Resident," *Journal Times*, 14 November 1919.
48. Primm, Clarence, Letters, 29 April 1919.
49. Dundon, Walter, in Moore, Joel, *"M" Company*, 1920. Stoner, George, *Diary*, 30 April 1919.
50. "Permanent Losses of 339th Infantry," Historical Files of the U.S. Expeditionary Force, 30 April 1919.
51. Whitehorne, Joseph W., *The Inspectors General of the United States Army*, 1998, 301–02.
52. Dundon, Walter, in Moore, Joel, *"M" Company*.
53. Stoner, George, *Diary*, 3 May 1919.
54. Dundon, Walter, in Moore, Joel, *"M" Company*.
55. Salchow, Hugo, PBOHP, n.d.
56. Dundon, Walter, in Moore, Joel, *"M" Company*, 1920.
57. Stoner, George, *Diary*, 5 May 1919.
58. Moore, Joel, et al., *History of the American Expedition*, 1920, 198.
59. Dundon, Walter, in Moore, Joel, *"M" Company*, 1920.
60. Steely, Skipper, *General Richardson*, 2013.
61. Stoner, George, *Diary*, 17–18 May 1919.
62. Davies, Crossley, "The Story of the Campaign in Northern Russia," *Detroit Free Press*, 6 July 1919.

Chapter 19

1. Lewis, Charles E., "339th Infantry: Strength of Regiment," Historical Files of the U.S. Expeditionary Force, 12 May 1919. Polar Bear Expedition Digital Materials, UMBHL.
2. *Centennial History of Michigan*. Polar Bear Expedition Digital Materials, UMBHL
3. Essery, Evan, "Commissioner of Schools," 7 May 1917. Freeman, A.F., "To Whom this May Concern," 5 May 1917. Ladd, Sanford W., "Department Adjutant, U.S. Army," 7 May 1917. Polar Bear Expedition Digital Materials, UMBHL.
4. *Centennial History of Michigan*. Polar Bear Expedition Digital Materials, Bentley Historical Library, UMBHL.
5. Lewis, Charles E., *Journal*, 31 August 1918, 2 September 1918.
6. Lewis, Charles E., *Journal*, 5–7 September 1918.
7. Lewis, Charles E., *Journal*, 28 September 1918.
8. Lewis, Charles E., *Journal*, 10 October 1918. Lewis, Charles E., *Journal*, 6 November 1918.
9. Lewis, Charles E. "Capt. D.A. Stroh," 29 December 1932. Polar Bear Expedition Digital Materials, UMBHL.
10. Lewis, Charles E. "Capt. D.A. Stroh," 29 December 1932.
11. Lewis, Charles E. "Capt. D.A. Stroh," 29 December 1932.
12. Siplon, James, PBOHP, 6 July 1977. Primm, Clarence, Letters, 25 May 1919.
13. Smith, Gordon, in Gordon W. Smith Papers, UMBHL. Anderson, Godfrey, *A Michigan Polar Bear*, 2010, 152.
14. Stoner, George, *Diary*, 20 May 1919.
15. Willett, Robert L., *Russian Sideshow*, 2003, 141.
16. Dundon, Walter, in Moore, Joel, *"M" Company*, 1920.

17. Moore, Joel, *"M" Company*, 1920.
18. Primm, Clarence, Letters, 25 May 1919.
19. Primm, Clarence, Letters, 27 May 1919.
20. Siplon, James, PBOHP, 6 July 1977.
21. Moore, Joel, *"M" Company*, 1920.
22. Moore, Joel, *"M" Company*, 1920.
23. Yohey, George, in Ward, William, *A Well Kept Secret*, 2010.
24. Costello, Harry, in Steely, Skipper, *Allied Intervention in Russia*, 2013.
25. Primm, Clarence, *Polar Bear Tales*, 2009, 109.
26. Moore, Joel, *"M" Company*, 1920.
27. Primm, Clarence, *Polar Bear Tales*, 2009, 109.
28. Stoner, George, *Diary*, 30 May 1919.
29. Moore, Joel, *"M" Company*, 1920.
30. Bozich, Stanley, *Detroit's Own Polar Bears: The American North Russian Expeditionary Forces, 1918–1919*, 1985, 97.
31. Steely, Skipper, *Allied Intervention in Russia*, 2013.
32. Stoner, George, *Diary*, 2 June 1919.
33. Lewis, Floyd, PBOHP, 29 June 1977.
34. Moore, Joel, *"M" Company*, 1920.
35. Primm, Clarence, Letters, 4 June 1919.
36. Stoner, George, *Diary*, 3 June 1919.
37. Stoner, George, *Diary*, 4 June 1919.
38. Yohey, George, in Ward, William, *A Well Kept Secret*, 2010.
39. Borzich, Stanley, *Detroit's Own Polar Bears*, 99.
40. Borzich, Stanley, *Detroit's Own Polar Bears*, 99.
41. Stoner, George, *Diary*, 5 June 1919.
42. Stoner, George, *Diary*, 8 June 1919.
43. Davies, Crossley, "The Story of the Campaign in Northern Russia," *Detroit Free Press*, 6 July 1919.
44. Anderson, Godfrey, *A Michigan Polar Bear*, 2010, 158.
45. Stoner, George, *Diary*, 11 June 1919.
46. Leitzke, Carl, in Ward, William, *A Well Kept Secret*, 2010.
47. Davies, Crossley, "The Story of the Campaign in Northern Russia," *Detroit Free Press*, 6 July 1919. Dundon, Walter, in Moore, Joel, *"M" Company*, 1920.
48. Grahek, Matthew, in Ward, William, *A Well Kept Secret*, 2010, 34.
49. "Heroism Without Rival on Frigid Front of Russia," *The Pontanezen Duckboard*, 21 June 1919.
50. Grobbel, Clement, Letters, 18 June 1919.
51. Marxer, Rudolph, PBOHP, 16 June 1977.
52. Borzich, Stanley, *Detroit's Own Polar Bears*, 160.
53. Nichols, J. Brooks, "Landing Return, 21 June 1919," U.S. Army WWI Transport Service, 21 June 1919.
54. Dundon, Walter, in Moore, Joel, *"M" Company*, 1920.
55. Stoner, George, *Diary*, 22 June 1919.
56. Crissman, John, in John Sherman Crissman Papers, UMBHL.
57. Dundon, Walter, in Moore, Joel, *"M" Company*, 1920.
58. Borzich, Stanley, *Detroit's Own Polar Bears*, 99.
59. Nichols, J. Brooks, "Landing Return." Lists of Incoming Passengers, 1917–1938. U.S. Army WWI Transport Service, 30 June 1919.
60. "339th Heroes Reach Boston," *Detroit Free Press*, 13 July 1919.
61. "339th Troops Barely Avoid Drifting Minefield," *Detroit Free Press*, 1 July 1919.
62. Hardy, William, "Detroit's Own Due Here Friday," *Detroit Free Press*, 2 July 1919.
63. Zacharias, Patricia, "Detroit's Polar Bears and their Confusing War," *The Detroit News*, November 1998.
64. "Polar Bears, Arctic Heroes Loudly Hailed," *Detroit Free Press*, 4 July 1919.
65. Tremaine, Roy, Michigan Heroes Museum, 15 September 2018.
66. "Sorrow as Well as Joy," *Detroit Free Press*, 6 July 1919.
67. Kooyers, Frederick, PBOHP, 13 June 1977.
68. Charles, PBOHP, 14 June 1977.
69. Siplon, James, PBOHP, 6 July 1977.
70. Lewis, Floyd, PBOHP, 29 June 1977.
71. Costello, Harry, in Nelson, James, *The Polar Bear Expedition*, 2019, 254.
72. Marxer, Rudolph, PBOHP, 16 June 1977.

Chapter 20

1. *The Evacuation of North Russia, 1919*. London: His Majesty's Stationery Office, 1920.
2. Cudhy, John, in Nelson, James, *The Polar Bear Expedition*, 2019, 254.
3. Primm, Clarence, Letters, 23 June 1919.
4. *The Evacuation of North Russia, 1919*, 1920. Beers, Henry P., "U.S. Naval Forces in Northern Russia (Archangel and Murmansk), 1918–1919," Office of Records and Administration: Navy Department, November 1943.
5. Primm, Clarence, Letters, 2 July 1919.
6. *The Evacuation of North Russia, 1919*, 1920.
7. *The Evacuation of North Russia, 1919*, 1920.
8. Primm, Carol, and Stuntz, Pete, *Polar Bear Tales*, 2009, 130.
9. Primm, Clarence, Letters, 12 July 1919.
10. Harzinger, Kyle J., *Democracy of Death: U.S. Army Graves Registration and its Burial of the World War I Dead*, 2020.
11. Harzinger, Kyle J., *Democracy of Death*, 2020.
12. Harzinger, Kyle J., *Democracy of Death*, 2020.
13. Primm, Clarence, Journal, 19 July 1919.
14. Primm, Clarence, Journal, 20 July 1919.
15. Primm, Clarence, Journal, 21 July 1919.
16. Primm, Clarence, Journal, 22 July 1919.
17. Primm, Clarence, Journal, 23 July 1919.

18. Primm, Clarence, Letters, 23 July 1919.
19. Primm, Clarence, Letters, 23 July 1919.
20. Primm, Clarence, Journal, 26 July 1919.
21. Primm, Clarence, Journal, 27 July–1 August 1919.
22. Primm, Clarence, Letters, 26 July 1919.
23. Primm, Clarence, Journal, 2 August 1919.
24. *The Evacuation of North Russia, 1919*, 1920.
25. Primm, Clarence, Letters, 4 August 1919.
26. Primm, Clarence, Letters, 15 August 1919.
27. Primm, Clarence, Letters, 4 August 1919.
28. Steely, Skipper, *Allied Intervention in Russia*, 2013. Primm, Clarence, Letters, 15 August 1919.
29. Richardson, W.P., "American Expeditionary Force, North Russia," 5 August 1919.
30. Primm, Clarence, Letters, 15 August 1919.
31. *The Evacuation of North Russia, 1919*, 1920.
32. *The Evacuation of North Russia, 1919*, 1920. Primm, Clarence, Letters, 4 August 1919.
33. Primm, Clarence, Letters, 29 August 1919.
34. Steely, Skipper, *Allied Intervention in Russia*, 2013. *The Evacuation of North Russia, 1919*, 1920.
35. *The Evacuation of North Russia, 1919*, 1920.
36. "Primm Lands at Hoboken on Thursday," *Manitowoc Herald*, 18 October 1919.
37. "First Dead From Russia Reach Here," *The New York Herald*, 23 November 1919.
38. www.rochestermedia.com.
39. Dundon, Walter, F., "A Personal Experience Unique in the History of the U.S.A. Wars." Walter F. Dundon Papers. Polar Bear Digital Materials, UMBHL, n. d.
40. "Five Michigan Veterans Hunt Bodies of Buddies," *The Tuscaloosa News*, 10 September 1929.
41. Dundon, Walter, F., "A Personal Experience Unique in the History of the U.S.A. Wars."
42. Dundon, Walter, F., "A Personal Experience Unique in the History of the U.S.A. Wars."
43. Dundon, Walter, F., "A Personal Experience Unique in the History of the U.S.A. Wars."
44. Mason, Herbert M., Jr., "Mission to North Russia," Veterans of Foreign Wars, 1999.
45. Mason, Herbert M., Jr., "Mission to North Russia," 1999.
46. Dundon, Walter, F., "A Personal Experience Unique in the History of the U.S.A. Wars."
47. Mason, Herbert M., Jr., "Mission to North Russia," 1999.
48. "Kistler Grave Bared 22 More," *Lancaster Sunday News*, 1 December 1929.
49. Dundon, Walter, F., "A Personal Experience Unique in the History of the U.S.A. Wars."
50. Mason, Herbert M., Jr., "Mission to North Russia,"1999.
51. Bushaw, Walter, PBOHP, 1978.
52. "Five Michigan Veterans Hunt Bodies of Buddies," *The Tuscaloosa News*, 10 September 1929.
53. Mason, Herbert M., Jr., "Mission to North Russia,"1999.
54. "Nation Honors 75 Doughboys Home from Russia in Coffins," *The Indianapolis News*, 29 November 1929.
55. *New York Times*, 29 November 1929.
56. Mason, Herbert M., Jr., "Mission to North Russia,"1999.
57. Zacharias, Patricia, "Detroit's Polar Bears and their Confusing War," *The Detroit News*, November 1998.
58. Dundon, Walter, F., "A Personal Experience Unique in the History of the U.S.A. Wars."

Bibliography

Books

Alumni Directory: The University of Chicago. New York: The Baker & Taylor Co., 1919.

Anderson, Godfrey J. *A Michigan Polar Bear Confronts the Bolsheviks: A War Memorial.* Grand Rapids: William B. Eerdmans, 2010.

Bozich, Stanley. *Detroit's Own Polar Bears: The American North Russian Expeditionary Forces, 1918–1919.* Frankenmuth, MI: Polar Bear Pub. Co., 1985.

Costello, Harry J. *Why Did We Go to Russia?* Detroit: Harry J. Costello, 1920.

Cudahy, John. *Archangel: The American War with Russia.* Chicago: A.C. McClurg & Co., 1924.

The Evacuation of North Russia, 1919. London: His Majesty's Stationery Office, 1920.

Francis, David R. *Russia from the American Embassy, April 1916–November 1918.* New York: Charles Scribner's Sons, 1921.

Gillett, Mary C. *The Army Medical Department, 1917–1941.* Washington, D.C.: Center of Military History, United States Army, 2009.

Gordon, Dennis. *Quartered in Hell: The Story of the American North Russian Expeditionary Force, 1918–1919.* Missoula: Doughboy Historical Society, 1982.

Helman, Francis B. *Historical Register and Dictionary of the United States.* Washington, D.C.: Government Printing Office, 1903.

Ironside, Edmund. *Ironside: The Authorized Biography of Field Marshall Lord Ironside.* Stroud, Gloucestershire, UK: The History Press, 2018.

Jones, Frank, and Atkins, H.E. *Souvenir: Camp Custer, Michigan.* Battle Creek: Atkins Engraving Co., 1918.

Kennan, George F. *The Decision to Intervene: Soviet-American Relations, 1917–1920.* Princeton: Princeton University Press, 1958.

Marquis, Albert N. (Ed.). *Book of Detroiters: A Biographical Dictionary of Leading Living Men of the City of Detroit.* Chicago: A.N. Marquis & Co., 1914.

Moore, Joel R. *"M" Company, 339th Infantry in North Russia.* Jackson, MI: Central City Bookbinding, 1920.

Moore, Joel, Mead, Harry, and Jahns, Lewis. *The History of the American Expedition Fighting the Bolsheviki: Campaigning in North Russia, 1918–1919.* Detroit: The Polar Bear Publishing Co., 1920.

Neft, Davis S., Cohen, Richard M., and Neft, Michael L. *The Sports Encyclopedia: Baseball 2001.* New York: St. Martin's Griffin, 2001.

Nelson, James Carl. *The Polar Bear Expedition: The Heroes of America's Forgotten Invasion of Russia, 1918–1919.* New York: William Morrow-HarperCollins, 2019.

New York Supplement Vol. 95 *(New York State Reporter, Vol. 129) Containing the Decisions of the Supreme and Lower Courts of Record of New York State.* St. Paul: West Publishing, 1906.

Pennington, Phil. *Fugitive Moment.* Boulder, CO, 2015.

Pixley, R.B. *Official War Record of Ozaukee County, Wisconsin.* Port Washington. Ozaukee County War Commission, 1919.

Primm, Clarence J. (Primm, Carol, and Stuntz, Pete, eds.). *Polar Bear Tales By a Soldier of the A.E.F. North Russia.* n.p., 2009.

Register of Officers Who Served in the U.S. Army, 1798–1969. U.S. Army Military Registers, 1918.

Steely, Skipper. *Allied Intervention in Russia, 1918–1920: General Richardson and His Role in the Withdrawal of American Troops from Northern Russia.* Paris, TX: Wright Press, 2013.

University of Wisconsin Alumni Directory, 1849–1911, The. Madison: University of Wisconsin Press, 1912.

Waring, George J. *United States Catholic Chaplains in the World War.* New York: The Chauncey Holt Co., Inc., 1924.

Weatherson, Michael, A., and Bochin, Hal W. *Hiram Johnson: Political Revivalist.* Lanham, MD: University Press of America, 1995.

Whitehorne, Joseph W. *The Inspectors General of the United States Army.* Washington, D.C.: Office of the Inspector General and Center of Military History, United States Army, 1998.

Willett, Robert L. *Russian Sideshow: America's Undeclared War, 1918–1920.* Washington, D.C.: Brassey's, 2003.

Williamson, William H. (ed.). *George Cullum's*

Biographical Register of the Officers and Graduates of the United States Military Academy. West Point, NY: U.S. Army, Vol. VIII, 1920.

Winslow, Horatio. *Rhymes and Meters: A Practical Guide for Versifiers.* Deposit, NY: The Editor Publishing Co., 1909.

Periodicals and Newspapers

The American Scholar. Washington, D.C.
The Baltimore Sun.
The Battle Creek Enquirer.
Brooklyn Daily Eagle.
The Buffalo Courier.
Chicago Daily Tribune.
Chicago Tribune.
Detroit Free Press.
Detroit News.
The Flint Journal
Homeland Magazine. San Diego.
The Indianapolis News.
Journal Times. Racine, WI.
Leelanau Enterprise. Muskegon, MI.
Michigan Heroes Museum. Frankenmuth, MI.
Monroe News. Monroe, MI.
Monthly Weather Review. Boston.
Morgan County Republican. Versailles, MO.
Naval War College. Newport, RI.
The New York Times.
New York Tribune.
The Paducah Sun.
The Palladium. Richmond, IN.
The Polar Bear Club. Detroit.
Polar Bear Memorial Association. Frankenmuth, MI.
The Pontanezen Duckboard. Camp Pontanezen, France.
The Railway Age. Chicago.
St. Louis Post-Dispatch.
Sanilac County News. Sandusky, MI.
The Sentinel, The. Archangel, Russia.
Sunbury Daily. Sunbury, PA.
Toledo Blade.
The Tuscaloosa News. Tuscaloosa, MI.
Veterans of Foreign Wars. Kansas City, MO.
Wall Street Journal.
The War Illustrated. London.
War Work Bulletin; Y.M.C.A. New York.

Government Sources

Beers, Henry P. "U.S. Naval Forces in Northern Russia (Archangel and Murmansk), 1918–1919." Office of Records and Administration, Navy Department, November 1943.

"Building Alaska with the U.S. Army, 1867–1965." Headquarters, U.S. Army, Alaska, 1 October 1965.

Extract from Discharge Certificate of Officer to Secure Victory Medal. 1920.

Foreign Relations, 1918, Russia, Vol. II, 1918.

General Orders: War Department. Washington D.C.: F.L. Winn, 1920.

Historical Files of the U.S. Expeditionary Force, North Russia, 1918–19. National Archives, 30 September 1918; 1 October 1918; 12 October 1918; 26 November 1918; 2 December 1918; 5 December 1918; 14 January 1919; 12 February 1919.

Leavenworth Papers, Fort Leavenworth, KS, December 1981.

Operations of the 339th Infantry Regiment in North Russia, September 4–April 1, 1919.

Red Cross Record of Manistee County Soldiers and Sailors in Service in the Great War. National Archives, 12 March 1919.

United States Army in the World War, 1917–1919. "Bulletins." GHQ, AEF. Washington, D.C.: Center of Military History, United States Army, 1992.

United States Army World War I Transportation Service, 1918. National Archives.

United States Census: 1910 Michigan; 1940 Michigan.

World War I Selective Service System: Draft Registration Cards, 1917–1919. National Archives.

Diaries, Letters, and Journals

Broadus, B.F. Papers. UMBHL.

Colburn, Cleo. *Diary, 1918–1919.* UMBHL.

Colburn, Cleo. "Letters from the Yanks." Ann Arbor: University of Michigan, 1918.

Douma, Frank W. "WWI Service, July 14, 1918—July 18, 1919." In Frank W. Douma Papers.

Grobbel, Clement. "Letters." Mike Grobbel Collection, 1918–1919.

Kooyers, Fred. "Diary, 1918–1919." In George Albers Papers.

Moore, Joel Roscoe. Papers, UMBHL.

Ramsey, Leon. "Two Points of View." Newspaper Clippings, Leon Ramsey Papers, 1917–1919. UMBHL.

Riordan, C.E. "Letters." Papers, UMBHL.

Stoner, George W. "The Diary of 1st Lt. George W. Stoner, Jr. Company M, 339th Infantry Regiment, 85th Division, U.S. Army, Part II." Transcribed and edited by George W. Stoner (his son), 2009.

University of Michigan Bentley Historical Library. UMBHL.

Manuscripts

Baldwin, Robert C. "The Allied Military Expedition to North Russia: 1918–1919." Washington, D.C: The American University, June 1969.

Beera, Henry P. "U.S. Naval Forces in Northern Russia." Navy Department Library, November 1943.

Bonnell, Jay H. "A Reminiscence of the Polar Bear Expedition to Northern Russia." Jay H. Bonnell Papers, UMBHL.

Grobbel, Mike. "Outnumbered on the Vologda Railroad Front—the Bolshevik Attack of November 4, 1918." 2007.
Harzinger, Kyle J. *Democracy of Death: U.S. Army Graves Registration and Its Burial of the World War I Dead*. University of North Texas, August 2020.
Moore, Joel R. "Record of Events," War *Diary, Company 'M,' 339th Infantry*. 1919.
Page, D.C.M, "A Chat with Ironside." 19 March 1919.
Polar Bear Digital Materials, NHLUM.
Primm, Clarence J. "Has Control of the Central Government Unduly Increased?" Thesis, University of Kansas, 1908. *University of Kansas Graduate School Theses 1888–1947*. Lawrence: University of Kansas, 1949.
Scales, Howard. "Alleged Mutiny of Company I, 339th Infantry." Washington, D.C., 25 June 1920.
Simmons, Christopher. "The Alleged Mutiny of Company I." Northfield, VT: Norwich University, 20 May 2011.
Ward, William S. *A Well Kept Secret: The Allied Invasion of North Russia, 1918–1919*. 2010.

Interviews

Bartels, Levi. By Johnson, Glen, 1978.
Colburn, Cleo. By Lenning, Deborah, and Johnson, Nancy L., June 17, 1977.
Grace, Charles. By Johnson, Nancy L., June 14, 1977.
Hershberger, Russell. By Lenning, Deborah, and Johnson, Nancy L., June 6, 1977.
Hope College Interviews. "Polar Bear Oral History Project." Holland, MI.
Kemperman, Radus. By Lenning, Deborah, and Johnson, Nancy L., June 23, 1977.
Larsen, Alfred. By Lenning, Deborah, Johnson, Nancy, 13 June 1977.
Lewis, Floyd. By Lenning, Deborah, June 29, 1977.
Marxer, Rudolph. By Lenning, Deborah, June 16, 1977.
Rotman, Martin. By Johnson, Glen, June 13, 1977.
Salchow, Hugo K. Hugo K. Salchow Papers, 1918–19. UMBHL, n.d.
Siplon, James. By Johnson, Nancy L., July 6, 1977.

Internet Sources

www.ancestories1.blogspot.com
www.ausableoscodahistoricalsociety.org
www.battleorder.org
www.canadiangreatwarproject.com
www.cmohs.org
www.fold3.com
www.grobbel.org
www.highbiemaxon.com
www.laborarts.org
www.military.wikia.org
www.mlive.com
www.pulpmags.org
www.recordpatriot.com
www.rochestermedia.com
www.2nd-division.com
www.valor.militarytimes.com
www.wikiwand.com
www.worldwar1gallery.com

Index

Numbers in ***bold italics*** indicate pages with illustrations

Abel, Henry (Co. I, Pvt.) 127, 131
Akutin, P.T. (Russian, Cpt./Maj./Col.) 109, 110, 111, 113, 114, 115, 116, 161
Alaska 24, 40, 154, 155, 157
Albers, George (Co. I, Pvt.) 76, 124, 125, 150, 151, 152
Aldershot, Camp, England 18, ***19***, 20, 21
Alliez (French, Cpt.) 55, 56, 58
Anderson, Godfrey (337th Field Hospital) 10, 11, 13, 16, 18, 19, 28, 33, 165
Andrews (British, Col.) 177
Antwerp, Belgium 181
Apsche (French, Cpt.) 67, 70
Archangel, Russia 25, 26, 27, 28, 32, 33, 38, 47, 48, 49, 50, 51, 58, 61, 67, 72, 73, 81, 83, 84, 85, ***86***, 87, 88, 89, 90, 92, 100, 109, 110, 111, 112, 113, 114, 116, 119, 122, 124, 125, 126, 127, 128, 129, 130, 131, 132, 134, 142, 151, 154, 158, 160, 162, 164, 165, 168, 171, 175, 176, 177, 178, 179, 180, 181, 182
Archangel-Vologda RR 32, 33, 34, 38, 49, 56, 62, 78, 79, 129, 130, 134, 176
Arlington National Cemetery 184
Armistice 68, 81, 82, 156

Bailey, Thomas (British, Cpt.) 145
Baker, Newton (Sec. of War) 123
Bakharitza, Russia 31, 33, 34, 36, 37, 39, 58, 60, 76, 81, 98, 127, 131, 165
Ballensinger, Richard W. (Co. H, Cpt.) 135, 145

Bartels, Levi (Co. K, Pvt.) 21, 28, 89
baseball game 166
Becker, Alfred (Co. I, Pvt.) 157
Bissonette, Harry (Co. M, Cpl.) 166
Bogacheff, Simon (Co. M, Cpl.) 70
Bolos 35, 38, 41, 42, 43, 44, 45, 47, 51, 53, 57, 58, 59, 62, 63, 65, 66, 67, 68, 69, 70, 71, 76, 78, 79, 80, 82, 90, 92, 93, 94, 95, 97, 100, 104, 106, 107, 108, 109, 113, 115, 120, 121, 124, 128, 130, 132, 134, 135, 137, 141, 142, 143, 144, 145, 146, 147, 148, 157, 158, 159, 161, 174, 176, 178, 179
Bolshevik government 25, 26, 27
Bolshie Ozerki, Russia 97, 98, 120, 121, 130, 134, 135, 136, 137, 138, ***139***, 140, 144, 146, 148, 157, 158
Bonnell, Jay (310th Engineers, Pvt.) 55
Bowie, Fort 155
Boyer (French, Cpt.) 62, 63, 66, 68
Boysen, John (Co. M, Pvt.) 71
Brest, France 168, 169, 171, 181
Brest-Litovsk, Treaty 25, 26
Broer, Edwin (Co. E, Lt.) 138
Brooks, Julia A. 49
Bullitt, William C. 122
Burr, Jane *see* Guggenheim, Rosalind

Caesarea (transport ship) 60, 61
Carey, Donald (Co. E, Pvt.) 13, 21, 137, 138
Carpenter, Milton (Co. M, 2nd Lt.) 36
Chekuevo, Russia 120, 130, 135, 136, 140, 141, 144, 145, 146, 177, 178
Cherry, Grant, Jr. (Co. L, Cpt.) 13, 37, 44, 45, 46, 47
Childs, Catherine (YMCA) 148, 150, 151
Christensen, Marguerite 7
Chu Chin Chow 20
Cialkowski, Tony (Co. I, Pvt.) 157
Colburn, Cleo (Co. I, Pvt./Cpl.) 20, 34, 35, 36, 42, 43, 46, 55, 75, 97, 119, 128, 133, 157, 158
Collins, Earl W. (Co. H, Cpl.) 134, 135, 137, 173, 174
Collins, Edmund (Co. H, Lt.) 136
Conway, John (Co. G, Cpt.) 98, 104, 105, 106, 108, 109, 113, 114
Conway, Michael (US, 2nd Lt.) 177, 180, 181
Corbley, James (1st Btn., Maj.) 12
Costello, Harry (MG Co., 1st Lt.) 21, 33, 117, 174
Couzens, Frank (Detroit mayor) 172
Craig, John W. (Col.) 24, 50
Crissman, John (Co. A, Sgt.) 172
Crook, Alva (Co. M, Pvt.) 142
Cudahy, John (Co. B, 2nd Lt.) 21, 34, 35, 36, 51, 54, 55, 65, 77, 88, 140, 142, 143, 144, 145, 181
Custer, Camp, MI ***8***, 9, 10, ***11***, 12, 13, 16, 24, 31, 40, 50, 60, 61, 78, 92, 99, 108, 119, 126, 134, 147, 164, 174, 181
Czar, HMT 168, 171, 181
Czech-Slovak troops 26

Danley, Gerald (Co. I, 1st Lt.) 41, 43, 45, 46, 67

Index

Day, Robert (Co. I, Pvt.) 45
Dequerte, Conrad (French, Lt.) 65
Des Moines, USS 167
Detroit, MI 9, 50, 79, 80, 91, 108, 134, 147, 158, 159, 163, 168, 172, 173, 181, 182, 184
Dial, Charles (Co. M, Pvt.) 142, 148
Division 85th 13, 19
Donnor, William (Co. M, Pvt.) 51
Donoghue, Michael (Co. K, Cpt.) 13, 37
Donovan, James (Co. M, 1st Lt.) 36, 43, 51, 57, 110, 112
Douma, Frank (Co. D, Pvt.) 18, 19, 20
Drews, William (Co. M) 58
Duff, Henry (Co. I, Cpl.) 169, 172
Dundon, Margaret 40
Dundon, Walter (Co. M - 1st Sgt.) 16, 17, 18, 19, 21, 33, 36, 37, 38, 40, 41, 42, 44, 47, 51, 57, 62, 66, 70, 71, 75, 76, 81, 89, 93, 94, 95, 98, 100, 101, 102, 103, 104, 105, 109, 111, 112, 114, 115, 116, 117, 139, 140, 141, 158, 159, 161, 165, 170, 181, 182, 183, 184
Dunlap, Rosa Sparks 50
Dusseau, Ora (Co. M, Pvt.) 70
Dyment, Schlioma (Co. M, Pvt.) 58

Economie, Camp (Russia) 165, 166, 168, 171
Ellis, Leo (Co. I, Pvt.) 79
Emtsa, Russia 123, 149
Esyevileva, Maria 168

Fisher, Roy (Co. M, Pvt.) 166
Fistler, Dwight (Co. I, 1st Lt.) 57, 78, 79
Francis, David R. (Ambassador) 25, 26, 27, 32, 73, 81
Fruse, John (Co. H, Pvt.) 135
Fulcher, Earl (Co. H, Pvt.) 134, 135

Gevers, Carl (Co. H, Cpt.) 134
Gordon-Finlayson, Robert (British, Gen.) 51, 72
Grace, Charles (Co. D, Sgt.) 10
Grahek, Matthew (Co. M, Sgt.) 9, 41, 57, 58, *107*, 108, 127, 142, 171
Graves Registration Service (US) 175, 176, 177, 179, 181, 182, 183
Griffen (British, Cpt.) 53, 54

Grobbel, Clement (Co I - Pvt./Cpl.) 3, 10, 62, 67, 71, 75, *77*, 78, 80, 89, 119, 127 158, 171
Grobbel, Mike 3, 77
Guard (British, Col.) 41, 43, 44
Guggenheim, Rosalind 16

Hager, Cecile 40, 41
Harrisburg, USS 17
Hasselvender, Alfred (French, Cpt.) 65
Hebner, Charles (Co. M, Sgt.) 162
Heil, Bernard (Co. H, Cpt.) 137
Henkleman, William (Co. B, Pvt.) 129
Hershberger, Russell (MG Co., Pvt.) 9, 41, 75, 88, 119, 125
Hicks, Donald M. (USN, Ensign) 31, 32, 33, 37, 38
Higgins, William (Co. G, 1st Lt.) 106, 108
Hoboken, NJ 17, 18, 172, *180*, 181
Hogan, Freeman (Co. M, Pvt.) 141, 148, *149*, 150, 153

Ironside, William (British, Gen.) *72*, 73, 74, 81, 89, *90*, 108, 130, 136, 137, 140, 144, 146, 156, 157, 159, 168, 176, 179

Jahns, Lewis (HQ, 1st Lt.) 46
Jerrain, John (Co. M, Pvt.) 58
Johnson, Adolph (Co. M, Pvt.) 101, 104
Johnson, Hiram (Senator) 130
Jondro, Benjamin (Co. M, Pvt.) 66

Kanada (icebreaker) 154, 156
Kantrowitz, Jacob (Co. M, Sgt.) 4
Karapuz, Joseph (Co. M , Pvt.) 58
Keith, Lawrence (Mortars, 2nd Lt.) 55, 56, 57
Keller, John (Co. M, Pvt.) 66
Kemperman, Radus (Co. E, Pvt.) 9
Ketcham, Harry (Co. H, Lt.) 137
Kildoman Castle (transport ship) 180
Kistler, Herbert S. (Co. I, Pvt.) 183
Kleiber, Richard (Co. I, Pvt.) 157
Kooyers, Fred (Co. E, Pvt.) 10,

11, 12, 13, 14, 17, 18, 20, 22, 28, 137, 174
Kroenski, Howard (Co. I, Pvt.) 157
Kurklewicz, Edward (Co. I, Pvt.) 46
Kwasniewski, Ignacy (Co. I, Pvt.) 45

Lachacki, Frank (Co. M, Pvt.) 95
La Follette, Robert 122
Lake Drago (transport ship) 181
Larsen, Alfred (Co. D, Pvt.) 26, 27, 28, 82, 87
Laursen, Jens (Co. M, Pvt.) 142, *147*, 148, 150, 152, 153
Lawrence, Ray (Co. M, Pvt.) 66
Le Havre, France 184
Leitzell, Glenn (Co. M, Sgt.) 139, 141, 148, *149*, 150, 151, 152, 153
Lewis, Alfred (Co. M, Pvt.) 10, 11, 12, 13, 16, 81, 86, 90, 116
Lewis, Charles E. (Staff, 1st Lt.) *163*, 164, 165
Lewis, Floyd (Co. M, Pvt.) 20, 28, 174
London, England 20, 108
Lucas (French, Col.) 135, 136
Lukovski (Russian, Lt.) 141

McCauley, Frank (Co. I, Pvt.) 157
McConvill, Edward (Co. H, Pvt.) 137
McCulla, Michael (Co. G, Pvt.) 182
McGuire, Whitney S. (Co. I, 1st Sgt.) 126, 131, 132, 133, 169
McKee, Forest (Co. I, 2nd Lt.) 67, 78
McLaughlin, Frank (Co. I, Pvt.) 68
Maitland, James (Co. M, Pvt.) 83, *85*
Malm, Clarence (Co. G, Pvt.) 109
Manders, George (Co. M, Pvt.) 143
Martin, Hugh (Staff, Cpt.) 128
Marxer, Rudolph (Co. E, Pvt.) 20, 27, 28, 171, 174
May, Albert (Co. M - 1st Lt.) 17, 44, 45, 53, 55, 56, 57, 67, 78, 79, 80, 122, 131, 132, 133, 156
Menominee (transport ship) 168, 175

Index

Merrick, Walter (Co. M, Pvt.) 66
Merritt, Camp (NJ) 172
Merwin, Eugene (Co. M, Cpl.) 171
Meyers, William (Co. L, Pvt.) 27
Miller, Clarence (Co. M, Pvt.) 58
Miller, Norman (Co. M, Pvt.) 159
Mills, Camp, NY 16, 17
Minteer, Harvey (Co. I, Pvt.) 157, 158
Moore, Joel R. (Co. M, Cpt.) 13, 17, 21, 26–28, **29**, 31, 33, 36, 37, 38, 41, 42, 43, 44, 45, 46, 47, 51, 53, 54, 55, 56, 57, 58, 59, 61, 62, 63, 65, 66, 67, 68, 69, 70, 71, 74, 75, 76, 80, 81, 83, 84, 85, 86, 88, 89, 90, 92, 93, 94, 95, 97, 98, 100, 101, 102, 103, 104, 105, 106, 108, 109, 110, 111, 112, 113, 114, 115, 116, 117, 120, 125, 127, 128, 130, 135, 138, 139, 140, 141, 142, 143, **144**, 145, 146, 152, 159, 160, 161, 165, 166, 168, 171, 181
Moscow, Russia 25, 76, 125, 149, 150, 151, 152, 153, 174, 182
Mosin-Nagant rifle 21
Murmansk, Russia 25, 26, 27, 129, 156

Nagoya, USS 164
Nelson, James C. 5
Nevasa (transport ship) 60
New York City, NY 16, 20, 23
Nichols, Jesse Brooks (2nd/3rd Btn., Maj.) 12, **49**, 50, 51, 56, 57, 59, 61, 62, 66, 67, 68, 75, 93, 120, 122, 137, 138, 139, 140, 157, 158, 161, 162, 164, 168, 169, 171, 172, 181
Nichols, Martin (Co. M, Pvt.) 143
Nielson, Susan 143
Niemi, Matti (Co. M, Pvt.) 58
Northumberland, USS 17, 134

Obozerskaya, Russia 32, 33, 35, 36, 37, **38**, 39, 43, 47, 51, 53, 72, 76, 80, 85, 90, 95, 97, 98, 112, 119, 120, 122, 125, 130, 131, 132, 133, 135, 136, 137, 138, 139, 140, 141, 142, 146, 148, 157, 158, 159, 160, 161, 162, 166, 177, 179
Olmstead, Frank (YMCA) 140
Olmstead, Mabel 29

Olympia, USS 31
Onega, Russia 38, 97, 129, 134, 135, 136, 145, 178
Onega Road, Russia 38, 97
Oslund, David (Co. M, Pvt.) 70

Paris Peace Conference 156
Parris, Silver (Co. B, Sgt.) 129
Pavlin, Joseph (Co. M, Pvt.) 101, 104
Peating, John (Co. F, Pvt.) 21
Peligora, Russia 115
Penningroth, Louis (YMCA) 152
Perschke, Dewey (USN, Seaman) 32
Pershing, John J. (USA, Gen.) 156, 157, 168, 179
Petrograd, Russia 152, 153
Petropoulos, George (310th Engineers - Pvt.) 9
Petrowskas, John (Co. I, Pvt.) 132, 133
Philippine insurgency 24
Phillips, Clifford (Co. H, Lt.) 136, 145
Pickard, Clare A. 50
Picard, Walter (Co. M, Cpl.) 159
Pinega, Russia 98, 100, 103, 104, 105, 106, 108, 109, **110**, 111, 112, 113, 114, 115, 116, 117, 161, 179
Pitts, Jay (Co. G, Pvt.) 109
Plattsburg, USS 17
Plesetskaya, Russia 176
Pocahontas, USS 181
Polar Bear Association 181, 182
Polar Bear Patch **167**, 169, 171
Polar Bears (American) **167**, 168, 169, 171, 172, **173**, 174, 182, 184, 185
Pontanezen, Camp 169, **170**, 171
Poole, Frederick (British, Gen.) 67, 73, 74, 164
Pratt, Robert (Co. M, Cpl.) 69, 141
President Roosevelt, USS 184
Primm, Clarence F. (Co. M, 1st Lt.) **7**, 8, 20, 26, 27, 31, 33, 36, 39, 47, 48, 54, 62, 63, 65, 66, 67, 69, 70, 74, 75, 84, 85, 87, 92, 94, 97, 98, 103, 110, 112, 113, 114, 117, 120, 123, 126, 127, 128, 129, 139, 140, 141, 145, 146, 157, 160, 166, 167, 168, **175**, 176, 177, 178, 179, 181

Quilpue (transport ship) 176

Rahn, Frank (Co. M, Cpl.) 57, 58
Ramotowske, Joseph (Co. H, Pvt.) 135
Rasmussen, Roy (Co. I, Pvt.) 68
Red Cross, American 18, 22, 87, 104, 111, 126, 127, 151, 174, 175, 181
Redmond, Nathan (Co. H, Cpl.) 135
Reese, Gordon (Co. I, 1st Lt.) 46, 67, 78, 79, **118**, 118, 120, 121, 123, 125
Revels, James F. (Co. I, Bugler) 46
Richardson, Wilds P. (USA, Gen.) **154**, 155, 156, 157, 158, 159, 160, 161, 163, 165, 166, 167, 168, 176, 179, 180
Riha, Charles (Co. M, Cpl.) 58
Roach, Father 151
Robbins, William (Co. I, Pvt.) 20, 125
Romanski, Frank (Co. M, Pvt.) 159
Roosevelt, Theodore (President) 15
Rosenau, Walter (Co. M, Cpl.) 171
Rowers, Will (Co. H, Pvt.) 25
Russell, William (Co. M, Cpl.) 142, 142, 159
Ryall, Bryant (YMCA) 140, 141, 148, **149**, 150, 151, 153
Ryan, Charles (Co. K, 1st Lt.) 34, 37
Ryduchowski, Joseph (Co. M, Cpl.) 143

Safer, Samuel (Co. E, Pvt.) 11, 12, 82, 121
Salchow, Hugo (Co. E, Pvt.) 11
Salvation Army 171
Samoylo, Aleksanr (Bolshevik, Gen.) 140, 146
Sanders, James W. (Co. E, Cpl.) 138
Sapp, Frank (Co. M, Cpl.) 142
Sarosiek, Jan (Co. K, Pvt.) 21
Sauter, Joseph (Co. K, Pvt.) 25, 85
Saeickis, Frank (Co. I, Cpl.) 160
Scales, Howard (Staff, Maj.) 160
Scheulke, William (Co. H, Pvt.) 135
Schillinger, Norbert (Co. M, Cpl.) 158
Seletskoe, Russia 32, 37
Seward, Fort William 155
Shackleton, Sir Ernest 21, 94, 104

Index

Shackleton boots 94, 102, 103, 124, 137
Shenkursk, Russia 113, 114
Sheridan, Philip (Co. F, Lt.) 111, 113
Sheridan, Fort, IL 16, 31, 50, 118, 119, 164, 181
Shreve, Paul K. 1, 2, 3
Sickles, Floyd A. (Co. M, Pvt.) *91*, 95, 97
Sieloff, Theodore (Co. I, Cpl.) 79
Signal Corps, US Army 67
Simpson, Charles (337th Field Hospital) 28
Siplon, James (Co. I, Pvt.) 9, 10, 13, 19, 26, 41, 54, 57, 61, 62, 67, 74, 75, 76, 81, 82, 87, 88, 131, 132, 166, 174
Slaught, Albert, AJ (Co. D, Pvt.) 21, 28, 81
Slavo-British Allied League (SBAL) 127, 176
Smaglick, Paul (Co. M, Pvt.) 58
Smolny barracks, Russia 83, 84, 89, 90, 92, 100, 117, 119, 125, 126, 128, 129, 130, 132, 136, 165
Soczkoski, Anthony (Co. I, Pvt.) 46
Sokol, Philip (Co. I, Pvt.) 45
Somali (transport ship) 28, 31, 33
Soyer (French, Lt.) 62, 63, 66
Spanish-American War 23
Spanish Flu 28, 33, 36, 40, 61, 164
Stalinski, Julius (Pvt.) 13
Stark, Louis (Co. G, Pvt.) 108, 109
Starr, Steven (Co. M, Pvt.) 65
Steigerwald (transport ship) 176
Steinhauer, Homer (Co. M, Cpl.) 66

Stemptzyk, Louis (Co. I, Pvt.) 157
Stewart, George (Lt. Col./Col.) 15, 17, *23*, 24, 28, 31, 45, 47, 48, 51, 61, 73, 84, 108, 109, 111, 113, 117, 122, 127, 129, 130, 131, 132, 133, 154, 156, 157, 164, 166, 167, 168, 175
Stoner, George (Co. M, 1st Lt.) 18, 20, 22, 36, 43, 51, 62, 63, 65, 66, 68, 60, 70, 76, 90, 92, 94, 98, *99*, 100, 101, 102, 103, 104, 105, 106, 108, 109, 111, 112, 113, 114, 115, 116, 117, 138, 141, 146, 161, 162, 168, 169, 170, 172
Stringham, Charles (Co. M, Pvt.) 63
Sutherland (British, Col.) 44, 58, 59, 128

Taft, William (President) 155
Taylor, Joseph (HQ Co., Cpt.) 128
Toboggan, Archangel 87, *88*, 127
Toornman, John (Co. G, Pvt.) 22, 75, 76
Tremaine, Roy (Co. M, Pvt.) 13

Ust-Pocha, Russia 114
Ustarboski, Joseph (Co I, Pvt.) 157

Venable, Carl W. (Co. L, Sgt.) 46
Vickary, Ray (Co. M, Pvt.) 70
Vologda, Russia 33, 74, 76, 125, 150
Von Steuben, USS 171, 172
Vrahoritis, John (Co. M, Pvt.) 168

Walker, Ralph (Co. M, Sgt.) 162

West Point, NY 155
White Chapel Cemetery 184
Wieczorek, Robert (Co. M, 2nd Lt.) 36, 43, 62, 63, 65, 69, 70, 98, 110, 114, 117, 143, 144, 162
Wildman, Elizabeth 24
Willett, Robert L. 5
Williams, Charles T. 111
Wilson, John B. (WI Supreme Court Justice) 15, 17
Wilson, Woodrow (President) 19, 26, 27, 123, 130, 156
Wing, Homer (310th Engineer, Pvt.) 181
Winslow, Horatio G. (Co. I, Cpt.) 13, *15*, 16, 35, 38, 44, 45, 46, 51, 67, 68, 71, 74, 75, 76, 78, 79, 80, 81, 82, 92, 95, 97, 119, 125, 126, 128, 130, 131, 132, 133, 158, 159, 171
Wright, Wesley (Co. M, 2nd Lt.) 36, 98, 100, 101, 102, 104, 108, 109, 110, 114, 117, 127, 141, 143, 158

Yasas, Andrew (Co. M, Pvt.) 58
YMCA, American 87, 92, 113, 116, 119, 120, 125, 126, 127, 129, 130, 132, 140, 148, 152, 175
Yohey, George (HQ Co., Pvt.) 12
Yopp, Herman (Co. M, Pvt.) *60*, 61, 102
Young, Charles (3rd Btn., Maj.) 12, 13, 31, 34, 35, 36, 37, 38, 41, 44, 45, 46, 47, 48, 51, 53, 56, 58, 61, 83, 129, 131, 132, 164, 165, 166, 167, 169

Zank, Richard (Co. L, Pvt.) 12
Zawacki, Martin (Co. I, Pvt.) 80

www.ingramcontent.com/pod-product-compliance
Lightning Source LLC
Chambersburg PA
CBHW080805300426
44114CB00020B/2831